# Revenue or Relationships? Win Both.

## A Customer Experience Primer to Shift Your Perspective of Business

Mary Brodie

Publisher: Gearmark
DALLAS, TX

Mary Brodie—Gearmark
1409 South Lamar St., Dallas, TX 75215
www.gearmark.com, www.mfbrodie.com

Editor: Jodi Brandon, Jodi Brandon Editorial
Cover design & illustrator: Melody Christian, www.finickydesisgns.com
Book Layout ©2015 BookDesignTemplates.com

Ordering Information:
Quantity sales. Special discounts are available on quantity purchases by corporations, associations, and others. For details, contact the "Special Sales Department" at the address above.

Revenue or Relationships? Win Both. / Mary Brodie -- 1st ed.
Library of Congress Control Number: 2019915919
Trade Paperback ISBN: 978-1-7341426-0-0
Amazon E-book ISBN: 978-1-7341426-1-7
Printed in the United States of America.

# Acknowledgments

There are many people who influenced me while writing this book. I'm almost afraid to list them all because I may inadvertently exclude someone, but here is a short list:

**All of my past employers and clients, through Gearmark or me personally,** have contributed to this book in some way. Working with you allowed me to learn how integral automation and digital transformation is to any organization. You also gave me the opportunity to discover what makes a successful customer experience.

**My editor, Jodi Brandon.** Without Jodi, this book wouldn't make it to the finish line. She showed me how to write a book, understand the structure, and made me sound far more intelligent than I am.

**My book designer, Melody Christian.** She helped me get the book to look professional and finished. And she created a professional, elegant cover that made the book super marketable.

**Dragonfly Editing.** They introduced me to Jodi. Very thankful to their support and recommendation.

**Jennifer Grace.** If I never took her course, Creative Insights Journey, and then subsequent courses in speech writing, public speaking, and lead generation, I wouldn't have had the courage to write this book.

**My parents.** They got me started in life so I could have the experiences that led me to write this book. I appreciate their guidance and assistance for me to get here.

**Susan Molthen (Sausan).** She has had such an influence in my life to help me overcome my fears and build my confidence. I learned how life should flow smoothly from Sausan.

**Shannon Muruli.** Her work in fear and courage helped me overcome my own fears, many of which were unknown to me until I met her. Her work inspired me to start writing this book and keep going.

**Sharon Miller.** Her support of me as a person is always tremendous. A beautiful cheerleader. Thank you, Sharon!

**Linda Forbes.** She volunteered to read my book and gave me the encouragement and energy I needed to complete the last mile of the journey. Without her encouragement, I wouldn't have seen that there really is a market for the topic.

**Julie Greene.** For many years we worked together to achieve the unachievable. We often raised each other up to meet the next challenge, creating mutually beneficial opportunities for each of our careers. For those, I am very grateful. Without Julie, I could not have had the experiences or opportunities to write this book.

**Roxana Damas.** Another life cheerleader who encourages me to be more. She has included me in many of her projects to help others be empowered, including her work with the UN.

**Jennifer Chase.** She read an early version of this book that inspired her to think about business a little differently. That feedback kept me going to finish writing the book and realize that it had value. Thanks, Jen!

**The Dallas Entrepreneur Center (DEC).** During my time volunteering at the DEC, I leaned the value of people and teamwork and discovered that business is really about conversations and connections between people. My experiences there has had a profound impact on my perspective of business.

**The faculty, the staff, and my classmates at IE University in Madrid for the Executive Master program in corporate communications (2018).** I had a number of gaps in my knowledge about corporate communications, research and measurement, and branding, but that changed after I completed the program. I received the formal education I was hoping to receive. I learned so much from the professors and my classmates. From some professors, I learned more about business. From others, how to better communicate to an executive. The best part of my education came from my classmates, from whom I learned what it meant to work with a true global team. By this I mean a team that develops its own culture based on the personality of the people in the team, not a corporate culture loosely defined by the company's home country. I am very thankful and grateful to have had such a memorable experience. Without it, I couldn't have written this book.

**All of my friends, colleagues, and extended family.** Again, there are too many to include without excluding important influencers. So many supported my work, read my book, and gave me the feedback I needed to finish it. I appreciate you all!

# Table of Contents

**Why I Wrote This Book............................................................ 1**

**Introduction | Automation by Any Other Name........... 13**

**Chapter 1 | Automation Paved the Way for Better Customer Relationships ...................................................... 36**

Conversations. Listening. Empathy. Engagement. Compassion. Relationships. ............................................................38

It's All Perspective ..........................................................................44

Focus on Relationships, Rather than Profits, as the Business Result.........................................................................47

Time to Look at Business Differently ....................................................51

My Personal Experience with This Idea .................................................56

**Chapter 2 | Vision: What Is the Value You Provide? .... 59**

Vision and Mission Statement Examples................................................61

Outline the Unique Customer Value.......................................................71

Define How Business Will Change the World and Create a Community......................................................................78

How Do You Know Your Destination if You Don't Have a Vision?.... 84

Inspire Improved Employee and Customer Behavior...........................87

Provide Meaning for Customers and Employees, or Provide the Why .... 93
Conclusion .... 102

**Chapter 3 | Brand: How You Communicate the Experience .... 105**
Brand: The Humanizing Element of a Company .... 107
The Experience of a Brand at All Ages .... 117
When a Brand Intertwines with Celebrity Executive Personality .... 118
Conclusion .... 127

**Chapter 4 | Plan: Activities Showing How You Provide Value .... 131**
The Role of Operations in Creating Memorable Customer Experiences .... 134
Agile: Designed to Improve Customer Experiences .... 142
Agile's Manufacturing Counterpart: Lean (or Just-in-Time Manufacturing) .... 151
Design Thinking .... 160
Sustainability Improves Customer Experiences through Transparency .... 169
Why Understanding People's Motivation Matters with Automation .... 185
Conclusion .... 190

**Chapter 5 | People: The Community, Making the Vision a Reality .... 193**
The Power of Employees: Interpersonal Relationships and the Value Employees Provide .... 198
Impacts of Company Culture .... 224
Accountability: The Agreement Experience .... 227
Corporate-Level KPIs Selected to Define Success Consistently across the Company .... 237

How a Culture Responds to Change....239
Curiosity: Identifying Problems and Situations....240
Creativity: Solving Problems....242
Conclusion....245

**Chapter 6 | Customers....248**
What's Old Is New Again....249
Employees vs. Customers....253
Research: Part of a Dialogue Whereby Sometimes You Need to Read Between the Lines....256
Product Adoption through the Familiar....258
Make Every Interaction an Opportunity to Get to Know the Customer....262
A Customer Journey, a Customer Relationship Lifecycle, or Both?....263
Why the Customer Relationship Lifecycle for Businesses?....272
Customer Relationships Begin in Various Ways....312
The Ultimate Ingredient for a Great Customer Experience: Trust....319
Accountability in Agreements....320
Mutual Respect....324
Conclusion....334

**Chapter 7 | Relationships Bring Revenue....337**
An Overview of Metrics by Programs and Tactics....339
Relationship Roles....352
Identifying KPIs that Map to Your Relationship Values....354
Engagement....356
Loyalty....362
Accountability....375
Public Relations Metrics Can Be Underrated....378
Brand and Reputation....380
How Revenue and Relationships Come Together....383
Conclusion....388

Chapter 8 | Conclusion .......... 391

Epilogue | Conversations: Not Just for Humans Anymore .......... 398

Chapter Notes .......... 411

Bibliography .......... 428

About Mary Brodie .......... 444

# Why I Wrote This Book

I didn't plan to write a book. Actually, I wanted to write a 10-page white paper to generate leads for my company, Gearmark. After a year of personal growth, my business model was no longer aligning with my personal goals and needed to change. I got a second advanced degree, did more strategic client work, provided leadership advice, and experienced many relationship shifts. I was in a new place and needed to work on different types of projects. After much consideration, I decided that Gearmark should work with larger companies in a more strategic capacity. That meant I needed to establish it as a thought leader. And writing a white paper is typically a great first step in that direction.

The white paper was going to outline the business issues that prevented companies from creating engaging customer experiences. I can't begin to tell you how many times I started a user experience project and later discovered that the real business problem to solve was completely different. A challenged user experience was often a symptom of other problems. I noticed how organizational, brand, or operational issues were driving the need for an improved customer or user experience. To help these companies, I would refine internal processes, help improve team dynamics, provide input to database improvements, or spark a brand refresh project in addition to the user experience work I was hired to do. The real work that needed to be done was usually business-related rather than related to building a great interface or software.

During the early years of web development (from 1995 to 2005), there seemed to be a misunderstanding of what automation really was. Professionals learned the hard way that it included far more than moving spreadsheets to databases or developing a website for ecommerce. You were reproducing your offline process in a computer system. If your offline process was ineffective, then it would be difficult, if not impossible, to replicate it digitally. It's only when you work on automating systems that you truly discover what's broken. People have a lot of power to make broken processes effective through conversations and collaboration.

As I worked on the user experience portion of the automation, I would escalate such issues because they interfered with creating a simple, clear, usable website or app. I figured users would eventually see what I was noticing—process gaps, inaccessible data, or inconsistent communications—unless we fixed the problems. Unfortunately, the employee conversations that served as the glue to keep challenged processes together couldn't be automated. Computers don't know how to create workarounds to get a job done unless that's in their programming. We would have to identify those workarounds and fix them with the intention of automating them. This became one of the most challenging tasks. We don't realize how many details need to be considered for effective automation. Conversations are easy. Documenting the decisions needed for automation is not.

As an example, let's say a customer calls your support or service team to resolve a complicated issue over the phone. A service agent can easily find a way to buy more time to find a solution to a difficult problem. An app or chatbot most likely won't spin that story to a caller because they don't have the appropriate information available for that type of response. When we automate such situations, we consider what should ideally happen. Then we implement that process in the call center, refine it based on feedback from its daily use, and later automate it so the app or chatbot can provide an appropriate response with the right information. Effective automation always starts with great real-world processes that solve issues. That human conversation element, the story to buy time, isn't part of that solution.

This is why I wonder if we are more forgiving of humans claiming that data isn't available than computers. One reason may be because subconsciously, we know people are fallible, while computers are presenting available information based on their programming. We may hear from a human that they don't know the answer, they can't find it in the computer, or another plausible-sounding excuse. We'll dismiss it as "human error." However, if we hear similar excuses from a computer interface, we don't believe it because we assume that the data must be "in there, somewhere." We'll believe that something, possibly the programming, isn't allowing it to be seen by the user. And if it's customer data, that's problematic because they feel they have a right to see their information (justifiably so). We subconsciously believe that the computer must know all when, ironically, it is the humans who program the computers and tell them what to display. Employees have the ultimate control to define digital experiences by determining which data points a customer can access.

Another side effect of the rise of the Internet, its adoption in everyday life, and automation, is that customers are becoming more active participants of a company's ecosystem and community. Customers can now experience your company in ways never previously considered through social media, the web, online chat, and apps. Rather than designated spokespeople in marketing, sales, and customer support and service representing your company's interest when communicating to customers, customers can go online and directly access information about your company when they want. They only contact you if they find discrepancies between what they found online and what they understand to be true. In this world, there are fewer opportunities to smooth over a story and resolve customer issues. This means that companies are no longer the sole owner of their message to the world, broadcasting to the masses. They co-create and share their messages with their customers, encouraging customers to share their stories too, all the while building a brand and community with them.

What hasn't changed with the rise of the Internet and automation is the need to understand your customers better. For years, customer researchers tried to understand their customers' needs and belief systems to sell more to them. Part of the job of those middlemen and spokespeople was to understand who their customers were, communicate with them, and build a relationship with them. But their roles shifted with the rise of the Internet and automation. Customers could access the information they needed on their own and didn't need human guidance to build a relationship. Over time, companies gathered information directly from digital experiences to understand customer choices. They encouraged customers to access the company through the phone, in person, or online. This opened direct communication, and a relationship, between customers and company employees so subject matter experts were able to answer more in-depth product and service questions. Why get an answer from a middleman when you can hear a response direct from the source? Why build a relationship with a middleman when you can build a direct relationship with the company?

The job of marketing, sales, and support/service has been slowly complemented through automation on websites and apps. We placed marketing information on websites, created forms to qualify leads, created mini-apps to complete operations, and developed support and partner portals to help communicate with those audiences. But as we developed these apps and sites, we quickly learned that the business didn't really know who their customers were and how they accessed or used that information. We discovered that users had a difficult time navigating apps and websites because they didn't see the company and its processes as the company understood them. There was a perception gap, and it was highly unlikely that customers would change their views to suit the company. Companies had to communicate to customers in their language if they wanted to be understood. And the only way for a company to understand their customer's language was to listen to them and understand how they communicated.

Most of the marketing information that companies had about their customers at that time was limited to demographic data. To develop a great app or website, that wasn't enough. User experience (UX) teams needed psychographic information about customer needs, desires, motivations, and thoughts. To access such information, UX teams did their own research to create personas and completed usability studies to understand how people were using the sites and products. Looking back, this response was short-sighted and not strategic. If I were an executive hearing that marketing didn't provide enough customer information to the development teams, I would have seen that as a critical problem. It illustrated that marketing didn't understand the motivations, wants, and needs of customers. They understood their customers as a group, but not as individual people.

As previously stated, understanding the customer has always been a vital aspect of business. Even in the early days of trade, merchants always knew what types of objects or materials their customers would purchase. Consumer products companies valued access to customer information so they could better meet customer needs with new products and services. Sadly, not all industries followed their lead. They forgot that their customers were people, and instead focused on satisfying different stakeholders: investors, shareholders, executives, and boards. These are vocal groups with high demands to achieve results. With such pressures, it's easy to forget that the customer is the real boss of any business. Let's face it: If customers don't like your product and don't buy it, then you don't have a business.

The harsh lesson that companies are learning through this digital automation process is that they sell to individual people, who have feelings, emotions, thoughts, and opinions. The sale is the result of a relationship with them. You can't force people to buy anything, but you can get them to like your company, recommend it to friends, and find a way to include it in their lives.

This lesson has evolved into a revolution in marketing, sales, support, and product design and development. These departments are merging together to become "customer experience," or simply "experience." How a customer experiences a company is related to how a customer perceives it through its communications and activities, including the product. The perception generated through the customer's experience is directly related to the customer's relationship with that company. Sales teams understand that the customer relationship is vital to make a sale and that a great customer relationship is the result of great customer experiences. Although the role of CXO is emerging as a key executive role, it should have been established long ago during the early stages of automation. Marketing involves more than convincing people to talk to sales and buy. Product teams need feedback from sales, support/service and customer insights from marketing to create the next innovation. Sales teams manage the relationship with customers as people and are ineffective if they don't work with marketing and product to access information and provide feedback. And customer service and support have always been the quarterback to resolve problems that fall through the cracks, collaborating with the other teams to make or break a customer experience, and, ultimately, a customer's relationship with a company.

Over the years, I observed companies sabotaging their success by creating sub-par customer experiences. Many of these companies shared similar organizational problems. I also saw companies create wonderful experiences because they didn't have these problems or managed to avoid them. Or there was a mixture in-between. But companies always had a pattern of issues and challenges that prevented them from creating amazing customer experiences.

Often in these challenged companies, the employees knew something was wrong. However, when you are in a difficult situation, it's hard to see what's really happening and easy to believe that you are experiencing a unique, isolated problem. No company is experiencing any of the problems I outline in this book alone. They are common management problems that exist across industries and markets.

Sometimes my clients asked me what I observed with other clients to gain perspective about their situations. This is a very courageous question to ask because you are admitting that you have a problem that you need to fix. When I told them that they weren't unique and other companies suffered from similar challenges, they always felt comforted knowing that they weren't alone. It created solidarity to understand that all companies are on a quest together to improve customer experiences. It's a united mission, even among competitors.

In this book, I wanted to share these insights with company leaders for two reasons:

- To help them feel comforted that their companies didn't have unique problems and
- To help them understand the impact of these issues on their organization and customer experiences

I figured that if they understood the issues and their implications, companies could make different decisions and choices, not just for themselves and their employees, but their customers.

Of course, the next question many of my clients asked me was, "Well, how do we fix this? How did they fix it?"

That was always a difficult yet important question that I often couldn't answer. Some companies didn't fix their problems and let them continue. Some companies may have shared the same issue, plus or minus five more, adding complexity to their situation. Sometimes the complexity created a necessity to resolve all problems at once or they decided to prioritize them to solve them sequentially. Sometimes, the root problem was one issue; sometimes, a collection of problems. It really depended on the company and its culture, products, and values. There is no single solution to fix these issues besides the executive teams and senior leaders collaborating to improve their companies, often by having a vision for how the company should transform their industry, if not the world. Employees can always highlight issues and make adjustments to day-to-day operations, but it's difficult for them to make the type of last change necessary for creating memorable customer experiences. A single employee or a team can only take change initiatives so far. For example, a marketing specialist in a large global corporation doesn't have the reach or influence to update a vision or mission statement, revise the brand, or create a new action plan for the company. This person can help a group improve, but they can't change a brand or culture alone. And they most definitely can't lead the charge to create a vision or mission statement by themselves.

That's why, while writing this book, I didn't feel that it was my place to tell readers how to solve their problems in their organizations. There are too many variables to solve strategic challenges, including a company's culture, teams and people, leadership, products, brand, services, and operations. Each company can be so different in how it defines problems and solves them that each requires a unique solution. I figured it would be more helpful for readers to identify an issue, understand the impact of it on their organization in relation to their customer experiences, and if possible, get inspired to fix that issue to ultimately improve customer relationships.

It's easy to see how the intention for a 10-page white paper grew to a book. The topics to cover in this piece expanded until I decided to outline:

- The impact of automation on businesses and customers,
- The ongoing importance of customer relationships, and
- The relationship between customer relationships and revenue.

Ironically, the business structure I outline to help companies create great customer experiences was the structure that existed long ago. Small, successful local businesses always knew their customers well and considered their needs in company decisions. As businesses grew into global organizations larger than most small cities, the direct connection between companies and customers dissolved. Middlemen filled the gaps. But everything changed again when business automation (especially marketing and sales automation) brought employees and customers closer together.

Relationships are built through shared experiences and information. With the rise of digital experiences, it became easier to track and observe customer activity. From that customer activity, a company could gather information about their customers and get to know them as individuals or as a customer segment, en masse. We are discovering that digital experiences can provide the information necessary to initially automate relationship building.

Business isn't just about numbers and revenue. It's about relationships. Somehow, that perception got lost along the way. We need to bring that back to business to be successful—and some companies already have. Companies like Apple, Airbnb, Uber, and Google have discovered that if you create great customer experiences, you will build solid customer relationships, which will increase your revenue. That's why we see them as the model digital businesses. And that's how your company can emerge as a model company as well.

INTRODUCTION

# Automation by Any Other Name

*Digital transformation. Modernization. Artificial intelligence. Big data. Algorithms.*

All of these words have different implications depending on how they are used in conversation. But they all have the same basic definition: automation.

Automation has always been an ongoing company activity, with no clear start or end date. The rise of the Internet and the adoption of mobile devices made computing and automation ubiquitous. We sometimes associate automation with installing a database or a customer relationship management (CRM) or enterprise resource planning (ERP) system. However, automation could be as simple as storing data in an Excel spreadsheet or sharing files with team members using Box.com or Dropbox.

Business teams sometimes believe that technology upgrades are a set of activities completed within a finite time frame. Once complete, the business is considered to be "modernized" or "digitally transformed" for the next "many" years. Today, all businesses support automation to the point that most are considered to be technology companies. Ironically, it isn't always straightforward for a technology company to get the necessary funding for upgrades. If you want to finance an upgrade, you may need to use the right terminology to describe the idea to your executive team or board. Often you can't use the word *automation* because, to them, that activity is complete. You need to be more specific about anticipated results and outcomes.

You may describe updating your organization's technology and systems as "modernization." Or you may describe updating your product-related systems and customer experiences as "digital transformation." If you are trying to gain insights from your data, you may describe your initiatives as a combination of "artificial intelligence" and "big data" activities. In all cases, the proposal must include a revenue number, or savings objective, to achieve as a result of the efforts. If the conversations with leadership go well, you implement the solution. If not, you wait until next year and hope that your competition doesn't complete their update first so they get an edge and make your company's approach outdated.

Technology companies, product teams, and IT departments typically see automation as an ongoing process. There are always new technologies to include in your company's infrastructure to improve employee productivity, accuracy, or to streamline communications and processes. And with the number of disruptive technologies emerging, there are always a handful of companies each quarter with innovations mature enough for commercial use. The Gartner Hype Cycle helps us discover where various technologies are in the maturity curve. For example, augmented reality and virtual reality (AR/VR) recently surprised us by approaching readiness for consumer use. Other innovations that we may have assumed were more mature, like AI, needed more development. But here's what's always true about the Gartner Hype Cycle: Innovation is ongoing and doesn't stop.

**A Brief History of Automation**

From my perspective, automation started with two core technologies:

- The abacus to help humans more accurately compute financial transactions
- Writing to track business and trade finances (AKA record-keeping)

Manual addition and subtraction and mental record-keeping left room for human error. People make careless mistakes when quickly computing arithmetic problems. And people don't always remember facts and agreements correctly. Memories aren't simply based on factual recollections but feelings and emotions, which can alter perceptions of an event or situation. Recording events as they occur, real-time, remedies reminiscence. These two innovations—abacus and writing—were the first steps in removing human fallibility from interactions, resulting in faster, more accurate, and therefore trustworthy, transactions.

Innovations in these areas continued throughout history, resulting in one of the more well-known productivity and record-keeping inventions of the modern era: the punch card computer. Originally developed in the 1880s by Herman Hollerith, later founder of IBM, it was used for the 1890 US Census.[1] Punch cards enabled that project to be completed three years ahead of schedule, saving millions of dollars.[2,3] Its use continued well into the 1970s as a standard of record-keeping and calculation for financial services, credit cards, and business records. Notable historic punch card projects ranged from positive humanitarian projects, like managing the Social Security program in the 1930s, to managing business activities in retail stores like Macy's and Lerner's or in the military's US Navy Medical Supply Office, to nefarious activities, like tracking individuals in the Nazi concentration camps.[4,5]

Punch card processing was promising, but computing's ultimate success was tied to hardware innovations to reduce equipment size and increase transaction speed to support more complicated processes. As vacuum tubes transitioned to transistors, viable digital technologies became commonplace. Moore's Law, or the observation that the number of transistors in a dense integrated circuit doubles about every two years, was introduced and allowed computing to mature.[6] Computers shrank from the size of several rooms to the size and weight of a notebook. The cost went from thousands to a few hundred dollars with a processing speed that produced almost immediate computational results. But computing improvements didn't stop there. The ultimate advancement for computing affordability and accessibility was the simultaneous emergence of the smartphone and the Cloud. Now everyone could own a computer in the palm of their hand and leverage the computing power and storage of multi-site data centers through the Internet. This innovation made Moore's Law no longer applicable.[7]

Meanwhile, the Industrial Revolution introduced machines, assembly lines, and eventually robots to consistently increase manufacturing productivity and improve product quality. Automation was no longer limited to storing information, but included physical activity to save human strength and energy. This became the better-known side of automation that gradually brought us machines that can build a brick wall, create a concrete house, and sort mail.

In conjunction with computing processing speed, the Internet was the one last technical development that emerged to complete the business automation story. With it came the ability to transmit information and conduct communications long distances without the help of a mail system.

Telegraphs could transmit signals. Telephones could transmit voices. But the Internet could transmit written words.

DARPA (Defense Advanced Research Projects Agency) researchers created the Internet in 1973 while looking for a new communications protocol. Instead, they discovered a way to facilitate transporting written communications long distance.[8] Through the Internet, someone could send a message, or later email, immediately to the receiving party rather than a typing a memo and distributing it through the mail for delivery in days or sending it via fax for delivery in minutes. It revolutionized written communication.

At that time, the alternative real-time communication medium that was most accessible was the telephone. You could make a phone call to complete similar transactions like we do through email today, but unless a call is recorded, calls don't allow you to track agreements. Each person would need to record their side of the conversation through audio or in writing. If this didn't happen, a decision made over the phone could later be debated. Summary notes listing meeting conclusions, unless made real-time, may include some bias based on memories and emotions. This is why after a call, documentation would always need agreement by both sides of a conversation to confirm what was discussed. That's also why calls aren't always effective business tools. They help resolve emotionally charged issues because they help people communicate through their tone of voice, but there's benefit in the permanence and clarity of direct written communication, even if it is based on 1s and 0s.

In addition to its work purposes, email allowed real-time communication and connection between employees and customers. Employees and customers could have a real-time record of their communications and interactions including coming to agreement, building consensus, and confirming commitments. Email was the first medium for digital conversations through correspondence.

Alongside the rise of the Internet and email was the rise of the web, which allowed companies to communicate to prospective customers by posting information that could be viewed globally, 24/7. It's obvious today, but in the 1990s it was incredible to think that putting your company's communication on a website allowed you to reach a global audience with real-time, up-to-date information. People only needed web access to discover your company. Your store location or hours no longer mattered in attracting store visitors. With the web, your store was always accessible. Being listed on Yahoo was better than being in the Yellow Pages.

If business is based on conversations with purpose, and the web is a medium for automating communication (and conversations), then it logically followed that business operations could be automated via the web. The most established business model that was already automated via telephone and computer systems was retail commerce, which is most likely why stores went online first.[9]

A sale is a conversation between two people agreeing to conditions regarding an exchange of goods for money. Phone calls can't achieve a sale in the same way that you can in person or online because you need trust, records, and agreements to formalize a transaction. A phone call also doesn't allow you to see a picture of what you want to buy. You need another medium, typically print, to support the sale. In the past, this was achieved by customers trusting that the catalog brand they were ordering from adequately represented its inventory.

Besides not fully understanding what you are ordering, there was an additional gap in phone sales: you can't get a copy of a receipt. After a sale, the company would need to mail a receipt for follow-up. The salesperson on the phone could tell you a delivery date, but there is no record of that unless the call is recorded by you or the company sends you that in writing. Catalog phone sales were popular before the web, but limited. And it is easy to understand why. But it is also easy to understand why the web first innovated and automated retail catalog operations. The catalog-phone store process was ready to model digitally.

These digital communications provided real-time records for trusted transactions that could be used as customer recourse for unfortunate sales circumstances, such as a challenging delivery or poor product quality. That receipt—the record for the buyer—is vital in the transaction process as proof of purchase and to set customer expectations. Along with website photos, such documentation created a type of accountability for the seller to deliver what was promised. And with a buyer rating system to validate the transaction and provide insights into accountability (like the one on eBay, TRUSTe, or the Better Business Bureau), this solidified trust. In turn, this trust allowed online purchasing to become more convenient than an in-store or phone experience. You could shop from your computer at home (and later from the phone in the palm of your hand), knowing that what you were seeing online what was you would be receiving once purchased.

### The Unintended Effects of Automation: Improved Customer Relationships

Automation through computing and robotics reduced the physical and mental burden on humans to complete repetitive tasks. The direct business results of these efforts included:

- Employee accuracy,
- Higher-quality product, and
- Increased productivity.

But there were unintended and unexpected side effects from automation that benefitted customer relationships and built trust.

**First, automation allowed employees to more effectively communicate company activities to each other.** (This is indirectly related to customer relationships, due to its results.) Once a company grows beyond two to three employees, word-of-mouth communications fail. It's difficult to track complex activity among many employees without record-keeping and maintaining a single "source of truth." The alternative is for everyone to maintain their own understanding of company projects. This requires colleagues to constantly check-in with each other for updated information. It's a cumbersome approach that discourages self-service and produces too many dependencies to understand what's happening in any situation. One dependency is opinions and memories, both based on people's feelings and emotions. A disgruntled employee may perceive a situation as a disaster whereas a happy employee could see a situation as a small inconvenience. The truth could lie somewhere in the middle. There may be factual evidence to support a perspective, but emotional understandings don't always help resolve company issues in a methodical, unbiased way.

Record-keeping removes emotions from historical understanding by recording facts. This improves information accuracy, which also improves consistency and creates this single trusted "source of truth." Employees can then work from facts rather than assumptions or a patchwork quilt of opinions. This increases employee confidence in their work, as well as product quality, consistency, and speed to complete tasks. Less time is spent validating or discovering information. Such wins encourage employees to continue recording their work activities to share their knowledge and multiplying efficiency and effectiveness gains over time.

**Second, because automation supports more effective internal communication, your company can develop more trusting customer relationships through consistent and accurate communications and improved accountability.** Trust is an integral component of successful relationships, often built through consistent accountability and mutual respect. Automation has the greatest impact on accountability. Respect is built through the honesty and truth that comes from accurately communicating facts during record-keeping.

Being accountable means that you are delivering on a promise to deliver value to customers or meet customer commitments. The most straightforward example of accountability using current automation approaches is online shopping, in which product photos and descriptions on a site match what is delivered to a customer. The photos set customer expectations for what they will receive when they exchange money for those goods. If the customer receives what the photo promised in the time line cited, that's a successful sale. If the customer's expectations don't match what they receive or when, then the company is perceived as not being accountable for the promises they made during their transaction and trust is lost. As are future sales.

Some accountability also lies in legal and transaction processes. Digital signatures and document scans using cell phone cameras have recently become acceptable, allowing customers and companies to make binding commitments online and offline easily. Payment tools like credit cards, PayPal, and automated purchase order processes allow more varied digital transactions to financially confirm agreements. Brand agreements can help streamline processes between complementary companies to improve accountability and operations, increasing trust. For example, the Amazon partnership with UPS has made returns easier. A customer can express intent to return an item on Amazon's site and then bring the item to a UPS store for processing and packaging. UPS handles the rest. The partnership extends the Amazon brand experience to UPS, and vice versa. As automation improves, there is a greater variety of digital transactions available that removes the in-person element previously required to maintain trust and accountability. Add to that complementary brands partnering, and companies can further extend their operations, capabilities, trust, and accountability.

Customers trust companies that consistently solve customer problems, produce quality product, have consistent behaviors, are responsible (do what they say they are going to do), and create accountable communications. Some examples:

- If you charge a fair price and your invoices are logical, customers will work with you again because they know you are transparent and honest.
- If customers know that you will deliver on your promises, then you are building a reliable connection to encourage additional transactions.
- If you consistently communicate the truth during your interactions, the customer wouldn't question what you claim because they don't see a need for you to lie to them.

- And if you include third parties in the process, the trust all brands bring to the experience will further confirm that customer perception of accountability through the partnerships.

Leveraging these ideas help us automating trust. We are seeing it happening—and succeeding.

**Trust online is also built through respect by understanding the customer's perspective.** It's hard to achieve this on a scale of hundreds, thousands, or millions of customers without automation. Today it seems second nature, but tracking how customers interact with your business not only gives it an edge, but it provides you with deep knowledge of who they are, and help you understand them as if they were a close friend. Friends share stories and experiences that you can later recall through shared memories. By tracking your customer interactions, you are also keeping a record of the memories they made with your company and sharing them with other employees in your organization. All employees have an easier way to understand the relationship this way. The benefits of this are tremendous:

- You can better support their purchase if a problem develops and it requires a recall or maintenance. You understand their situation based on their purchase history.
- You can better communicate to them through marketing activities, anticipating what they like and don't like based on their interaction history and transactions.
- You get to know who they are as people, how they respond in different situations with your company. You can learn

what can give them joy and satisfaction through various platforms, like their responses to the site and social media posts.

It's almost as if automation today supports the connection aspects of the "mom and pop" business, enabling you to respect your customer more because you can more easily understand their situation and motivations. Automation allows you to see your customers as people.

We often refer to the "mom and pop" business as the defining standard of customer relationships and connections. Why? They treat you as a respected friend by connecting through memories from shared experiences. For example, in a "mom and pop" business, one of the owners may ask how you liked that new soda you purchased the other day. Or remind you how that cake is just like what your mom picks up for your birthday every year. Or ask about your new car. Or even see you at church or a community event and just say hello. You may have felt close to them because they knew you: They remembered what you purchased, the stories you shared, or your preferences, and they may have tried to find ways to stay connected. Often, such business owners become friends with their customers because they consider their customers' best interests for more than a sale. They would recommend products that may help you or your family in a tough situation or tell you the best times to come to the store because you will be better able to find parking. I have countless stories of how my connections at small businesses keep me returning—and not just to buy great products. I'm sure you do as well. The connections and relationships the owners and employees in these stores make with customers matter, sometimes more than the products. The more personal the connection, the more likely you are to return. And not just return to buy a product.

Today, we can leverage automation tools to track and record relationship-building activities, like customer site activity, to discover patterns and preferences. By sharing such customer memories with employees across your organization, you can achieve a similar result as you would with a close friend. We could say that this type of automation has evolved into personalization.

Personalization emerged as an automated way to build a relationship with a customer. It's often misunderstood, but personalization technologies anticipate customer needs based on past behaviors and preferences of similar customers. The personalization system may appear to make the right selection for you, but the algorithms leverage purchase and behavior trends of thousands of people who share similar behaviors, purchase similar products, or have similar interests. But it's not a simple one-to-one mapping. Your behavior pattern may overlap with multiple groups. Based on the actions of others similar to you, the system can predict the next few options you may likely take. So a company could confirm with a customer that yes, you purchased our product, we saw you at the trade show booth and recorded that in our CRM, and we know that you just downloaded the white paper, so we will now show you this white paper next because other people who exhibited similar behavior to you found this paper helpful.

There's an additional benefit of personalization technologies—they demonstrate to a customer that you are listening to their actions and you can offer them the best next step solution to improve their lives. With the customer insights and knowledge your company has based on mass scale, you can do more than provide them with potential solutions to their problems. Through predictive technologies, you can anticipate their needs. Additionally, you can guide them on how to interact with you better in the future by encouraging them to use features like online chat or call for a better experience. Not all interactions can be automated; some require a direct connection. But knowing what works best with specific audiences can improve the relationship building process.

The accuracy of the information you have about your customers is vital to respect them, be accountable, and ultimately develop trust. It's embarrassing to make assumptions about someone, especially a customer, based on inaccurate information. It shows that you aren't listening. One personal experience of a company not using the data available to them is when my car had to get significant repairs six months after I purchased it. It was a certified pre-owned MINI Cooper. The dealer told me that I didn't buy it at that dealership when my original warranty paperwork was attached to the bill. Not only was it embarrassing for them to deny it, but it communicated to me that they didn't want to take responsibility for selling me the car in the first place. They later corrected the error, but the event made them seem unaccountable at the time, which resulted in my decreased trust in that dealership. They later redeemed themselves so I trust them completely, but at the time I wondered if the purchase with them was the right decision.

Every business has a risk determining how information that it collects could be used:

- To understand customer motivations,
- To know and use (but not repeat) to help a conversation progress, and
- To be collected and the knowledge that this information exists shared with the customer.

There are times when you don't completely understand the motivation behind a customer action, and it's not your business to know. All businesses need to develop discretion regarding data collection to avoid being the "big brother" and cause a customer to feel violated. This destroys trust. Customer activity is a communication method that provides feedback to a company, but not all customer activity tells you about who they *really* are. Some activity may be done on behalf of someone else or based in pure curiosity, not the desire to solve a problem. Some examples include searches for sex toys, "edibles," or even luxury goods like high-end fashion, cars, or jewelry. Someone could be configuring a luxury car with no intention to buy, only to dream. Every business needs to consider this factor. It's like the teen buying condoms in a "mom and pop" business. The condoms may be for that teen, for his friend, or for a sex education class discussion. The business doesn't know, and it's not their business to share or use that information, even with the parents. This is why privacy for business transactions is important and not all data communicates purchase intent or something specific about the customer.

As a more common example, many people will search for the costs of a trip to Las Vegas but will never book because it is a dream trip. So showing Las Vegas in personalization preferences may be a fool's errand because it most likely is not part of that user's true interest. Same with outlier searches that fall outside of a customer's search pattern. They may not represent a customer's true interest. But such data provides an opportunity to help a company automate discretion in a customer relationship. Today, this is a current gap because there are many factors to consider, even though discretion builds almost immediate customer trust for repeat business.

**A third benefit of automation is the ability to abstract individual information gathered so you can understand your customers as large groups.** Communicating with each customer individually is important, but if you have millions of customers, it may be challenging to communicate with everyone using individualized, personal messaging. As we know, personalization is often based on the patterns of thousands of customers and their transactions and activities. A single customer often represents the intersection of many groups. Understanding how these customer groups think and act can help your company understand customer trends and gain insights into their motivations. From this, a company can determine what's best to offer customers. But a company can only reach this point by listening to customer actions.

Customers communicate to companies directly and through an activity feedback loop recorded through metrics and results. That's why we should approach them with curiosity: It's a way for us to listen. And sometimes in business we get so focused on understanding how we can increase the bottom line, or we want to prove that we were right in that last report or recommendation, that we miss what our customers are really telling us in data.

We may overlook trends that may not fit our narratives or contradict our understanding of our customers. We may dismiss outlier data as a fluke because it doesn't support the main story that we or our managers want to see. But in doing this, we miss key insights that could increase connection and strengthen our relationship with them.

We have a luxury through automation that businesses never had regarding customer relationships: the ability to gather everyone's data and understand who our customers are at macro and micro levels. It's an opportunity that we shouldn't waste.

**The fourth unexpected and unintended consequence of automation was businesses placing an increased value on satisfying customer needs by creating digital experiences that they could use.** Software effectiveness wasn't always based on its usability. Often, it was based on what was possible technically. Keyboard commands ruled the computing world until Apple developed the 16-bit color monitor and the LISA computer. The LISA computer was innovative at its time because it was one of the first "affordable" consumer computers that offered a graphic interface.[10] No longer was a computer experience driven solely by commands or function-digit keys. A user only needed to select an item with his mouse and keep going. Later, Microsoft Windows took graphic interfaces mainstream on the PC, improving ease of use. This made computing more accessible for people.

But nothing transformed computer interfaces as much as the world wide web.

In addition to the web being used as a communications tool or ecommerce platform, we realized that the web was technically a new platform for software, and user experience was born. The web made the idea of software and automation accessible to any business with a developer and Internet access. Employees could use web apps internally for work and customers had the ability to interact directly with a business on its public site.

This opened a conversation for customer-centric thinking in the digital world that could be divided into two movements:

- Design Thinking
- Agile Methodologies

Design Thinking is a methodology that focuses on what "future customers really want instead of relying only on historical data or making risky bets based on instinct instead of evidence."[11] Tim Brown, CEO of IDEO, described it best:

> *Design thinking is a human-centered approach to innovation that draws from the designer's toolkit to integrate the needs of people, the possibilities of technology, and the requirements for business success.*[12]

This idea continues to drive web innovations.

In many ways, Design Thinking held businesses accountable to their customers. It drove a different conversation for the business, asking: From a customer-centric perspective, does the business requirement describe a set of functionality that benefits the customer? Or the business? Hopefully, it's both.

A new perspective of the customer emerged with this approach: Why not create what will benefit customers most, especially if they are the ones paying your company money to buy your product and covering your bills?

This balance of power and business accountability extended to development teams. With the adoption of the Internet, there was a need to produce high-quality custom software faster. Developers realized that if they produced not what the ***business wanted*** but what the ***users needed***, then they would be more productive. When businesses defined software requirements using Waterfall Methodology, they contained many hopes and dreams, but the time lines required to turn those requirements into software weren't realistic. Products were often partially developed to meet a deadline, containing fewer features than necessary. The developers just didn't have the time to make those visions reality. They needed the business to prioritize what the customer really needed to be successful. Sometimes the business knew; sometimes the business needed to research what would help the customer most. By developing what the customer needed, developers could accelerate their work and focus on developing the most important features that would allow them to be productive. That's why Agile methodologies gained wide adoption.

Over the years, business methodologies have been shifting toward customer- and employee-centric approaches. I like to think of them as being people-focused. You could also consider them community-focused because they bring people together, united by a common purpose. Through Design Thinking, people come together to create a product that customers will love. Through Agile, a team comes together to create a digital product that will help a customer. There are two other methodologies that follow this system: Lean and Sustainability.

Lean brings teams together on the assembly line to develop processes that increase customer value. Sustainable approaches allow teams to repeat and reproduce activities regularly over a long time, reducing waste and optimizing resources so you don't use more than necessary. Like Agile and Design Thinking, these methodologies have been seeing increased adoption. You could consider them all cousins. Lean and Sustainability are methodologies typically used to produce hard products; Agile can be used for digital products; and Design Thinking used for all products and services.

What do they all share in common?

- They encourage teams to create products and services that the customer wants, delivering them when needed.
- Although the customers were king, employees emerged as a type of king as well. All of the methodologies included approaches, tenets, and belief systems that ensured teams were respected for their knowledge and time. An individual's time emerged as a valuable commodity when achieving efficiency. This is why a key question emerged from these methodologies: How could an individual (or other resource) contribute optimally in an eight-hour day?

- Companies became an ecosystem—a network of customers, employees, and various stakeholder companies—as well as part of a global network. Their impact reached not only employees, but local communities, the environment, and governments.

In the digital world, user experience started as a way to enable web transactions to be experienced with simplicity and make business processes understandable to customers. As the customer came back into the business ecosystem, its strategic sibling, customer experience, struggled to gain prominence. Customer experience is now emerging as a discipline because customer engagement is the next ingredient for automating businesses (record-keeping and communication) to encourage growth. In many ways, what is old is new again, because what made businesses great is what is needed for a business to grow:

- Understanding your customer
- Involving them in your activities
- Connecting with them emotionally, as people

All with the intent of building a relationship with them.

Modern automation approaches, such as digital transformation, modernization, and AI, benefit business by directly improving customer relationships. As we automate conversations and similar complex processes, we'll be deconstructing them to examine how they work, reconsider what we want to them achieve, and then determine how we can use them to improve employee productivity and allow customers to be more included in the business. Revenue is always a result of solid customer relationships. And ongoing automation updates will help us achieve that through more accurate data records, higher-quality products, and accountability. If we create approaches and tools to build great customer relationships, the revenue should follow.

CHAPTER 1

# Automation Paved the Way for Better Customer Relationships

We hear about successful companies that everyone wants to model and copy every day: Apple. Airbnb. Uber. Facebook and Instagram. Google. Bumble. Amazon. Dropbox.

They inspire us. We study them closely. We use their ideas and approaches in our own businesses with the intention of creating better companies and products.

They resemble what a traditionally successful business looks like in many ways. They earn high revenues, see amazing growth, and have a large customer base. But there is one exception that makes these companies stand out from the rest: Their customers love them and go to them first to solve their problems.

Most businesses today covet this, but they aren't quite sure how to get it for themselves.

Some reasons (or excuses) people use to explain why these companies succeed, and more traditional companies don't, include:

- They target and appeal to millennials or Gen Z.
- They have better social media, SEO, and content marketing programs.
- Their brand is emotionally engaging and they have great brand awareness campaigns.
- They're one of those pesky disruptor startups.
- They use Lean/Agile methodologies to get results fast.
- They do a great job with empathy (whatever that may mean).
- They incorporate Design Thinking (or another buzzword du jour) into their strategy.

**All of those reasons are valid, but none address the single reason why their customers love them: These companies interact with their customers directly.** Automation and digital systems enabled companies to directly connect with purchasers, or customers, removing the middleman (distributors, resellers, even salespeople). This drastically changed how companies reached, contacted, and engaged customers. New companies emerged, resetting expectations and quality standards by using convenience and connection to solve complicated communications and transaction problems.

**These companies simplified life.** Without the middlemen, they were able to streamline information exchanges and transactions, further simplifying customer experiences.

Through hyper-transparency, they elevated customer expectations for how they can access information and experience services.

This movement made personalized and individually crafted customer experiences an inevitable next step for how companies interacted with customers. Companies are now able to take advantage of every customer touchpoint along a journey as an opportunity for the customer to interact with and experience the brand—and for the company to communicate with the customer, learn about them, and build a relationship. In a world of best practices to streamline transaction flow, these companies quickly realized that success lies in not what you do, but in how you do it. A transaction became not just an exchange of money for service but a type of conversation to gain information and build a relationship.

A **conversation** is an interaction between two entities that builds a relationship. A **transaction** is actually a type of conversation to gain information and, consequently, build a relationship.

## Conversations. Listening. Empathy. Engagement. Compassion. Relationships.

Once reserved for psychologists, these words now describe how businesses can be more customer-centric and provide great customer experiences. This isn't a new business trend. Companies have always been customer-centric, but for larger companies, their first-line customer contact was a defense shield that included staff (marketing, sales, customer service) or third-party partners (distributors, resellers)—those to whom I refer as "the middlemen." The middlemen acted as the face of the business, connecting to customers and protecting dutiful employees from the public. Their job extended to creating messaging and customer communications. Internally, departments like marketing, sales, and public relations were the envy of the company because they were allowed to talk to customers. They crafted carefully worded marketing collateral, sales scripts, and press releases, and they were specially trained in how to address the public. Customer service and support spent hours in training, learning how to use guidebooks and scripts during challenging calls to keep customers happy. Outside partners received communications from these internal teams and created their own to achieve the same. They were part of an extended sales and customer service force for the company.

With the rise of the Internet and automation, the need for distributors and resellers declined, unless they offered a service that could add value. Inside staff became the line of defense from customers for the company. And the work was overwhelming.

Customers were empowering themselves to interact directly with businesses not yet prepared to engage with them. Previously, these companies didn't have the knowledge of what they wanted from customers or how to best talk to them except through sales channels and call centers. Customers suddenly wanted to talk to experts to get solutions to their problems or talk to operations to resolve an issue directly. This change required a new approach for how leaders viewed their businesses.

Traditional "mom and pop" businesses are more closely related to the rising Internet company stars because they constantly researched their customers and maintained very close relationships with them. Remember going to the corner store? When I went, I always had a conversation with the owners, if they were available. They would notice what my family and I would purchase, ask if we'd be interested in trying something similar that was better, or just share a sample. In a few days, we'd return with feedback and input so they could carry it in their store. We definitely had more than a transactional relationship, since we gave them input into what their business should be. They had a number of data points for each us: They knew everyone in our families, what we liked for lunch, how we talked, and what we did for fun. Don't think they didn't use that information to develop a great customer relationship!

I frequent a French bakery in Dallas every few days to get a box of four morning breakfast treats and a cold-brew iced coffee for my drive home. Needless to say, they know me well. I also place special orders with them, like breakfast treats as holiday gifts and birthday cakes. They know what I like, what I don't like, and what I'll buy. Sometimes, they let me taste new products they are developing to see how I like them. (Who says "no" to cakes or pastries?) They probably know which monthly flavor they will choose during the tasting, but letting me give feedback and feel like an insider helps me feel like I'm part of their community. And that relationship keeps me coming back, choosing them all the time.

Many businesses struggle to be customer-focused mainly because they define success using metrics that highlight transactions, revenue, and information distribution. They are focused on the end result of business, that culmination of the journey: purchase and revenue. This is the traditional measure of a successful outcome of what is believed to be an established customer connection. But is it?

In the Mad Men advertising era, we believed that building brand awareness required widely distributed information through media ads. With the rise of content marketing, we followed a similar belief pattern—that providing the public with information that uses the right keywords would help readers find our company or product using a search engine or sharing content through social media. But this philosophy still missed the key factor that brought companies success: getting customers to love them. Some achieved it through great ad campaigns that were emotionally engaging; some through great products or services that solved a core customer problem. But there are companies that don't know how to do this or where to start. To achieve a goal, you need to target a metric to achieve. That's easy for revenue. But what are the tools and metrics you can use to measure relationship success? And even if you have that number, how can you measure a great relationship with your customers if you are overly focused on the bottom line? Which metric comes first? Or do both matter equally?

**Why Customers Matter in a Company's Operation**

- **They pay the bills.** Without customers in a company's ecosystem, a company won't earn revenue and it will be doomed to fail. And without revenue, companies can't pay the employees, keep the lights on, and pay the bills. Most likely, the shareholders will wonder what happened. **Customers are a key element of any company.** As an example, Facebook struggled for years to identify paying customers. You can have a product, you can have users, but you need someone who finds enough value in your products and services to pay for them. Sadly, Facebook's product became its users because identifying another type of customer proved difficult and a fee-based model may have dissuaded users from logging into the site. But I often wonder would that have happened if Facebook considered how they were going to monetize their value before they started their business. Facebook probably would have been a very different company.
- **Without customers, you are creating without receiving feedback.** The difference between artists and designers is that artists create to express themselves and designers solve a problem. The problem could be based on a challenge observed in communication, transportation, financial areas, healthcare, or any industry. In many ways, companies and product teams are like designers.

> They are solving problems. When you solve a problem for someone, you need to understand how they see and experience the problem, which we can do through research and testing. However, in most companies, employees often aren't solving new problems; they are creating solutions that are competing against existing solutions. And although you may approach your problem and solution differently than a competitor, customers have an expectation for what the product should be, mainly around industry best practices, baseline product, and parity. If those aren't met at a minimum, most likely, your product won't be used. Jeff Goins at *Fast Company* summarized this best: "People tend to evaluate their experiences of a product or service based on what's expected, so creators first need to understand how they're serving others' needs. But we can't stop there. Innovation begins with identifying people's expectations and ends with exceeding them."[13]

### *Today's Customer Feedback Indicates Success. But is that enough?*

The feedback we get today from customers could be through direct contact or through digital metrics. From there, we learn how to create a solution that better meets their needs.

That's why customers are a key element of a company's team. By customers expressing their needs to employees trained to gather requirements, these employees can identify solutions that will change their customer's lives. However, we often don't see customers that way and sometimes discount what they bring to a discussion, further separating them from the business. It is confusing why companies treat customers as a distant stakeholder even though they are contributing money toward the company's survival. Customers should always be at the heart of a company's community.

The best way to include customers in your company's community is to build relationships with them by winning their hearts. Automated transactions and information distribution aren't enough to capture customer attention and affection. Including customers in the company's business community makes them feel like they are contributors to something larger than themselves. This will encourage them to be part of the company to innovate, create, and build better solutions.

## It's All Perspective

What you measure is what you pay attention to, so if you continue to count leads, contacts, sales, and support calls, in a way you are saying that your company solely exists to create revenue. This indirectly devalues your product and your employees, highlighting only one result of the value you are providing customers. From another perspective, this highlights a value you are providing shareholders, not even customers.

Isn't it more fitting, and rewarding, to look at some key performance indicators (KPIs) that reflect the relationships between your employees and customers through the business? Wouldn't that be more helpful for you to understand what's happening with your business regarding your customer relationships and increase your revenue?

What if we apply the quote: "If a tree falls in a forest and no one is around to hear it, does it make a sound?" to products in the market: "If a product exists in the market, and you don't have a customer community to buy it, does it matter?"

According to Seth Godin, the most successful companies today started by solving a specific problem for a specific group of people. They created an experience for that particular customer and developed a relationship with them that turned profitable. By looking at their business from a slightly different perspective, they were able to rethink how they delivered value by revising their view of business and how they measured success. Through this process, they were able to find a better way to achieve revenue.

We may consider this to be a non-traditional approach, but in many ways it is supported by a business-school standard—Michael Porter's value chain.[14] From Porter's perspective,

> *Competitive advantage is a function of either providing comparable buyer value more efficiently than competitors (low cost), or performing activities at comparable cost but in unique ways that create more buyer value than competitors and, hence, command a premium price (differentiation). You win either by being cheaper or by being different (which*

*means being perceived by the customer as better or more relevant). There are no other ways.*[15]

The goal of value chain analysis is to optimize processes for decreased costs or to get a better valued product into customer hands. According to Porter, there are two groups of activities:

- **Primary**—five activities related to producing products and getting them into the hands of customers: operations, inbound and outbound logistics, services, marketing, and sales
- **Support**—four activities related to ensuring that the products get to market: HR, procurement, technologies, and infrastructure[16]

By documenting activities like these for analysis, business strategists can easily understand how a business operates and identify opportunities for improvements. Coincidentally, this is what businesses do when they are automating processes and why automation is a beneficial activity. To automate a process, you need to document it first so you can fully understand the dependencies and implications related to each step and then identify efficiencies. In a way, the automation process and digital transformation require that you perpetually work in Porter's value chain model, finding ways to increase efficiencies and bring more competitive and valuable products to market for customers. This passage from ***Investopedia*** best summarizes Porter's model: "If a company can create an advantage . . . through a value chain analysis, it captures a competitive advantage and increases its overall profit. To capture a competitive advantage, a company maps out its specific activities within the five generic value chain activities and looks for ways to create efficiencies."[17]

To connect this back to creating engaging customer experiences, what better way to create a competitive advantage than to put your customer at the center of your business ecosystem and create solutions specifically for them? That not only makes your company different and noteworthy, but ensures that how you solve your customer's problem cannot be reproduced. How your company solves their problem, your approaches, your thinking, and your views are unique to your company.

## Focus on Relationships, Rather than Profits, as the Business Result

**Value**, *noun.*

- Worth or quality as measured by a standard of equivalence.
- The material or monetary worth of something; the amount at which something may be estimated in terms of a medium of exchange, as money or goods, or some other similar standard.[18]

**Worth**, *noun.*

- Senses relating to monetary value.
- The material or monetary value of something; the amount at which something may be estimated in terms of a medium of exchange, such as money or goods.[19]

Value and worth have recursive definitions, which makes discussing either difficult. We falsely assume that they are related to money, especially regarding the measurement of value or worth, but money is only a small part of the purchase equation.

Customers purchase products because they have a high-priority problem that they need to solve.[20] They place value on a solution by determining how strongly they feel they need that problem solved *in relation to* how much the product or service costs.

Customers don't determine value through your marketing messages telling them how much you tell them they need it (although that helps). They want to know what value the solution will add to their lives.

Customers perceive the worth of a solution based on what they can gain in their life from it (time or energy saved) minus how much time and energy it will take to regularly use it—from acquisition to installation to training to use. There isn't really a mathematical formula for it, just a ballpark perception. Customers don't care how much a product or service costs the company to create, produce, support, or sell. The value and worth of a product are based on what that means to the customer: how it will solve their problems and ultimately improve their life.

## VALUE AND WORTH: INVESTMENT AND COMMITMENT

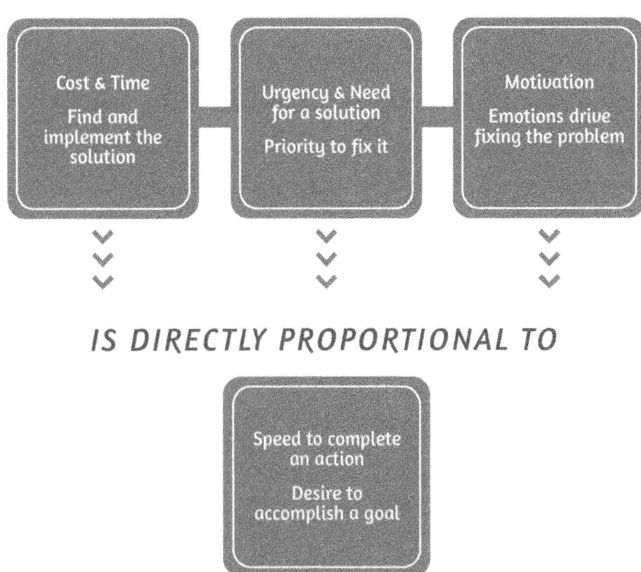


*Figure 1: The Value and Worth Perception Equation*

I see the equation to be like this:

- If a product will save a customer time, money, and worry

  ***plus***

- If it costs little (time and effort) to implement

  ***plus***

- If it is easy to use with great results,
- Then it is a winner.

This is why free products that are difficult to use don't always succeed. The purchase decision for a customer isn't based purely on product cost; it's based on the problem it solves (or job to be done) and the time to learn how to use it.[21] A customer determines the priority of this problem, and solution, in their lives. Then, the customer determines at a high level how much time and energy (including costs) it will take to learn how to use and implement the product. Those two factors will lead to a *yes* or *no* decision.

- If a product is easy to use and solves a priority problem in the customer's life, the product will be used—free or paid.
- If a product is difficult to use, and therefore will take time to learn, and solves a low-priority problem for the customer, then the free product isn't worth it.
- If a product is simple to use and a low-priority problem for the customer to solve, it may be worthwhile for the customer to use it.
- And if the product is difficult to use but the problem is a high priority for the customer to solve, there's a 50/50 chance they will use it.

Usage depends on the product usability and the priority of the problem in the customer's life.

Customers always have four options when they purchase, which map to why they exit a buyer's journey:

| PURCHASE OPTIONS | WHY THEY LEAVE THE BUYER'S JOURNEY |
|---|---|
| Do nothing | Lost interest to solve the problem ***OR*** not ready to solve the problem |
| Create their own solution | Reprioritized the problem's urgency in their life ***OR***<br>Lost interest ***OR***<br>Not ready to solve the problem |
| Buy your solution | Didn't leave (experienced the journey successfully) |
| Buy a competitor's solution | Chose the competitor's solution (despite a free option being available) due to changed urgency, problem redefinition, lost interest, or something else. |

## Time to Look at Business Differently

Companies used to provide customer value through the products they sold. This meant that success was demonstrated through sales. Selling more products meant gaining more revenue, which meant providing more value to customers. Customers were the target ***object*** of this activity. However, today's successful businesses are providing customer value through their **solutions**—a hybrid combination of products and services. The customer and the solution to their problem are now the ***subject*** of business, and businesses need to create experiences that involve customers in their activities.

This shift of customers from being the target object to the subject creates a new view of how business works. Before we look at the new view, we should review how businesses have interacted with customers to date.

Traditionally business operations occurred outside of the customer experience, inside the company. They were separate entities and actions, usually siloed in an organization. Employees rarely interacted with customers, except for a select group in marketing, sales, and customer service (or support). As previously discussed, those were coveted positions, trusted by the company to manage potentially challenging conversations. Naturally, over time, sales, marketing, and customer service became the gatekeepers. For retail, it was the distributors. Due to their increased interactions with customers, these groups began to represent the customer and became their mouthpiece.

But in this structure, there was little sense of a company community; operations and customer-facing teams were separated and didn't really need to be joined or connected to the other teams. Employees from the customer-facing teams provided those connections as needed and remained the "face of the company."

The businesses that inspire us today use a different view of how business works. Rather than looking at value in terms of revenue earned by products sold, businesses look at how a company connects to people first. Profits become the outcome of the relationships. It's a small yet important shift, with revenue measuring the success of a relationship to solve a problem. Rather than marketing and sales activities focused on driving revenue, conversations with customers would be focused to further build relationships through emotional engagement and shared interests. The messages would ideally promote trust and accountability, and encourage interaction

*Figure 2: Traditional View of Business and Customers*

between the customers and the company. These interactions and conversations would develop relationships that would allow the company to more fully understand its customers and their problems. The company could use this knowledge to create better solutions for its customers. These solutions would be more attractive to customers, which would drive sales and build loyalty and more trust. Of course, all these actions combined would increase profits. However, we don't have many effective ways to measure relationships versus revenue, which is part of the problem as we transition to new, automated business models.

## New Approach: Business When You Focus on Relationships

VISION

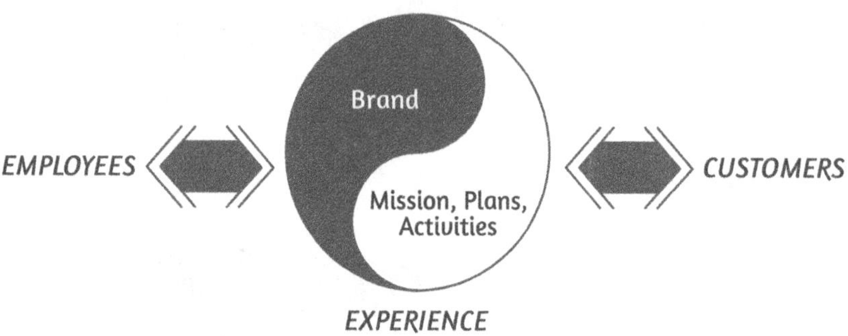


Relationship REVENUE

*Figure 3: New Approach—Business When You Focus on Relationships*

This new model produces the same business output—revenue from relationships—but it creates an environment that better supports customer experience and results in stronger customer relationships. How does it do that?

**Vision:** As always in business, the vision identifies the value you provide and shapes how the company will evolve.

**Business Experience:** This is a departure from the previous model. The business experience combines business activity with the brand and the business community (which includes employees and customers).

**Experience (the transactions and activity):** Processes/ action plan combined with the brand. All processes are branded in how they are expressed and activated.

- **Brand:** Communication and expression for value (emotional)
- **Mission/Plan:** How you will provide value outlined in the vision/mission through action (operations)

**Community/ecosystem:** Employees create the solutions and customers purchase them. They are a type of team in which the creator (employees) receives direct feedback from users/consumers (customers).

- **Employees:** The people who will provide that value
- **Customers:** The people who choose a solution based on the value it offers—and how much they value the solution

***Defining customers:*** *Customers are officially individuals who purchased a product or solution from a company. This definition includes prospects and "friends," or influencers, bloggers, and those who support the company through marketing, thought leadership, and word of mouth. Other stakeholders could also be an extension of this community, like shareholders/ investors, analysts, the press, investors, and partners (channel and strategic), but they have a complex relationship with the company, so for simplicity, we exclude them. We'll refer to the company's community as customers and employees.*

**Relationship and Revenue:** The end result

- **Relationship:** A valuable feedback loop to improve the solution, making customers an active part of the company ecosystem, or community.
- **Revenue:** The result of a great relationship.

The vision, brand, action plan, and business community (employees and customers) are the key elements of any business. By looking at them in a slightly different way, removing the middleman, and creating a branded experience between your employees and customers, your company can create a deeper relationship and connection with your customers, and become one of the companies you always wished to emulate.

## My Personal Experience with This Idea

While consulting through my company, Gearmark, I noticed the trends outlined in this chapter happening at almost every client site. Companies thought they would do some light automation or create a simple website, but even those automation processes exposed all of the flaws that employees covered. Companies with challenged messaging strategies discovered their challenges when we were trying to create content for a site. Sales may have covered the messaging problems by developing great customer relationships or by creating their own presentations based on what worked for them for past sales. Sales funnels were re-examined and evaluated for efficiencies during sales automation activities. Criteria were more accurately defined between steps. In apps, different workflows were re-examined. It was as if every problem of a company was exposed during the automation process. We got to see what worked and what didn't work. And we got to repair it.

I discovered that almost every problem encountered related to a change in the company structure in some way. We didn't realize it at the time, but people did a lot of work to cover problems in companies. Automation exposed what worked and what didn't work, uncovered challenges, and exposed issues. Marketing's distance from the direct customer drove the need for more refined customer and user research. Sales knew a lot about the customers, but they were motivated by commission. Support knew their customers, but they only saw the problems with, and rarely the benefits of, the product. Original customer research—market research, customer research, user research, and digital metrics and research—became a necessity to understand who these customers were. This became even more important when customers went online to solve their problems rather than call. Everyone was now in some way a customer service representative.

Gearmark stood for Process + Brand = Experiences, but customer experience wasn't a "thing" in 2000. Neither was digital transformation, really. People just put things online. In those early days, we believed that you could have an online and brick and mortar business. Now, such sentiments sound sophomoric.

The recommendations included in this book are based on my experiences with companies and clients through Gearmark and independently over the years. I often started projects doing some type of front-end update, which ended up including workflow updates and more. I'd sometimes be included in identifying and managing the teams to produce these interfaces. Measurement was frequently a last-minute discussion, when it should have been the first conversation related to goals. Vision and mission statements weren't always taken seriously in business until we started working on automation projects. Even then, sometimes they were seen as unimportant. Brands were misunderstood and seen as graphics, colors, and fonts, when they have so much more value than that.

Through the automation process, many companies and business leaders formalized their structure. Automation exposed flaws that made businesses overcome the shortcuts that were previously supported as "efficiencies."

With the rise of automation, the business ecosystem changed. Customers gradually became a more active participant in a company's ecosystem, which prompted them to shift their operational approaches and how they perceived their brands and experiences as being part of their identity. This shift also exposed the customer relationship as being a key component for business success. Rather than directly finding ways to achieve revenue that may be disconnected from the company and brand, companies were building customer relationships through branded digital experiences, which resulted in revenue. The shift was the powerful result of automation and continues to fuel a number of business changes and technical innovations today.

CHAPTER 2

# Vision: What Is The Value You Provide?

As we all know, a company's vision defines who the company is, what it does, and where it wants to be in the future. Rather than outline a plan to achieve goals, it outlines the value the company will provide now and in the future to various stakeholders, including customers, the industry, and society. A company's vision is timeless, rarely changes, and is usually transformative and inspiring.

We hear about visions constantly, and it seems like everyone wants to develop one—to the point that it feels like everyone is a visionary. It's great that leaders and aspiring strategists have a vision, but is it a vision that can be realized?

Some companies have the opposite problem: They could easily implement a vision—if they only had one. Some companies don't place value on creating a vision for their company, or they have a vision that is too tactical and only defines what success looks like today.

A company's lack of vision becomes clear in its operations and product strategy. A company with a vision will have clear, targeted goals to achieve. It isn't afraid to take risks because it is being guided by its vision to drive the company forward. Conversely, a company without a clear vision may make half-hearted attempts at launching products or expressing its brand. There is an uncertainty about its actions. It is most likely hesitant to act because it doesn't know exactly what it is working to achieve.

**Characteristics of Companies with Strong vs. Loosely Defined Visions**

| STRONG, FOCUSED VISION | LOOSELY DEFINED VISION |
|---|---|
| Clear identity that defines what it does and doesn't do | Unclear focus of what it is trying to achieve |
| Ability to set trends | Chases trends |
| Defined target audience | Broad target that includes almost anyone |
| Targeted way to get revenue | Revenue comes as needed or earned |
| Takes a risk and accepts challenges | Risk-averse and avoids challenges; looks for an easy solution |
| Strong focus and direction driven by the company | Focus and direction driven by market trends |
| Clear, defined values leveraged in the organization | Unclear values and organization doesn't represent the values listed |
| Does something specific | Does everything |
| Sense of purpose and mission | No purpose; just a job |

Not only does a vision define what's important for a business, but it also defines what is important for the customer experience. Here's how a vision will guide customer experiences:

- Outline the unique customer value it provides, which becomes the basis for the brand and action plan
- Define how the business will change the world (or at least an industry)—and inspire how that should be communicated through the experience
- Inspire changes in customer and employee behavior
- Provide meaning for customers and employees, or provide the *why* for a company's existence

**Don't Forget Your Mission Statement**

Often a standalone vision doesn't provide enough detail to give someone a strategic picture about what your company does or how it does it. The mission statement will fill in the blanks with that additional layer of detail.

- **Vision** addresses the value you provide.
- **Mission** addresses how you plan to make that a reality strategically.

Together, they provide what you need to align your communications and experiences.

## Vision and Mission Statement Examples

Some companies have great vision and mission statements that help drive what they do by clearly defining the problem that they solve, while others don't provide clear direction (and sadly, we see the results of that in company operations and revenue). Following are some examples of successful companies with inspiring vision and mission statements.

*Cisco: Changing IT*

The data center supports all of the innovations we have today for IoT, Big Data, AI, and more. But what supports many data centers? Cisco's equipment.

> **Vision:** Changing the Way We Work, Live, Play, and Learn.[22]
>
> **Mission:** Shape the future of the Internet by creating unprecedented value and opportunity for our customers, employees, investors, and ecosystem partners.[23]

The vision is definitely aspirational and the mission outlines clearly how it plans on achieving it. From my perspective, the mission is a little too specific by addressing how Cisco wants to change the Internet specifically. It is possible for new technologies not yet developed to displace the Internet as a driving force behind automation and require Cisco to create a new mission.

However, its mission statement does limit the scope of how the company will change our lives. It's open enough to encourage creativity and innovation among employees, but it is specific enough to keep employees focused to work on specific types of projects and tactics. It also informs customers about who Cisco is and what it does. If you are looking to apply innovative robotics technology in your factory, Cisco may not be the right partner—unless, of course, you are looking for those devices to communicate with each other via Wi-Fi.

### *Airbnb: Where the Hosts and Guests Are the Customers*

Airbnb is one of my favorite companies for many reasons, especially because it has a clearly defined vision and mission.

> **Vision/tagline:** Belong anywhere, people can live a place, instead of just traveling to it.[24]

> **Mission:** Airbnb's mission is to create a world where people can belong through healthy travel that is local, authentic, diverse, inclusive and sustainable.[25]

Like Cisco's, Airbnb's vision is inspiring: belong anywhere; live in a place instead of just traveling to it. It's a vision that hits the heart of every traveler. You don't want to just experience being in a new country; you want to experience what living there *feels* like. For the true traveler, everywhere you go becomes home for a short while. And the more comfortable you feel, the more memorable the trip.

It is unusual that the vision statement and tagline are the same (typically those are different). However, the vision is clear and succinct, so it makes sense why Airbnb would have a dual-use for its vision as a tagline.

What's great about the mission statement is that Airbnb clearly states how it plans to help travelers feel that they belong anywhere. It is working to create a world where people feel that they belong through "healthy travel" (and they define what that means) within the community that Airbnb has created through its products. Notice there is no mention of technologies Airbnb plans to use or how it plans to implement this idea. This leaves Airbnb open to solve this problem in various ways—through technology, through government policy, or through new community-based products.

What I like about the vision and mission statements is that they don't specify Airbnb's flagship hotel-like product. They are larger than that. Airbnb is creating solutions to solve the problem of travelers feeling a sense of belonging or connection to a city. This may be because many travelers don't feel that there are people like them there, or they have a difficult time finding something they like to do, or they don't feel "at home" where they are staying. Traveling can include exciting adventures, but also exclusion because you aren't part of the community or culture you are visiting. The targeted openness of Airbnb's vision and mission has enabled it to expand its "places to stay" business to include designed experiences, in which local residents "sell" a package of events and activities that presents what they like most about their city. Airbnb understands that belonging comes from a sense of community, which it has been building over the years through its hotel product and is now extending through its host-designed experiences.

Airbnb requires a sense of community in its products to not only support its unique business model, but to support its mission and vision statements. The original hotel product allows hosts to connect with guests, making them both a type of customer. The hosts post vacancies to attract a guest; the guest is looking for a place to stay. Airbnb needs them both to offer a wide variety of booking options. Strangers come together to create a safe, affordable travel experience (a place to stay or local experience in a city) in a type of community. By focusing on customers as people and community building in its vision and mission statement, Airbnb was able to brilliantly create a product that brings people together who crave travel experiences as a host, a guest, or both.

*TED: Spread Ideas*

Who doesn't like to spend 10–20 minutes learning a new perspective through a TED Talk? TED is a successful organization because it has a very clear purpose:

> **Vision:** We believe passionately in the power of ideas to change attitudes, lives, and ultimately, the world.[26]
>
> **Mission:** Spread ideas.[27]

TED has developed inspiring vision and mission statements. It is clear how TED wants its business to change the world: by sharing ideas that change people's attitudes. TED doesn't say how exactly it plans to do this, which is appropriate. Today, TED has the TEDx franchise, its website, and other media and communication channels. If a new communication method emerges, such as virtual reality or holographic transmissions, it will be easy for TED to incorporate that into its business without upsetting its core goals. TED is built for scaling, and has been for a number of years.

*Google: A Revolutionary Mixed Bag*

Google is massive. It has evolved to become "Alphabet, Inc." to encompass all of its various initiatives. So let's look at Google's vision and mission statements on their own:

> **Vision:** To provide access to the world's information in one click.[28]

> **Mission:** To organize the world's information and make it universally accessible and useful.[29]

Both statements are inspirational. I love how Google plans to execute its vision through the mission statement. It's specific yet general. It could make information universally accessible and useful in many ways—through AI, through ubiquitous Internet access, or even through a library.

However, I'm challenged by Google's vision because it is too specific by using the word *click*. With the rise of mobile, clicks are now taps. And with the rise of voice interactions, clicks are now commands. So what happens when AIs evolve to support a statement to access the right information? That's not addressed here. In some ways, Google has limited the innovation of its employees with the word *click*. Google is working around this by embracing the intention of click to mean user desire with their voice AI and similar products. This works today, but may be limiting in the future in the same way Cisco is limited with the word *Internet* if new technologies emerge.

Following are some examples of vision and mission statements that have a narrow focus to illustrate the difference between a vision and mission statement that can encourage your employees to innovate by solving a defined problem versus simply delivering value to the bottom line.

*Macy's: A National Brand*

I was surprised and not surprised by Macy's mission and vision statements. One wouldn't expect a retailer like Macy's to have an aspirational vision. However, unless I missed something or found the wrong vision/mission statement, it shocked me that Macy's vision was focused on achieving a bottom-line goal.

> **Vision:** A premier omnichannel retailer with iconic brands that serve customers through outstanding stores, dynamic online sites, and mobile apps.[30]

> **Mission:** Our goal is to be a retailer with the ability to see opportunity on the horizon and have a clear path for capitalizing on it. To do so, we are moving faster than ever before, employing more technology and concentrating our resources on those elements most important to our core customers.[31]

Operating iconic brands as an omnichannel retailer and serving customers through stores, sites, and apps describe Macy's operational strategy. That's not an inspiring vision of the future. Like the vision, the mission statement is too tactical and limiting. It's unclear how Macy's contributes to its customers' lives or creates value in the world besides selling "things." Is seems Macy's hasn't defined the problem that it is solving in the world. In many ways, its vision and mission statements reflect the aspiration of Macy's operational organization.

It's not surprising that Macy's may be a great store with a great reputation, but is often challenged in maintaining revenues. It may earn money from its sheer size and sales volume, but its mission and vision don't provide employees with the inspiration or direction to develop innovative solutions and new approaches to problems. It also doesn't allow a customer the ability to become a better person. Macy's sees the customer as a buyer of commodities, but there is more to people than that. A focus on the bottom line is not enough to succeed in business today. A vision needs to be more inspiring.

### *Disney: An Entertainment Leader*

Disney has innovated the entertainment and media industry for years, but lately, much of its innovation is predictable through amazing movies, exciting park rides, or media expansion through acquisition. The drive to acquire companies may seem obsessive and unnecessary, unless you read Disney's vision and mission statements from 2013:

> **Vision:** To be one of the world's leading producers and providers of entertainment and information.[32]

> **Mission:** Using our portfolio of brands to differentiate our content, services and consumer products, we seek to develop the most creative, innovative and profitable entertainment experiences and related products in the world.[33]

This iteration of Disney's vision is not particularly inspiring for a customer or employee. Like Macy's, it reflects an operations plan that is focused on the company's economic health, but it doesn't show how it will change the world or inspire customers to change their behaviors or thoughts.[34]

Recently, I noticed Disney updated its mission. It is a hybrid between its previous mission and its original mission statement: "Make people happy."[35]

> **Mission:** Entertain, inform and inspire people around the globe through the power of unparalleled storytelling, reflecting the iconic brands, creative minds and innovative technologies that make ours the world's premier entertainment company.[36]

This mission statement doesn't really focus on the customer and employee community that Disney is creating through entertainment. It describes how to create an entertainment company that will "entertain, inform, and inspire people." It's a step in the right direction toward inspiring people to be and do more rather than increase bottom-line results. Disney has a way to go before it returns to its original mission statement: "Make people happy." That was probably one of the best mission statements ever to build community because it encourages employees to explore what happiness means and demonstrate that through their work. Such a simple mission statement naturally encourages employees to think bigger than themselves because it is a simple *how* response.

Some considerations when you are creating your company's vision and mission statements:

- **How does your company impact the world? That's an inspirational vision.** A vision is a call to change the status quo. Although the status quo changes every day, a well-written company vision should adapt to that change. A vision describes a goal that represents a larger community or industry transformation that is rarely achieved. If a vision is achieved, then the company will either naturally close and have no customers or it will need to revise its vision.
- **A great vision focuses on what you are providing to the world and to your customers, not only what you want your company to achieve.** Focus your mission or vision too much on your company's goals, and you may be inadvertently reflecting your operations plan. Your vision should state how you can provide *value* to your customers—or the world at large. This perspective can instantly inspire your employees and customers to see your company as a leader with a larger goal in mind.
- **A great mission isn't specific for how exactly you'll make your vision come to life.** Provide direction. Including the mention of technology approaches may limit your company in the future. Innovation can come

from anywhere and be anything. Allow your employees to dream and create new ways to achieve the vision. Encourage employees to have conversations with customers for new ideas too.

**What if this isn't happening in your company?**

If the vision is too broad or general:

- **Few will understand what your company does or the value it provides.** It will appear that your company isn't focused on providing a specific solution to a problem.
- **You may have a hard time creating experiences that resonate with customers.** These experiences may not communicate the company's brand, and in the end, they may cause confusion.

If the vision is too specific:

- **Your business may be limited in the experience that it can create through the brand and the action plan/ products.** The teams may feel constrained to work in specific mediums, using recycled ideas or approaches to achieve their goal. The company may appear mundane without the inspiration necessary for creativity.

## Outline the Unique Customer Value

A company's vision doesn't outline specific solutions. Technologies, industries, and solutions change frequently, but the value your company provides your customers shouldn't change.

Typically, the values outlined or implied in a vision provide the basis of an organization's core three to five values that drive all operations in a company, identify action plan priorities, and define a brand. Different teams can interpret the values and vision differently as they apply to their discipline.

- **Product teams** can use them to create unique solutions for customer problems, going beyond a best-practice transaction.
- **Marketing teams** can be inspired to create experiences that appeal to new stakeholder groups or build emotional ties with existing groups and customers to shift their perception about the company or products.
- **HR** can use the vision and mission to create experiences and messaging that attract new talent and keep the existing talent onboard.
- **Finance** could use the vision to provide guidance for negotiations, terms, and policies.
- **Support and customer service** could use them to help define call center availability metrics, resolution turnaround approaches, and representative attitudes on the phone.

A company's customer and employee experiences (processes) should communicate its values and its vision. One could say these contribute to defining the company culture. They provide signals regarding how the company perceives a specific activity. For example, how a company implements login for an app not only shows how it values security, but how it values your personal information while you are in its app. If it provides the bare minimum security, it is a rule follower, willing to do what it takes to meet industry requirements. But if it implements the latest technology and features that go well beyond industry requirements and best practices, it obviously values secure information for everyone and may be an early adopter of new ideas or innovations.

Another example is how companies communicate payment structures. If a company is direct about how it wants to be compensated, that means the company embraces transparency and clarity, and values what it is offering. If there is confusion, then the company may be hiding information, isn't as organized as you may assume, and subconsciously may not value its own product enough to clearly communicate to the customer how much it believes the product is worth.

Actions and transactions are themselves messages and a type of communication. You learn a lot about a company's values based on how it interacts with you. Actions always speak louder than words, and actions often subtlety communicate a company's values in their expression.

### *Why Can't I Just Call?*

In the early days of the web, sites like Hotmail and other digital tools occasionally required technical support, especially for issues like passwords. Like most technology companies, they tried to automate customer service with online help. This was generally successful despite occasional textbook usability issues. Companies built searchable solution libraries or forums in which users were encouraged to post questions so employees could answer and provide clarifications. But there were times when a five-minute phone conversation may have been an easier approach to solve a problem that emerged while using the app.

Many sites with free, or even paid, solutions provided no phone number to call or email address to send a message. These companies created a situation in which there was just no way to contact them. This implied that there was no call center available to respond to any customer needs. It seemed like they saw digital business as a business that existed only in the digital world, where human interaction wasn't necessary. To add complexity to this perception, it seemed like a free or low-cost product meant that a customer wasn't entitled to support services. The attitude communicated by many of these companies was "If the free product doesn't work, well that's too bad." It may not have been true, but that was the perception they were communicating by not offering a direct support channel.

Submitting an online form became many people's only option for help. Sadly, these often seemed to go un-tracked and unanswered. There would be few confirmation emails or ticket numbers to use for follow-up. Certainly, some companies may not have been able to afford a call center or a way to manage all of the issues. However, not having a call center of any type communicated a very direct message to customers: Their problems didn't matter.

A shift seemed to happen when Apple started building retail stores, hosting the Genius Bar, and supporting an 800 number for its products. Apple communicated to its customers (paying or not) that their experiences were important, their problems were valid and required resolution, and they needed to be heard. Further, Apple wanted customers to be successful and enjoy using Apple products on- and offline. What better way than to provide support and care?

Apple understood that customers are necessary for business and always found a way to support them best. In the early days of Apple, it sold products through distributors rather than opening direct-to-consumer stores. However, Apple didn't just let anyone have a store; you needed to be certified and understand how its products worked. These resellers often provided training and services to help customers get their computers up and running. And Apple always had some type of 800 number/help line to offer customers assistance whether the warranty applied or not.

Shortly after Apple launched its dedicated product stores with documented success, Microsoft launched a store and 800 number to support its products. Being a free or paid customer didn't matter: The successful customer experience of the product mattered more.

Today, when I see companies not post a phone number, I wonder if they really want me to contact them. If they only offer a digital form, I know my answer: They don't really care about my experience as a customer, paying or not. Usually, I will leave that business behind and find a company that cares about its customers' satisfaction with their experiences.

**What if this isn't happening in your company?**

- **Your customers and employees will have a different experience with each department.** When your company's vision and mission don't speak to company values but to company achievements, each department will determine how to do their jobs differently to achieve those bottom-line results (achievements). Guiding principles across the company won't be present to define the *why* or *how* behind internal processes or customer experiences. There will be little consistency. Customers will feel that every interaction with a different department is like working with a separate company to satisfy their own needs. Communications, activities, and general operations will be disjointed and unexpected, which is confusing. Interactions with the company will be functional, but not consistent.

- **Mixed messages are inevitable when your company doesn't have clear values expressed in the mission and vision statements.** Does your company say one thing in its marketing and sales messages but act differently through its activities and tactics? Again, without values and principles to guide the *why* or *how* behind the actions and communications in your company, each department will do what it wants and construct their own experiences. Branding will become a visual, and hopefully a communication, element. This won't help bridge the gap between departments functioning like different companies with their own values, making mixed messages from departments inevitable. Departments will only appear similar. If you don't clarify your company values and why it exists, how can you help your employees share that with your customers?
- **Fast, easy, and functional experiences meet requirements, but something more is missing.** Your digital experiences help users achieve their goals, but they have difficulty seeing your company's products and

solutions as contributing more to their lives than the base function. What is the value that your company provides customers? What is the impact your employees have in the world? To society? The consistent value offered becomes easy to understand when there is a more aspirational goal to achieve.

- **There isn't a single brand, but the possibility of an internal brand in each department and an external brand.** Because every department works differently, the company is fragmented. And a fragmented brand will soon follow due to the different values exhibited.
- **Customers will think you don't care about your product—or their problems.** It will appear that your company isn't focused on providing a solution to a problem. If the teams in your company aren't aligned to solve a core problem, then each will solve what's important to them. Your customers will get lost in the process. Your company may mean well, and each department may mean well, but that won't come through to your customers as a unified message. Again, it's a disjointed experience and can be confusing to customers.
- **Customers will find your competitors and use them instead.** This happened with Gmail. When Google launched Gmail, a number of people fled Yahoo and Hotmail to use Gmail. Was Gmail superior? Not really. But Google felt easier to use and appeared to care more about the customers' experience. They had fewer problems and challenges, it was easier to access help, and it was set up so you understood that it would be self-service, free, and

standard. People understood what to expect. There was nothing to lose to move your account to a new system.

## Define How Business Will Change the World and Create a Community

As a visionary, you are inventing the future. You are looking to change your industry and the world, but you can't achieve a vision alone. To be truly visionary means that you can develop a collaborative environment and create a community that supports the vision.

When a company describes the future, it's not only communicating that it wants to be around a while, it's communicating "This is how I see the world. Want to help me change it?"

Visions, by their nature, are inspiring. They pull us out of our day-to-day activities, in which we are focused on achieving bottom-line results, to think more strategically. When you are focused on the day-to-day, it is easy to lose track of the innovations and changes happening in the world and to consider their impact on your business. It's also easy to lose sight of how your contributions achieve goals larger than a weekly paycheck or status report. Visions remind us of the true motivation for our work—and that motivation isn't tied to profits or creating presentations or reports. We should be motivated to create value and meaning for our customers and toward a greater mission in the world.

Customers buy into your company's vision when they purchase a product. They have identified a problem, perceive it as necessary to solve, consider your company's solution, and select it if they feel it is valuable to them. Your product or solution and vision inspire them to make a change, possibly in more ways than one.

Solving a perceived problem changes us. When we purchase a car, we make a change. We now have transportation available when we need it. When we purchase food, we are satisfying a craving and to go from feeling hungry to feeling satisfied. It's a change. When we buy a new shirt, we are making a change. We have a new way to represent who we are by the clothes we choose to wear. It could be a different style, or the same style.

To encourage people to purchase, you need to help them visualize what their life will look like when they use your product and make the change, and possibly what life would be like without it. Changes like these aren't hard or difficult. They're just uncomfortable because they are introducing something new into your life.

Dr. Srini Pillay tells us that we need to see change as essential to our lives or we simply won't do it.[37] That's why at times when you decide to make a change, events move quickly. It's not that you are ready for change, but you require it for your existence. A customer needs to be convinced that the benefits of the change far outweigh the pain of *not* making the change. This is why creating a vision for a customer and the customer community is so important. It helps someone experience the change through their imagination, giving them time to get comfortable with the new idea and fully realize why such a change is so important to their lives and existence.

To create a community that wants to collaborate and build your vision, executing a great communication or marketing plan or having a phenomenal product is not enough. There has to be a way for your community to experience your company and vision to best understand it. The best communication plan includes actions as well as words because, as we know, actions always communicate more than a sentence can. This means you need to create a great customer experience that communicates two key points:

- You are encouraging customers to work with you to achieve your vision.
- You are helping customers to experience a better life.

There are a number of ways to invite your customers to collaborate with you to fulfill your vision and embrace change as part of the larger company community. For example, they could be included in a customer council or participate in a brainstorming forum. These opportunities would:

- Blend the customer experience with the business experience.
- Cement a relationship with customers.
- Create community.
- Develop a forward-thinking business that solves key customer problems.

By including customers in your company's experiences, you not only strengthen your business relationship with them, but you make them active members of your company's community and ecosystem.

To create a great experience, introduce elements from your brand that reflect the broader thinking expressed in your vision. Experiences are the ultimate form of communication. Let's say you are developing a solution that requires customers to shift how they think about computing. Some solutions might include:

- Creating a thought leadership program in which employees speak publicly about these new ideas and introduce them at conferences.
- Creating a content marketing program with a publication or blogs that provide a voice for anyone writing about this subject matter online.
- Introducing your approaches and programs into schools to teach students your new approach so they can bring it with them to their employers.
- Encouraging your support teams to discuss the methodology behind the solution during calls. Make the solution less instructional than "do this or that." Teach people how to think differently about the problem to get to the optimal solution.
- Encouraging your customers to share their stories about their journeys and changes to a new life with the solution. Include the emotional changes that the solution brought them and what it means to be part of the company's community.

- Creating programs in which your employees become active in the surrounding community, working on activities that are related to your company's solutions. It's even better to include your customers in these activities too.

**What if this isn't happening in your company?**

- **Your team won't be inspired to deliver value—only a product—and you'll become a commodity.** Your employees and teams will only see how your product solves problems customers have right here and now. If this continues long-term, your product will no longer be perceived as a solution, but a commodity that has limited value. This happened in the airline industry. Airlines and their employees knew that airplanes solved a transportation problem: They moved customers across long distances quickly. What they missed was that this transportation solution created a different problem: one or more hours of "free time" in a literal tin can. Each flight lasts at least an hour in a confined space with a large number of people you possibly don't want to know. What could you do during this time? And how should the space and experience be constructed? Airlines defined flying in the 1950s as a lounge experience—with a meal, drinks, and time to read or visit with other passengers in a relaxing setting. With the desire to increase profits in the 1970s and 1980s, airlines tightened their belts regarding the experience and fit more passengers into the planes. Seats got more cramped, food got less appetizing, airlines offered fewer free perks, and once onboard, you couldn't wait to land. Richard Branson noticed this trend but saw the flight experience differently. To him, a flight should be an affordable treat—almost like spending an hour or more in an upscale lounge. It was a retro yet modern vision, bringing customers back to the 1950s and 1960s when travel was elegant. To achieve this in his various labels, including Virgin America, he offered guests ubiquitous Wi-Fi, outlets at seats, high-quality food, personal video viewing at your seat, and a purchase-driven seat upgrade system, to name a few amenities. Virgin's influence on the airline industry has been felt far and wide; all airlines saw this innovation as a new baseline for them to meet. Even Alaska Airlines, which acquired Virgin America in 2017, uses colored lights to set a lounge-y mood in the same way Virgin America did. (They considered blue to be a more current and fashionable color than purple, but the concept still applied.)

- **Your team will be solely focused on day-to-day activities and not create value for the future.** Sure, your employees and teams will be productive, and you'll be creating a product that customers need today, but what about tomorrow? You can't forget about your future. Through your vision statement, you have an opportunity to define that for your customers so they can support you and help you explore new solutions.
- **Your company won't be perceived as an industry influencer—a game-changer.** Is delivering value today enough? How does your company plan to contribute to the industry and change the world? That's what

customers want to see and experience. They want to solve their immediate problem, but they want that solution to exist and be supported in the future. Companies that embrace new technologies and understand how they impact business and the world overall are seen as leaders. Customers also don't want to implement a solution that will be considered dated in six months. Most customers want to be associated with innovators to be part of the cutting-edge future—or at least, the future that is coming soon.

- **Your company won't be perceived as a strategic, long-term partner.** If a customer is making a large investment in a solution, he wants to be sure that the company will be in business for years to come. Plans for the future are a key element in those discussions. If a company isn't thinking about what they will create in 10 years, customers won't perceive the company as a long-term partner. And this issue becomes apparent during the sales cycle. How salespeople and marketing talk about a product communicates if there is a future vision with product updates and changes or if the product will stay as-is for years to come.

## How Do You Know Your Destination if You Don't Have a Vision?

I have worked with a number of companies at various stages with different visions.

Unanimously, the companies that had a vision of where they wanted to go long-term were the easiest to work with when developing customer experiences. When it came to creating a road map and understanding their customers, that work almost fell out of the sky. The customers who were most challenging to work with didn't have a very clear vision of where they wanted to go.

One large corporation I worked with wanted me to create a program road map, but didn't provide me with a clear vision. The company told me to create one. I found this perplexing. As a consultant, I felt that I could provide strategic recommendations and options, but I wasn't ultimately responsible or accountable to achieve specific business goals or to live with those decisions or consequences. I understood how I could help the program, but I had dozens of questions regarding how the program fit into the organization. I hoped that the recommendations I offered sparked discussions to answer my questions to get the direction I needed. Without these discussions, I wasn't sure if I was moving in the right direction.

Sadly, these discussions never happened. I realized that I didn't have a clear understanding of the other priorities and initiatives throughout the organization that could impact or benefit this initiative. I also didn't have a complete understanding of all business goals impacted in the short- and long-term. There were budget implications as well. How could I create a solution that balanced all of those factors as a consultant with no senior management discussions? Understanding how all of the various customer programs and activities fit together from the customer perspective is vital to creating a new program.

I tried my best and provided a number of potential visions for feedback. Some were simple and others more complex, but every idea was rejected for vague reasons. I wasn't sure if the problem was with my suggestions or that they weren't sure what they wanted. Eventually, I spoke with a related team and we quickly aligned ourselves regarding the project's direction. I then realized the problem wasn't me or my ideas. The original group simply didn't have a vision and didn't know where they wanted to go.

We could have pursued any strategy at all and it wouldn't have felt right for this client because they didn't have an end goal in mind for what they wanted from the program regarding customers, the experience, the industry impact, or revenue contribution or expectation.

Creating a product or program without a vision is like creating a list of directions with Google Maps without a destination in mind. You can go anywhere you want and take any pattern of roads to get there, but if you don't have an endpoint, how can you create a plan to get there? A vision is your destination. You don't always need to know the exact street address for your endpoint, but you do need to know the general geographic area or town.

**What if this isn't happening in your company?**

- **Every idea is a possible idea. The possibilities are literally endless.** How to implement an idea best in an organization is based on the culture, operations guidelines, company values, and brand, which originate from a company's vision. It's hard to decide the best approach to create a program if there isn't an overarching vision for what the company, never mind the program itself, should do. A vision provides guidelines to make your company unique. A vision and mission together provide a competitive edge. It helps differentiate what success looks like. What is defined as successful for your organization is different somewhere else. That means your programs and products cannot be easily reproduced because you would need to have the same team, operations design, and vision of where you want to go and how you see this solution as helping you get there. That's a lot to copy.

- **You are never sure if you are on the right track to achieve a goal.** With the possibilities being endless, the goalposts are constantly moving. It's hard to achieve a goal and work toward a vision if the vision is a moving target. No vision, mission, or goals allows a team to drift and doesn't provide them the certainty they need to deliver results.
- **Customers can be easily confused.** If various teams aren't aligned and there is no vision everyone is working toward, then each team is doing what they believe is best. This is an opportunity for teams to do as they wish, confusing customers even more.

## Inspire Improved Employee and Customer Behavior

A company that solves a problem well typically has a great product or service. The product usually enables the company, its employees, and its customers to solve a problem larger than any of them individually. It not only solves a problem in society but provides inspiration for people to improve their lives.

One example is Martha Stewart and her media empire. Stewart left Wall Street to become a caterer years ago. She did a phenomenal job creating delicacies for fantastic parties. She refurnished her home to be comfortable yet elegant, and she became the master of how to live a quality life with just a little extra work. However, she noticed a problem in America: We knew how to live inexpensively, but not well. She decided to show America how to live better, like she did, even on a budget.

By developing a media empire based that distributed tips and tricks through TV, Internet, and books/magazines, she inspired her employees and customers to not only live differently, but to look at their lives differently.

- We learned why the microwave wasn't optimal for heating leftovers quickly.
- We learned why cooking with a stove and a convection oven to create quasi-gourmet feasts in less than an hour gave us a better life.
- We discovered recipes to have great-tasting food at home on a budget that rivaled fine dining.
- We were instructed how to entertain with grace to develop friendships over dinner parties, helping the businesses of Crate & Barrel, Restoration Hardware, Pottery Barn, and Williams-Sonoma expand.
- We learned what makes a better sheet to improve our sleep.

- We discovered and appreciated the qualities of effective cookware. Her homeware line at Kmart and later Macy's helped us experience her definition of a quality life in our own home.

Martha Stewart not only created a media and retail empire that sold a lifestyle, but she also instructed us, her customers, and her employees how to live better.

LinkedIn took a similar approach when it came to careers. Before LinkedIn, creating resumes and networking had always been manual processes without a lot of guidance. There were a few resume writers but many Microsoft Word formatters who could make a mediocre resume look good. Career coaches were difficult to find—or afford—unless you were an executive. People did their best to research a company and job when there was no Internet available, using the library and publications. Access to Hoovers and similar databases was a luxury that only sales and marketing professionals had through their jobs.

Most of us wouldn't get a job and never really understand why. HR never offered us a straight answer; we only got a polite "No thanks. We chose another candidate." What was missing? What could we have done better? Those were the greatest questions we would ponder with our friends and colleagues, guessing an answer, which was often completely wrong.

The same was true with networking. You'd go to an event and gather a collection of names and positions. You might send a letter or two or make a call, but there were no real connections unless you knew someone through a friend or colleague. After an event, you'd take your stack of business cards and put them in a box, never to be seen again. Or add them to your Rolodex file and remove them after a year or two because you couldn't remember who the person was or what they did for work. And you doubted that they remembered you as well.

We all knew that there had to be a better way to get a job.

LinkedIn decided to automate not just resume creation, but networking and career building, and guide us on the "best" way to do this. Some examples:

- It gave guidance to people on how to create a great career by promoting themselves better to find the ideal job.
- We learned what it meant to truly have a personal brand and create a great impression online and offline.
- We were inspired to learn more about networking and the job search.
- We discovered concrete reasons why we were rejected from the job interview process for a position, which helped us prepare better intellectually and emotionally the next time.
- We were able to access content by executive coaches to understand how we can get ourselves to the next level, and with that actionable advice we were inspired to take those next steps in our careers.
- We could more easily connect with past colleagues and others in our industry, bringing networking to a click.
- Keeping in touch with people became as easy as a wall post.

- We were encouraged to be thought leaders ourselves. For example, if we didn't have a blog, LinkedIn provided the infrastructure so we could write posts as we wished.

LinkedIn inspired us to challenge ourselves to be better people, push harder, and define not only new careers but a new vision for what our careers could be.

These customer experiences inspired employees and customers to be better people. They showed how a great company doesn't just automate a process or find a way to improve efficiencies or effectiveness. Rather, it helps people understand how to be better at their jobs, in their families, at life. Employees learn what this means through their innovative work that reflects the company vision. Then they educate customers about what they learned.

With the right vision, a company becomes an influencer for customers, employees, or other influencers. It will also provide advice and directions for how to improve. A company inspires us to understand how it is changing the world, starting with you as an individual.

**What if a company doesn't have this?**

- **It will excel at automation, but it will have a difficult time helping customers and employees connect to its vision and messages.** Martha Stewart was able to influence millions to connect with her perspective of good living because she showed how easy her vision was to obtain. With a few extra steps, anyone could live in luxury, even on a budget. LinkedIn had a similar impact. It influenced thousands on how to find a job and manage a career in a better way. And it embedded advice in its online resume posting tool to make this process simpler. The results spoke for themselves, and more people got an account and joined the network.

- **People won't learn why you are needed and see the value you offer.** This is related to the next point. Customers understand the value you offer through their experience of your company. A benefit is an immediate solution; value is experienced over time after multiple problems have been resolved. If your company solves an immediate problem, you will find customers quickly. But if your company is solving a larger industry problem, customers may require a greater commitment to buy into your company's vision because it is solving many problems, while also providing a number of benefits.
- **You will be replaced by a competitor.** Jail time slightly damaged Martha Stewart's brand, but it didn't damage her business. No one replaced her company's vision or message. Monster.com was once the king of the job search market, listing almost every company's position. LinkedIn was in the career and networking market and people found jobs through networking. Monster.com has faded into the background of relevance and LinkedIn now lists job posts. LinkedIn is the leader because it provides a way for people to improve their careers—not just get a new job, like Monster.com. LinkedIn provided value for the larger goal rather than filling an immediate need (filling and applying for jobs) as Monster.com did.

- **The company produces commodities, not value.** Without providing customers inspiration, a company could provide a product or service that solves a problem without adding value. Before LinkedIn, you could find a job through a search. However, LinkedIn allowed you to post your resume for others to see and find you for jobs in their company. It solved the problem of getting ahead in your career by helping you connect with others who could help you expand your network. And that's really the problem you need solved when you look for a new job. ***The job is the endpoint, but it's the journey to get the job, your career, and network, that matters more.*** LinkedIn was solving that problem.

## Provide Meaning for Customers and Employees, or Provide the Why

Victor Frankl founded the psychiatric school of logotherapy, which is,

> *. . .based on the premise that the human person is motivated by a "will to meaning," an inner pull to find a meaning in life. The following list of tenets represents the basic principles of logotherapy:*
>
> - *Life has meaning under all circumstances, even the most miserable ones.*
> - *Our main motivation for living is our will to find meaning in life.*
> - *We have freedom to find meaning in what we do, and what we experience, or at least in the stand we take when faced with a situation of unchangeable suffering.*

*The human spirit referred to in [l]ogotherapy is defined as that which is uniquely human. Though in no way opposed to religion, the term is not used in a religious sense.*[38]

How do we find meaning?

*According to Frankl, "We can discover this meaning in life in three different ways: (1) by creating a work or doing a deed; (2) by experiencing something or encountering someone; and (3) by the attitude we take toward unavoidable suffering" and that "everything can be taken from a man but one thing: the last of the human freedoms—to choose one's attitude in any given set of circumstances."*[39]

This existential branch of psychotherapy grew out of Frankl's experience in the concentration camps during World War II, as documented in his book, *Man's Search for Meaning*. He had a profound insight into what drives human survival. Alfred Adler and Sigmund Freud previously claimed that power and reproduction, respectively, drove humans to survive. Adler's views around humanity's drive for power were proven irrelevant in Frankl's experience because there was no way for the men of the camps to have power of any sort. The power structures were centered and focused with the Germans, not the prisoners. Yet the men in the camp continued to strive toward survival. Due to an extreme lack of food (and energy) and intense physical activity, most of the men's sex life was gone, which made Freud's view of the all-consuming human drive to procreate irrelevant as well. Frankl noticed that many in the camps clung to hope, prayer, art, relationships—anything that would give life meaning in their dire circumstances. This "meaning making" kept them alive, willing to wake up every morning and maintain some humanity in horrific living conditions. He discovered that we need meaning to survive such truly unbearable moments.

This is why we flock to religion. It's a human need to understand truths around why we are here, what we are meant to accomplish, and why we wake up and get out of bed in the morning. We need to make sense of life to navigate the unbearable and feel that we have a greater purpose.

How does this all relate to a company's vision and customer experiences? Employees and customers need meaning to be happy and productive. They need to understand how their work will contribute value to the company, to society, and to the history of the world. A vision helps us achieve this by helping us understand what we are part of and what we are working toward, allowing us to strive to be better people.

One way companies can achieve this through a customer experience is by implementing a corporate social responsibility (CSR) program. CSR programs elevate the mission and vision of a company from changing individual habits or an industry's transformation to changing government policies, raising awareness of ethical values, and supporting human rights and environmental issues. When we hear about the challenges citizens of various nations face globally, it is difficult to determine how you personally can make a difference in the world. CSR programs allow companies to participate in the community to provide change, while at the same time inspire their customers and employees to participate in change globally and locally in their corporate ecosystem. It is an opportunity for a customer to choose to be part of a greater transformation or movement—not just a personal or industry transformation. The experience of buying a shirt could become a political statement through the action of choosing a brand that tries to improve labor conditions in its manufacturing operations (for example, eight-hour days paid at a living wage). Or by choosing a brand that reduces waste or requires humane treatment of animals. The customers and employees see how their choices to purchase from such a company has a direct impact to change government policies in ways that petitions often fall on deaf ears. It's corporate influence being used for positive cultural and government change.

Patagonia is a great example of a company that is able to inspire customers to be aware of what's happening globally through its brand and programs. Patagonia continues to positively impact the environmental and economic situations of thousands globally through government policy and human rights activities. And Patagonia achieves this through the customer experience it offers in its products and services.

**Patagonia's mission:** We're in business to save our home planet.[40]

Fair trade and humane factory conditions in the supply chain are two examples of how Patagonia has impacted government policy globally. Patagonia recently assumed a larger role to prohibit human trafficking and labor exploitation in the supply chain. By partnering with Verite, Patagonia completed an audit to gain greater transparency about its supply chain. It wanted to truly understand how its supply chain worked on all levels to identify where the ethical labor issues were occurring. With these issues identified, Patagonia built awareness around the subject and has started making concrete changes internally and globally with government support.

There can be many hidden buyers and brokers to produce clothing and materials that are difficult to track. Some countries have practices that are considered legal but unethical to Americans, such as labor brokers overcharging for labor. It is difficult for an American company to dictate to these countries what is right or wrong, but it can help build awareness of the ethical implications of these practices. American companies can also work with countries to change their policies to find an approach that works for everyone. In the meantime, Patagonia does what it can to support its own brand values and ethics internally and with vendors. To expand on the labor broker example:

> *The use of labor brokers is common practice in Taiwan. The country has had a long-standing labor shortage and many companies rely on brokers, who solicit recruits and bring workers from places like Thailand, Vietnam, Indonesia, and the Philippines to work in the country's numerous factories and mills. The practice itself is legal, as is the ability to charge a limited fee for it. But in its audits, Patagonia found that labor brokers were charging workers astronomical sums for the service—as much as $7,000, well in excess of the legal limit. In addition, many workers are charged a monthly fee just to hold onto their jobs, a practice that is also considered legal. Often, between the illegally high initial fees and monthly fees, many employees find themselves in so much*

*debt that they are unable to repay brokers with the meager $630-a-month salaries (the required minimum wage) that factories pay.*[41]

Practices like this may sound shocking, but this is a common practice in offshore manufacturing. Often, the only way to reduce costs in those manufacturing plants is through labor exploitation. Companies such as HP, Apple, and Cisco are fighting human trafficking and forced labor in their supply chains in partnership with organizations like KnowTheChain.[42] As you can see, this exploitation can include more than debt servitude, including withholding passports and other legal documents, forcing workers to pay for their own job, or, more commonly, workers will receive low pay and be forced to work excessive hours. This was the topic of a recent controversy around the Foxconn suicide headlines for those working on the Apple product lines.[43] Apple has since set standards to improve its supply chain working conditions, which has produced measurable improvements. Although the number of suicides has been reduced, the company continues to have labor issues, such as forced labor for underage workers and illegal overtime while producing the iPhone 10.[44,45]

Certainly, Patagonia could return its manufacturing to the US and have direct control over factory operations, but additional challenges have been introduced with off-shoring manufacturing.

- The decline of skilled labor in the US, which makes bringing jobs to the US inconsequential because people would need to be trained to complete the work (which adds cost and time to production).

- The opportunity loss for these countries. Although there are labor challenges, there are job opportunities created. Why not improve the policies and working conditions to improve life for those there?

As companies try to improve the conditions of their supply chain, they are discovering that the true opportunity for lasting change happens through compensation and contracts (longer-term agreements across manufacturers) rather than factory-by-factory investigations. Investing in the suppliers long-term builds trust, certainty, and stability. Together, the partnerships drive improved work environments.

In addition to human and labor rights, Patagonia manages the environmental impact of its work by choosing natural, recycled, or humanely sourced fibers for its clothing. PETA has exposed animal cruelty in Patagonia's wool supply chain in the past, causing it to replace its wool garments with clothing made from synthetic fibers. After intense research to find new wool sources and developing a new 26-page standard for animal treatment, it has re-introduced wool fibers responsibly sourced into its clothing.

To further support its environmental causes, Patagonia created a store to sell used clothing and repair broken garments, a customer experience that encourages recycling and environmental awareness. Customers no longer feel they need to choose between supporting the environment through zero-footprint or purchase quality outdoor gear. Patagonia provides options that meet personal life goals as well as higher life meaning goals.

When a customer chooses to purchase a Patagonia shirt, they can feel that they are in some way helping to improve the supply chain and labor conditions for possibly at least one manufacturer in southeast Asia, support more humanely sourced fibers, and contribute to a clean environment. It may feel like a small contribution on behalf of an individual, but combined with many other individual consumers, this contribution becomes a larger social change effort with tremendous impact.

By balancing environmental and ethical concerns with profit margins, Patagonia is able to provide a meaningful customer experience that achieves a greater goal. It listens to protestors and responds with action, as it did with the supply chain and PETA. And Patagonia communicates to customers and employees that the experience of *how* it makes its products holds just as much meaning as *what* it produces. Customers and employees are changing policy globally through their purchase and manufacturing decisions by contributing to a larger cause, providing meaning for their purchase decisions. The larger Patagonia ecosystem is on a mission to create a more equitable and humane manufacturing business environment globally, to produce better quality hiking products, and to offer customers more ethical purchase options all in one place.

**What if a company doesn't have this?**

- **The company will be flat and not dynamic.** You need to inspire employees to go that extra mile. What are the employees working to achieve? Patagonia is literally changing the world through clothing production, how people make a living, and helping other businesses get started that can keep the spirit of change alive. That should inspire any employee to contribute to change the world. In some ways, they are working for equality globally as much as an activist.

- **Customers won't feel as if they are part of a larger initiative.** Sure, you can offer them a great product experience and solution, but are you really transforming the world? Take Apple and the RED Program as an example. Yes, Apple's innovations and insights transformed how we perceive technology. But has Apple changed global policy? Apple participates in the RED Program to support AIDS research and treatment globally. But does experiencing RED products change your behavior—how you think about social issues and perceive the world? Not really. Apple contributes money to RED, which makes it philanthropic, but it isn't involved in the day-to-day changes that the program coordinates. Intel contributes to social change in a different way. They incorporated CSR and an honest supply chain into chip manufacturing (Intel has been manufacturing conflict-free microprocessors since 2013).[46] Intel is involved in changing how operations and processes work in the industry and in manufacturing. Both are involved in contributing to social change, but Intel has changed how it works to inspire greater changes economically, environmentally, and in global policy.
- **You'll miss the opportunity to communicate that the experience of *how* a product is made is just as important as *what* is being made.** Sometimes companies forget that their operations and manufacturing choices contribute to more than the bottom line. These choices matter to

the customers and employees in this new company ecosystem, where third-party manufacturers are partners and customers are included in the company community.

- **Customers notice how you conduct business and actively work to keep the business alive.** They want to know how you are making your products because it has meaning for them as well as your employees. Every time they purchase, they have a choice: They can purchase any shirt, but they can always choose a shirt that is made from organic materials by people paid a fair wage that is responsibly sourced.

## Conclusion

As part of a class I took with Jennifer Grace, a Hay House author and life coach who teaches a program based on a Stanford University master's degree class in transformation, I got a one-on-one coaching session to talk about my business. She told me to write a business plan. She expected me to write something short with the goal to organize my thoughts on paper so I could be clear about what I'm doing, why, and what I want to achieve.

The irony of this recommendation is that I tell everyone to create a business plan, sort out their brand, and have a vision and mission statement. And yet this cobbler wasn't making herself shoes.

During the exercise, I created my own vision and mission statement for Gearmark:

> **Vision:** Customers become active participants in every company's community.
>
> **Mission:** Empower companies to build great customer relationships.

Writing this down helped me be clear about what I do and who my company is. It took a lot of reflection for me to realize what Gearmark really does, what I really want Gearmark to do, and how I want to position Gearmark for future growth. I recently updated my resume and LinkedIn profile to define who I am and what I offer clients so I could take this next step and separate me from Gearmark. Now I clearly tell people what I personally can contribute to their business, versus how Gearmark can contribute. This will be helpful when I add a new employee or contractor to my business.

I still review my vision and mission statements from time to time to help me write new messaging, create new courses, or write blogs. It keeps me focused on what Gearmark should and shouldn't be doing. Without a vision, I would continue to be a consultant, merging myself with my company and taking on client projects to help me pay for my lifestyle. I wouldn't be thinking about how exactly I can add value to customers' companies. However, with a vision, I can broaden my business to include new products and develop a customer community long-term. I already was partly there with a customer community that was a result of my business being primarily driven by word-of-mouth. But I failed to help customers see a larger picture of how being part of the Gearmark community will transform their business.

I look forward to adding employees to my "team of me" who can also help other companies create great customer relationships. They can help communicate Gearmark's vision to customers and prospects more clearly through their words and actions. And this allows Gearmark to develop its own identity and personality, providing employees the space to contribute more to the world and impact the lives of people they touch.

Having vision and mission statements provides your company with the direction needed for your action plan, your brand, and your customer experiences. They can help you differentiate your company by defining the value you provide customers by transforming an individual's life, an industry, or even public policy. Essentially, a company's mission and vision help customers understand why a company exists. And it's not always just to solve a problem. Some companies decide that the experience of how a product is made as meaningful as the solution that is created. Those companies embrace what it means to provide a customer experience that transcends business interests into social change and public policy, making a difference in the community. Their community doesn't stop with customers. Everyone is a member of their ecosystem, and their solution touches the world.

It makes you wonder if, at times, our businesses think too small and we need to consider how we all can contribute to the global bottom line. With the automation technology available today, all companies can contribute to improving the world in some way.

CHAPTER 3

# Brand: How You Communicate The Experience

My favorite way to describe branding: It's not what you do, it's how you do it.

Branding is often misunderstood. Many see it as colors, fonts, and logos, but that is only the visual expression and communication of a product or company. Branding goes much deeper; it represents the soul of a company—its essence. It is the foundation from which many business decisions are made, and it plays a significant role in mergers and acquisitions, corporate cultures, and determining company value. If you observe companies and their deals, many decisions are driven by their corporate vision and brand values.

Although branding is an intangible asset, according to Jan Lindermann in *The Economy of Brands,* it accounts for

30–80 percent of shareholder value, generates expectations of future financial performance, and positively impacts share price performance.[47] Lindermann further explains, "A powerful brand is more likely to attract and retain consumers/customers in the future, and can be leveraged into new channels, geographies, and businesses."[48] Strong brands contribute to consumer quality perception, allowing for organic growth with a lower risk.

> "Consumers' quality perception of a brand provides information about a firm's stock returns quantifies the direct and indirect brand influence on all the factors that determine the share price, such as cash flow, earnings, and share price growth, at around 70 percent."[49]
>
> —Jan Lindermann, *The Economy of Brands*

**A Short History of Branding**

Brands started by individuals branding their cattle, to associate a herd with an owner. Over time, this association expanded to indicate the quality of the cattle this owner maintained, evolving into a method to identify and classify merchandise without the owner being present. Brands indicated the quality a customer should expect in a product and served as a way to identify a seller for products and, more recently, services.

When mass manufacturing went mainstream and national companies were further removed from customers through middlemen (distributors, retailers, salespeople), they needed a way for their products to be remembered over the regional and local competitors. They used images, colors, and language to help create a consistent visual experience for a brand identity, which, in conjunction with the product and its quality, became the product experience.[50]

## Brand: The Humanizing Element of a Company

Branding and brand personality can be difficult to discuss because they are intangible. To make branding more accessible, we can compare an individual's personality with a company's brand personality.

Before we compare the two, we must shift word usage from calling a business a *company* to calling it an *organization*. This way, we are using words that describe organic structures, focused more on the people component rather than the legal entity. The word *company* does officially include "organization" in its formal definition, so they are equivalent words in that respect as well.

Then we need to consider the definition of *personality* to provide a baseline for the analysis:

> **Personality:** the complex of all the attributes—behavioral (the actions or reactions of a person or animal in response to external or internal stimuli[51]), temperamental, emotional and mental—that characterize a unique individual.[52]

Using this definition, we could say that if people express their personality (intangible) through their behaviors and actions or action plan (tangible), then you can get to know someone's personality through your more tangible experience of their behaviors and actions. If we impose that idea on an organization, we could say that an organization expresses its brand personality through its action plan (with the tangible components being operations, products, marketing, and procedures). This leads to a customer experiencing and understanding a company's personality, or brand, through the customer experience, which includes transactions, activities, and communication through activities.

**How People and Organizations Express Their Personalities**

| PERSON | ORGANIZATION |
|---|---|
| Personality | Brand personality |
| Behaviors | Processes and workflows outlined by the action plan |
| Temperament (Mental, physical, emotional traits of a person) | Corporate values, brand values, brand attributes |
| Emotions | Tone of communications for expression (Could include word choices and color options) |
| Mental attributes | Decision-making processes and company culture |

As we know, everyone has a personality, although they express it differently. Some are gregarious, others shy and withdrawn. And we experience this through their being, words, and actions. The same is true for organizations. All organizations have a brand or personality. A brand may not be emotional or clearly defined and communicated, but every company has one. To say that a company doesn't have a brand or has a weak brand would be like saying that someone doesn't have a personality or has a weak personality, which isn't true and, frankly, is insulting. All customers experience a company's brand in some way through its activities and communications, just as someone experiences an individual's personality through their speech and actions.

How someone experiences a brand in an organization (internal or external) is based on the person's relationship with the organization. Many communications professionals will separate external and internal brand communication functions. The challenge with that approach is that there isn't an external and internal brand. It's all the same brand communicated to different audiences. Typically, external brand communication focuses on customers and outside stakeholders, whereas internal brands often communicate a company's culture to employees. Some argue that an internal brand communication should be different from an external brand communication. But if employees and customers are part of the same community, as proposed earlier, and the brand reflects the company's culture (internally or externally), doesn't it follow that they should share a similar communication approach?

If an internal brand communicates a different culture than the external brand, then the customer will experience the discrepancy in its interactions with employees. Brands are successful when they are consistently communicated to all audiences. This doesn't mean that a brand needs to use the same approach speaking to the audiences and stakeholders;

in fact, that would be disastrous. The same values and personality need to exist in the communications to everyone, just expressed differently. If a brand has a separate value system and personality externally than its brand expression internally, that demonstrates a brand conflict. Such a conflict will emerge in all company communications, including phone calls, emails, and other communications.

Here's an example. Let's say a company communicates internally that it has the best talent and hires the best employees. The company isn't just lucky to have them; they are making a company that everyone wants to work for and be a part of, and customers are eager to be part of that ecosystem. Then let's say externally, the company communicates to customers that the company is there to provide them with the best service possible.

If employees believe, due to the internal messaging, that everyone wants to be customers of that company and is dying to work with them, why would they think that servicing customers matters? It's not a culture of service. It's a culture in which employees believe that they are in high demand, so one result may be that their behavior doesn't matter. They believe that they will achieve the numbers required for the bottom line whether they are customer-focused or not because customers desperately want their solutions.

However, based on the external marketing messages, the customers believe that the company will serve them and expect the employees to do so. That highlights a conflict in expectations. This conflict will appear in the employees' attitudes toward the customers and in the communications between the employees and customers.

This is an extreme example, but this is why having a separate internal and external brand is similar to having a brand for customers and a brand for partners. It doesn't make any sense. The same brand should be communicated so an audience will best understand what it represents. The communication medium or approach may be different, but the main brand story and experience should be consistent.

We rarely discuss the impact of brands on internal operations and workflows, but there is a strong branding impact on automation. We forget that every workflow and process require communication elements to function well. Either the communication is automated, or employees and customers directly communicate with each other. And company communications always reflect the culture or the company's brand personality in some way. Communication may be consciously constructed to fit with the company's approach (usually driven by marketing communications) or more closely reflect the employees' personal communication style with a hint of company culture included. Company culture is typically communicated through a customer's experience of working with employees and the employees' experience working with each other. This is usually demonstrated through word choice, requests, next steps, and actions, or simply how they summarize an event.

Here are some examples of how brand and culture impact employee actions in your companies and teams:

- **If employees tend to build consensus when making a decision,** this could represent a company culture that values collaboration. This value could be expressed by an employee outlining the situation, seeking options for a solution from the team, and sending a meeting request to discuss the issue.

- **If a team of employees looks to a team lead or manager for guidance** and you notice that the team stops discussion after the leader provides his or her feedback, which may seem like a decision, you may be working with a culture that values hierarchy, structure, and internal guidance. This is the opposite of a team that continues discussion until everyone in the meeting comes to consensus.
- **If a team is focused on doing the activities that achieve bottom line–related goals,** then the company is probably revenue- and achievement-driven and values profits and organizational results.
- **If a team ensures that everyone is *feeling* that they are making the right decision**, then it is a culture that values collaboration and consensus, and values the people of the organization.
- **An accountable team** will focus on what it needs to do to complete activities to achieve a larger goal. There is less focus on assigning people to complete specific tasks and time lines because everyone on the team will contribute toward the goal in some way. There are roles already established and the team expects everyone to pitch in and assume their contributing role to achieve an end goal or result. Completing the project isn't enough; the project has to make an impact on the bottom line and in the larger organization.

- **A responsible team** will focus on a time line and activities, and then designate specific team members who will complete the work, holding them responsible. The team is focused on completing the project. The larger organizational goal is important, but that's not the mission. Individual responsibility to complete your own work is more important.

You could also consider the relationship between brand and internal culture using radical transparency as David Mattin has suggested. In the article, "In 2017, Your Culture Is Your Brand," Mattin wrote:

> *Back when your business was a black box, the brand was whatever you painted on the outside of the box. You had control over that...Now, thanks to the radical transparency made possible by a connected world, your business is a glass box. People can see all the way inside. And that means that now the brand is everything they see. Every person. Every process. Every value...There's a single word that sums up what a person sees when they look deep inside your business: they see your culture.*[53]

In many ways, Mattin and I are saying something similar from a slightly different perspective. There is only one brand. It includes what's inside and outside your company. From his perspective, transparency through the connected world caused your company to become a glass box. From my perspective, automation created a community between employees and customers, in which customers are now an integral part of your company. I disagree with Mattin in that I don't believe that there is a transparent box around your company, only a thin membrane where customers enter and exit. I'm more aligned with Phil Terry and Mark Hurst in their book, *Customers Included,* who believe customers need to be at the center of a company's thinking to serve them and embrace them more fully in their business. I see customers in the middle of that company membrane with your employees, creating an ecosystem.

A company's brand is intertwined with every process, expressing values that provoke an emotional response by customers. It's through these processes that a company allows customers to experience a company. As previously stated, although many companies are working on creating corporate customer experiences that reflect the brand and its values, another way for a company to communicate its brand is in how employees communicate with its customers. Although customers and employees are in the same organization community, the customers always maintain their personal brand (personalities) outside of the company. The employees are challenged to maintain their own personal brand and internalize aspects of the organization's brand to reflect that personality while at work as well. The employees are part of the company community with the customers; however, because the employees are members of and represent the organization, they need to be closely aligned with how the brand is communicated and experienced.

**What if your brand is not communicated well?**

- **Companies will implement the latest "cool" technologies, thinking that will make them stand out.** It could. However, a disconnect happens when the digital or online experience doesn't match the brand identity and other company experiences. It's almost better not to be memorable than be remembered because the experience was sub-par or confusing.

- **You won't be understood by your target market.** If people don't understand what your company does, you may miss key opportunities for expansion and growth. They won't understand the problem you solve and how you can help them. It's like the saying "If the tree falls in the forest and no one is there to see it, did it fall?" If your target market doesn't understand what you are doing and doesn't comprehend how your solution can help them, do they know your company exists?
- **Internal and external brands will emerge that are very different and, subsequently, confusing.** What happens inside a company should be consistent with what happens with customers. It's a single entity. By communicating and expressing the brand differently in these situations, your employees could communicate your organization differently than intended and potentially, yet inadvertently, reset customer expectations.
- **Your employees won't be able to internalize your company brand and culture and not communicate it well.** If your employees don't understand your company brand or culture, how will your customers? This is especially important if your employees are the main brand ambassadors to communicate this to customers.

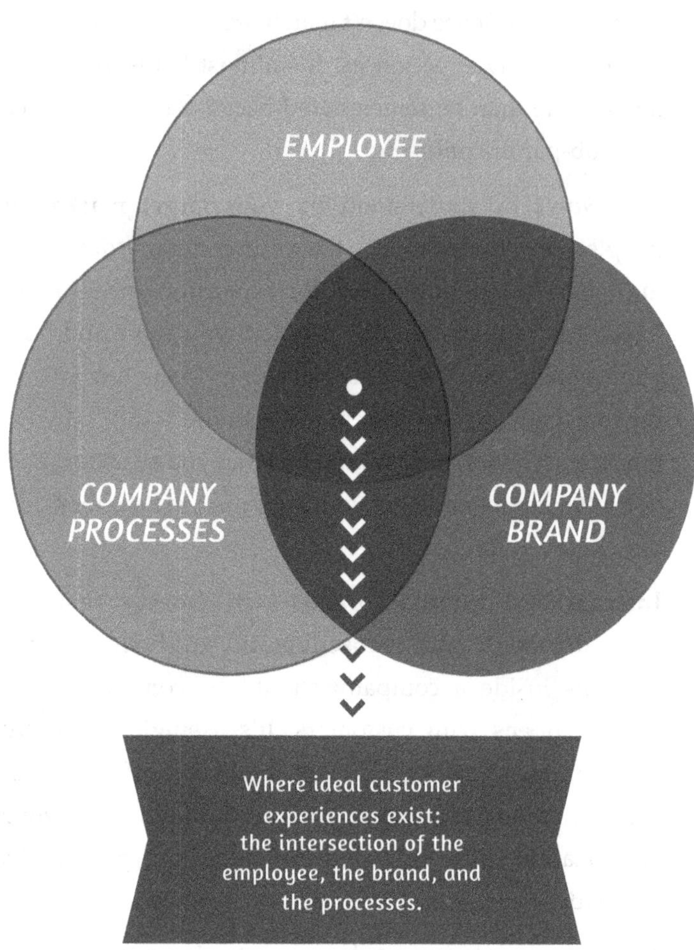


*Figure 4: The Sweet Spot for Experiences*

## The Experience of a Brand at All Ages

When I was a child, I remember going to McDonald's, Burger King, Howard Johnson's, and Holiday Inn with my family when we traveled because we knew the experience to expect. The food quality was about the same each time, the hotel room experience was close to the same, and the bathroom experience was mostly the same. When it wasn't the same, that was cause for concern.

It wasn't that my parents didn't want to experiment and try new things. The challenge of traveling with a kid during mealtimes is knowing whether that kid will like a restaurant. This sounds odd, but children having a calm restaurant experience helps the family to have a fairly peaceful, enjoyable trip. My parents learned this lesson during a family trip when I was two years old. We went to a restaurant that my parents often enjoyed when they visited this particular small town in New Hampshire. My two-year-old self had a different take. From what my parents told me, I made it abundantly clear that I hated the food and was having a challenging time. Our waitress, luckily, took pity on my parents and kept me occupied with a restaurant tour while my parents ate their meals in peace.

In this case, the problem wasn't the restaurant. The problem wasn't my parents. The problem was my customer expectations during my terrible twos. I wasn't expecting a nice, sit-down restaurant with elegant pastries and food choices. I wanted HoJo's toast and jam and to make a mess. By going to places that offered an experience that my parents knew I would like, my parents could more or less be guaranteed that we'd have a peaceful time that met everyone's expectations.

Chain restaurants achieve this. They offer a consistent atmosphere, food, and service. As a very young customer, I needed a place where my messiness wasn't an issue, there were a lot of distractions, and the food wasn't complicated. I got what I was expecting. And those brands delivered.

## When a Brand Intertwines with Celebrity Executive Personality

Sometimes, a company doesn't develop its own brand personality and instead adopts the personality of a celebrity executive. This may happen in early-stage startups when the founder has a strong, defined personality. He or she may not understand that it is important for a company to have its own identity or brand, separate from him-/herself and the employees. However, in all cases this usually happens because branding is not valued or understood.

Sadly, over the years, I've noticed that most leaders don't understand what a brand is or how it works. I've heard CEOs talk about colors and tone in terms of what they like or don't like, rather than how they reflect and communicate the company's cultures and values. Same with word choices. Suggestions are based on personal preferences rather than on business communication needs. There may be no discussion about what colors represent culturally around the globe. Or the communication value of a serif (tradition, stability) versus a sans serif (modern, innovative) font. Or the meaning of select words. These may seem like minor concerns, but they represent three issues:

- The executive doesn't understand what branding and brand communications are.
- The executive can't communicate business needs.
- The executive can't separate his personal needs from his business needs.

However, I have talked to founders who understand how company values and culture should be integrated with brand communications. These companies always succeed.

As we know, a company's brand and culture are reflected in customer experiences. If the brand reflects the personality of the founders and celebrity executives, then the customer interactions reflect how these company leaders, rather than the company, would act with customers directly. In these cases, you have to wonder: Is the leader creating a community between customers and employees through the brand? Or is that leader encouraging a direct relationship with employees and customers? If the company answers *yes* to the later, that means that the company doesn't have its own brand personality; it reflects the personality of the leader.

A great example of a company that developed a brand that reflected the personality of its key executives is Uber. Travis Kalanick has a strong and unique personality. He was very successful in a number of peer-to-peer (P2P) ventures and made a number of industries reconsider how they conduct business. He was considered a P2P business genius. When the opportunity to be CEO for Uber became available to him in 2010, it only made sense for him to accept the challenge and start their shared and intertwined history. Uber was a company that had a concept in line with his thinking; it was a company that seemed like something he should have founded.

There were many shared histories and traits that made Kalanick the perfect leader for Uber. Uber was a technology service for independent drivers, challenging taxis; Kalanick had previously founded numerous P2P businesses, challenging existing norms and regulations. This gave Kalanick a reputation as a rebel hero.[54] Uber was seen as a maverick company; Kalanick's personality traits of recklessness and arrogance were the legendary reasons behind his success—another reason why he was the perfect leader for Uber. Uber was well-funded to start; Kalanick made a fortune from his previous company and was independently wealthy. Money wouldn't be an issue for their shared success. The match seemed uncanny, fated for success. At the same time, these similarities provided a basis for the intertwining of Uber's and Kalanick's identity, which in the end, didn't serve either well. Uber had the brand potential to revolutionize short-distance travel (it did) and become an industry leader (depending on your perspective, it did) or use its irreverence as arrogance to challenge an existing industry and its employees and customers (it did this instead).

How Uber was described at its founding almost foreshadowed its fate, mainly due to the influence of the leaders' personality on its brand: "Back in 2010, Uber's founders launched an app that let wealthy bros summon BMWs and Lincoln Town Cars at the push of a button. It was an elegant, elitist way for Kalanick, his friends, and people like them to 'roll around San Francisco like ballers.'"[55,56]

From 2010 to 2012, Uber had a reputation of being an innovator and disruptor, causing chaos in the market while creating a new status quo with Kalanick as its rising, irreverent star. When Uber became mainstream after 2012, so did the expectations for how a company and CEO should behave. It needed to mature.

As a company grows by increasing its employees, customers, and revenues, its investors, customers, and employees expect it to adopt more formal practices, procedures, and industry leadership. A company transforming from being a startup into an established firm is expected to assume a personality of its own, more formal and separate from the founders and leaders. And the leaders are supposed to help in that transition.

"Bill Gates and Mark Zuckerberg went through something similar," said Uber board member Bill Gurley. "They were the young entrepreneurs who were allowed to kind of say anything, and do anything, and then all of a sudden their companies had this kind of influence on the world. That responsibility gets thrown at you quickly."[57]

That transition didn't really happen between Uber and Kalanick. Uber and Kalanick went from being the challenger to setting the new standard. But the new standard of Uber's culture was considered by many insiders and outsiders as sexist, irresponsible, and at times, above the law. This reflected on Uber's transportation solution from being perceived as innovative to simply unsafe.

Kalanick tried to shift this and change Uber's culture and brand, decoupling it from his personality. At an Uber employee meeting in Las Vegas, he famously introduced Uber's 14 core values. Sadly, they weren't unique to Uber and were loosely based on Amazon's values.[58] The Uber 14 included terms like *superpumped* and a *champion mindset*, and mentioned embracing "principled confrontation," which resulted in creating a culture more reflective of Kalanick's personality than the employees.[59] It seemed that his attempt at defining Uber as separate from himself didn't work.

News stories continued to prove that Uber wasn't maturing as a responsible company. Scandals around sexual harassment, poor treatment of drivers, drivers raping women, and Kalanick's personal shenanigans filled the news cycle. But then again, how could Uber mature on its own? Kalanick never created a true brand, identity, or culture for Uber besides using himself as the role model.

The company continued to have ridiculous revenue growth yet hemorrhaged cash. There was no structure, no CFO, and no COO. There were no checks and balances between executives. Its ethics were in question. It didn't resemble a stable company by any stretch.

Sheelah Kolhatkar wrote in an article in ***The New Yorker***, "Nick Beim, a partner at the venture-capital firm Venrock, told me, 'This particular company was so far out on the spectrum. It has cast such a shadow over Silicon Valley.'"[60] But with the money Uber was making, its continued financial success reinforced the idea that ruthlessness will be rewarded. Kolhatkar continued in the article: "'Is it O.K. to condone unethical behavior if you make a lot of money?' Beim asked.

'It shouldn't be, but that's the looming question Silicon Valley needs to take a stand on.'"[61]

Finally, in 2016, Uber rebranded itself in an attempt to "redeem" its reputation. "There's an evolution here, for the founder as well as for the company," [Kalanick] says, "because really, they're very connected."[62]

After a number of iterations and side steps, Kalanick and his design team created and launched a logo for Uber/ Kalanick that met Apple's app deadlines. Unfortunately, the logo produced could not meet the business requirements to scale for holidays and regions, so Uber decided to create a style guide and logo implementations globally. This was a severe workaround for the problem of Kalanick not understanding corporate branding and a brand communication being based on personal taste instead of being based on business requirements.

"The warmth, the colors, those things," he says, nodding to the new brand. "That happens, when you start to know who you are."[63] Whenever I read this quote, I wonder if Kalanick was referring to himself or to Uber. Their existence was so intertwined, it's hard to separate the two. And this quote makes you wonder if Kalanick suspected the same.

But in many ways, Kalanick and Uber were more than intertwined. They had almost the same identity. Uber's values, aesthetics, and personality were a mirror image of Kalanick. Uber was a creation in Kalanick's image and never had the opportunity to get its own identity separate from him and mature as a global brand.

Eventually, Kalanick was ousted after one too many scandals inside and outside Uber. Dara Khosrowshahi entered as new CEO. Not surprisingly, one of his first tasks was to rebrand Uber and establish new core values. He hired a firm. It utilized a creative brief that outlined business requirements to consider when creating the new brand. Khosrowshahi set Uber on a new path to mature, which it has been doing ever since.[64]

**If what happened in Uber is happening in your company:**

- **Expect massive culture change in your company after an executive leaves or a new one is added.** In most companies, when an executive leaves, most certainly the employees will feel the impact of his or her departure. However, the company's culture often doesn't change much. Neither should the brand or the strategy. The same is true if a new executive is added. But in companies in which there are major shifts after an executive leaves, the company may have never shifted to have its own identity. The question you need to ask yourself in these situations: Is this a company represented by the executive or everyone? A company should be bigger than a single person and include the perspectives of many. An executive carries a lot of influence in the company's culture—but it shouldn't be so much that his departure causes a complete culture shift. If it does, you may be in a company like Uber.
- **Your company may have celebrity followers willing to buy your product—not customers.** Customers purchase a product from a company because it solves a problem. Followers are fans of specific people or companies. They may purchase products from the celebrity owner, but I would argue that the driver to purchase from such a

company is based on the customer's affinity for the celebrity and not the problem that the product solves. The question to ask your business in this situation: If you removed the celebrity, would there be interest in the product or the problem it solves? Although Kalanick was controversial, he did get press for Uber, which drove additional interest in it. Lyft has an equally good product but doesn't have the same brand awareness as Uber. Uber reached a ubiquitous brand status whereby the brand name has become a noun representing a car ordered through an app, almost in the same way that Kleenex is a noun representing facial tissues. Even Lyft customers use Uber as a noun. A factor for Uber's market prominence is most likely linked to the public's awareness of Kalanick. People would try the product to see how it works. Or boycott the product because of something he did. His relationship to the brand drove his followers to use it (or his detractors to boycott it). In that regard, Uber's success could be directly related to him as a person. And is that healthy for a company?

- **Customer and user experiences reflect the preferences of the executive rather than the company.** When leaders express their preferences as personal likes and dislikes, a company is being guided by an individual rather than a leader. Ideally, business requirements, a brand, and customer insights should drive how an experience is designed and built. When personal preferences are driving a project, you have to wonder if you are creating an asset for the company and its customers or that person and his followers. Most likely, it's being made for the person and his followers.

- **The celebrity executive needs to be involved in every detail.** When a company reflects an executive personality rather than its own, the executive needs to be present in every decision because he or she is the company. Brands empower employees to make the right decision because they are participants in the organization and each participant represents brand interests. But in the case of a strong celebrity leader whose personality is the brand, since we don't really know what others are thinking, we don't truly know what the brand of such a company really is. An employee has no idea how to address this in his or her work and may not make an appropriate decision. So when creating customer experiences in this environment, there is a lot of micromanagement, little sharing and input, and typically, whatever the leader says, goes.

Brands empower employees to make the right decisions.

## Conclusion

For the longest time, my company, Gearmark and I were commingled into the same brand. I didn't realize how much of a problem this was until I wanted to build Gearmark's social media presence. I realized that how people experienced the Gearmark brand was really how people were experiencing me. Most of my customers perceived Gearmark to be just a legal entity for me to do business with larger companies. And for the most part, that was true.

Mary Brodie ran projects a certain way and had a communication style that should have been different from Gearmark. But it wasn't. Or at least it wasn't clear how it was different. If there was a second employee, maybe that would have helped build a differentiation. In many ways, Gearmark didn't have its own voice.

This raises the question if there is really such a thing as a one-person company. And it explains why a solopreneur will often blend their personal brand with their company's brand.

It's difficult when starting a company to create a culture that's separate from you. It requires a very conscious effort to do that. Often when you start a company, it's a "team of me." And that may last for a while as you build a product, hire contractors, and try to establish yourself in the market. It's difficult for people to have two aspects to their personality: One part stays true to who they are, and the other part is true to reflect corporate values and voice. It's inevitable for a startup's culture to reflect some aspects of the executive personalities involved, either communication style, leadership style, or values. However, as a company grows, it needs to transition to become its own entity.

I found this quote while reading an *New Yorker* article by Sheelah Kolhatkar about Uber:

> *Simon Rothman, a partner at the venture firm Greylock Partners, told me that the culture of a company often reflects the personality of its founder. "Here's an analogy: If you have parents, their DNA is in you," he said. "If someone else raises you, you'll be different, but you won't be radically different. I think the longer a founder stays at a company, the longer it will take to change the culture at that company."*[65]

I agree and disagree with that statement. Leadership most definitely influences a company's culture. But if a brand is established, and a company's brand includes its culture, then the leadership could change and there would naturally be an impact (because people create the company's community), but it shouldn't cause so much discord because the company's brand should be defined enough to embrace and include the new leadership influence. This is why founders need to acknowledge that a company needs a brand, its own identity, and that it is not an extension of him- or herself.

Sadly, I don't believe that any of my customers experienced what it is like to work with Gearmark, but they knew what it was like to work with me. This is a learning lesson for any entrepreneur and small business owner. I want to change that in the future so working with Gearmark will provide customers the same experience each time, and employees won't become clones of me. Each time I hire someone, I look for someone with a personality different than mine because I want to create a company, not have clones of me telling me that I was right.

Branding is an important nuance to establish in a startup, and we can't excuse founders for having a company's brand reflect themselves. If you ask me, it's a sign of lazy leadership.

It was a powerful experience for me to work with a resume writer who also worked on personal branding. I created a site for myself that was based on my own personal style, which I worked with a stylist to develop. During these branding processes, I realized that my Mary Brodie brand was completely different from Gearmark. Now when I create Gearmark branded materials, I create simple interfaces with illustrations and geometric patterns. The Mary Brodie brand uses animal prints, flashy colors, and fun photography. Both can and should be different and coexist. We are separate entities, and Gearmark is entitled to have its own personality.

I look forward to the day that I can meet with one or two employees and discuss the vision and mission statement of Gearmark, list its values, and discuss its personality. That's the only way Gearmark as a brand can grow and mature.

You can only understand who a company is by experiencing its brand. It's the same as saying you can only understand someone else by engaging and interacting with them. Many leaders misunderstand branding, believing that it's about a graphic, colors, and font choices, but it is much more than that. Branding represents the personality of a company. A brand allows a company to be an independent entity, separate from its leaders and employees. Customers who work with a company have expectations for the interactions and experiences based on the brand values and the interactions it creates. Employees express the brand, the culture, as well as their own personality, when working with customers. It is inevitable. But the main brand expression emerges in all company activities and customer experiences. It is this brand experience that binds the community, the ecosystem, between the customer and employees.

CHAPTER 4

# Plan: Activities Showing How You Provide Value

It's not enough to have a vision, mission, and brand. You have to provide customer value and earn revenue. During the dotcom boom in the 1990s, many companies had a vision and a brand, but not a clear, well-defined plan. How they were going to bring ideas to life and generate revenue beyond creating a website wasn't clear—and that was the problem.

If you don't have a plan, then how can you create an effective customer experience for your business operations? The plan provides the operational, tangible steps for executing your business.

There are four considerations to include in your plan so it is successful to implement:

- Flexibility
- KPIs and targets
- Risk management through internal communications
- Planned exit strategies

This may seem heavily focused on company operations, and in some ways it is. Marketing, sales, and customer support should be the teams supporting the revenue- and relationship-related KPIs. Product creation and production will have its own set of KPIs. You can't create successful customer experiences without knowing what you are creating, why, and what you expect to achieve from the effort.

If an operations plan doesn't include these areas, it will be more difficult to determine if it is successful. Some of these areas help you consider details and alternative approaches to what you may have originally planned to make a stronger business.

| CONSIDERATION | WHY YOU NEED IT | WHAT IF YOU DON'T HAVE IT? |
| --- | --- | --- |
| **Flexibility** | • Respond to industry trends, customer preference changes, and innovations faster.<br>• Shift from limitations to opportunities and improvements faster.<br>• Acknowledge that there are many ways to solve a problem. | • **Stagnation:** unable to quickly change a plan for growth and improvement<br>• **Limits:** believe there are limited solutions<br>• **Missed opportunities:** chase trends rather than lead them |

| CONSIDERATION | WHY YOU NEED IT | WHAT IF YOU DON'T HAVE IT? |
|---|---|---|
| **KPIs and targets** | • Define success for your organization, which should complement your vision, mission, and brand.<br>• Identify the value you and your team bring to your organization.<br>• Support team-building. People can work toward specific goals and ideas together.<br>• Maintain focus on organization goals. | • **No way to determine success:** no way to know if your plan is a success, a flop, or somewhere in between<br>• **No tangible way to unify a group:** Goals help direct a team to achieve results. Without a goal, people drift, unfocused. There needs to be a way to unify people on a team. |
| **Risk management through internal communications** | • Increase clarity and transparency so employees understand risks and how to avoid problems.<br>• Provide a feeling of inclusiveness. People like to know the "inside scoop."<br>• Strengthen accountability so customers know what's happening and why, and build trust.<br>• Build a customer community:<br>  • Allow customers to share their opinions and ideas.<br>  • Provide customers inside knowledge so they feel part of the larger company ecosystem and community. | • **Murky processes:** difficult to identify and solve problems without clarity<br>• **Faulty customer perception:** If a customer doesn't know what's happening, they will fabricate a story that makes sense for them.<br>• **No community:** It's hard to build a sense of community if there isn't a common goal to work toward. |
| **Planned exit strategies** | • Programs don't last forever. Sometimes, ideas need to be retired when they aren't meeting specific criteria or goals:<br>  • Not producing results<br>  • Not meeting customer needs (market changed or trends emerged)<br>  • Organization changes<br>• How do you exit managing the program/product?<br>• How do you transition to something new? | • Continue with an initiative that isn't successful<br>• Witness painful downfalls |

## The Role of Operations in Creating Memorable Customer Experiences

There are two ways an experience can be memorable: It's exceptionally well-done or exceptionally poor. This is why sometimes I think that if companies can't invest in creating a stellar customer experience, it's almost better to create a well-done basic experience that meets customer needs. It's functional, customers are able to complete the tasks needed, and they remember that your product helped them get the job done. The customer win in this case is that she isn't frustrated. That sounds like a low goal, but it's actually not. If you consider the peak-end rule, where people remember an experience as the average of the most intense part of the experience and what happens at the end, being mediocre is a great goal and leaves the user remembering a generally positive experience.[66] The average of a mediocre experience with no disappointments and a successful result is a great, positive memory. The user completed their task easily. It may sound easy to do, but it's challenging to create a basic experience that allows a user to successfully achieve their goals. A user experiencing a system without frustration is the first step toward a customer building a great relationship with your brand.

Many sites don't consider a user to be a converted customer until they purchase at least two or three times. Usually during the first site visit, the user is learning how your site works. If a first-time customer experiences a frictionless experience, that creates a positive memory and is a great first step towards a happy, returning customer to repeat that experience. After that first experience, your company has the opportunity to show the customer how else you can help them through content, social media, and support.

> If you don't build a customer relationship through actions like engagement and accountability, it will be challenging to build emotional engagement, trust, and loyalty in your company community. If you can't do that, then you may never sell a product.

VISION

Brand

EMPLOYEES

CUSTOMERS

Mission, Plans, Activities

EXPERIENCE

*Figure 5: New Approach—Business When You Focus on Relationships*

As we know, a company's customer experience is the combination of its action plans and brand within a community of employees, customers, and partners.[67] It's in this community space that a relationship is developed between the customer and the company (employees plus partners). The brand provides the company's *why*, its essence and reason for existing, and the action plan defines the *what*, the solution (product or service) and the experience activities. The experience activities could include the product or service itself, marketing activities from awareness to lead generation, and interactions with sales and support. However, customer experience activities don't only include what the customer experiences directly. They can include operational areas like:

- How products are manufactured,
- How management decisions are made,
- How processes are designed, and
- How customer experiences are identified.

These activities are the result of actions blending with the brand and company values in the company community. And as we saw in the branding section about bringing meaning to a brand for customers through CSR programs, how an activity happens is just as important as the activity itself. The interactions among people, teams, resources, materials, and activities speak to your company's values and its solutions to problems.

To be competitive in business today, you need to meet customer needs in a more inclusive way. Although inclusive approaches have a perception of being costly, it's becoming a fact that including customers, employees, and partners in your business is highly effective and just good business sense. Inclusion results in happy customers with happier employees and business partners. To achieve this, we all need to think about business differently. Switching around an assembly line, revisiting your ad spend, or tweaking your lead gen process isn't enough to reswizzle your business to be focused on your customers. Although these activities produce results, they aren't ultimately including employees and customers in your processes. To do this, you need to take more drastic measures that involve changing how your company operates.

There are four major methodology approaches that ***will*** shift your company to focus on your customers, as well as employee and partners:

- Agile
- Lean
- Design Thinking
- Sustainability

These methodologies are revolutionizing businesses and creating exceptional customer experiences because they focus on the relationships people have with each other and how they work rather than what they do to achieve a goal. Through these approaches, companies can experience benefits like increased revenue, improved cost savings and organizational efficiency, and decreased manufacturing time so customers can get what they want and need faster.

## How These Methodologies Help Customers, Employees and Partners Build a Relationship and Contribute to the Bottom Line

| METHODOLOGY | HOW IT HELPS CUSTOMERS | HOW IT HELPS EMPLOYEES AND PARTNERS | BOTTOM-LINE CONTRIBUTION |
| --- | --- | --- | --- |
| **Agile** | Customers can access features when needed. | Employees work on the highest-priority work at any time.<br><br>Employees feel that they are contributing value to the company in their daily work. | Highest-priority, top-value work is completed first.<br><br>Steady flow of work so the team isn't exhausted and functioning optimally.<br><br>Optimize time and budget to develop what's necessary. |
| **Lean** | Customers receive products they want faster. | Employees contribute feedback to optimize processes and output.<br><br>Employees feel involved in the process and that they are contributing value. | Increased employee satisfaction and improved turnaround times for product distribution. |
| **Design Thinking** | Customers are involved in defining the problem, suggesting solutions, and testing the results. | Employees involved in the process to define the problem and suggest solutions. | High-level of innovation (up to +200% increase above S&P).[67,68] |
| **Sustainability** | Customers are able to purchase products that are environmentally friendly; feel like they are part of something larger than themselves (meaningfulness). | Employees and the surrounding community provide feedback and structure for how work should be done as a global corporate citizen. | Millions saved by a company able to consider its role in the world, local communities, and in people's lives. |

### *Do Business Activities Always Have a Direct Connection to the Bottom Line?*

We often believe that operations are directly related to revenue savings or earnings. There are countless business books with case studies and ideas for how to "win at business" by optimizing operations. It seems that there is a solution to almost every problem. We implement these best practices as if they are the magic wand to increase profits and improve customer engagement. We'll measure every aspect of a production line to reduce time, reduce costs, and increase efficiency (whatever that means for an organization). But should we be looking at only those impacts as indicators of success? Or should we consider how improving relationships between people during these optimization processes can help us reach our goal instead?

There's an art to creating a great action plan (or business plan) that involves much more than implementing best practices for an operational area. You may notice that some founders will form a successful startup and leverage a similar business plan for their next venture yet experience failure. Or an organization will implement the same processes as another company and see different results. The target market and audience could be the same for the businesses. The product could be solving a similar problem in the same industry. But the differences between these organizations usually lie within the team, the business partners, the investors, and other stakeholders involved in the business.

It becomes clear that success lies in the people involved and their passion for the vision, mission, and brand values, not necessarily the business plan.

This would explain why a process that was successful at one company's location may be implemented at another location without corresponding gains and improvements.

Describing how to make a great action plan is like trying to describe to someone how to walk. You can outline the mechanics of walking—you put one foot in front of the other, heel to toe, bend your knee, and propel yourself forward. And that's what these books about best practices describe: the mechanics of doing business. But there could be mannerisms or gestures you make when you walk that are unique to you. Walking is a personal identifier. How you walk makes you, you. The same is true for how a company does an activity.

You could argue that walking is a fairly solitary activity, and companies have more than one employee so this is an inadequate analogy. So a better example may be an assembly line to put papers into folders for an event. There are many ways to achieve this goal. A line of people could pass pieces of paper to each other, each adding a new sheet, and the last person places this collection of papers into a folder. Alternatively, each person could put a sheet of paper into a folder and pass a folder down the row. Or you could have multiple people doing this assembly line by themselves or multiple lines of people in a row passing papers. There is no right or wrong answer. **However, I would propose that the most successful approach for that assembly line is the one where the people participating are happiest and agree that they are using the best approach.** If a team can come to consensus to determine which approach is most efficient, harmonious, and efficient *for them,* then you have a winning process and team.

Let's say you want to add people to your folder assembly line from another team. They could be considered partners in your company's community. These people would need to be brought into your production community and either use their own lines or their staff is integrated into your lines. But in the end, it doesn't matter. The approach that works best is the one where everyone is involved in the process, comes to agreement about the best way to work, and there is harmony in the community.

In Agile, Lean, Design Thinking, and Sustainability, the company's community (customers, partners, employees) is involved in the organization's decision-making and process-improvement recommendations. Everyone is engaged to improve the processes and to achieve the vision and goals. No one in the company's community is left out.

Sadly, companies sometimes misinterpret what it means for their customers and partners to care about their products and how they make them. They may assume that this is their business only, but in a way, it's not. Customers have a right to care about how a product is made. They are team members in the new world. How you respond to them about their concerns, as well as understanding the product, process, and results, is part of the customer experience. Transparency is a key element of all four methodologies and a vital component in companies of the new world. Some questions you should ask yourself about your customers to ensure you are ready to include them in your business community are:

- If your customers knew *how* you made your product, all of the details, do you think they would still buy it?

- Do you think your customers would approve of how you treat employees? How about partners?
- Would your partners agree that you treat your customers well?

However, a challenge with such relationship-driven methodologies is that most companies measure effectiveness through work completed and bottom-line revenues (or savings). But in this new world, these are only a few indicators of success. If work isn't getting done, these metrics don't always help identify what is causing the problem. We need to measure more "soft" criteria to improve productivity, like employee happiness, engagement, accountability, and transparency. We need to somehow measure the quality of culture and relationships to determine if an environment has the emotional health to succeed and correlate that with the desired productivity.

To have a great customer experience, you need a great employee experience. This will be explored in future chapters about employees and customers. In all of the examples included in this chapter, the operations that support memorable customer experiences require employees and customers to feel valued for their contributions and ensure that everyone is making a difference.

## Agile: Designed to Improve Customer Experiences

It's now popular for organizations to incorporate Agile software development methodologies (an approach in which self-organized and cross-functional teams collaboratively and iteratively build software) in other business teams, like marketing and finance, to increase flexibility and respond quickly to changing markets. Because you are responding to issues that are higher priority and working on what is truly needed for the business to succeed, you are essentially reducing waste. This can be a positive shift, allowing a business to pivot as new customer needs appear in the market. Although this sounds ideal, such a disruptive approach can create business challenges.

Often, Agile methodologies are misunderstood and misinterpreted. I often say that some teams don't understand the difference between Agile and chaos. Agile calls for iterative development focused on providing business value today. It also promotes culture changes to incorporate transparency, improved communication and team dynamics, and clarity. It's process-driven based on priorities, which is healthy for most companies. According to a McKinsey report in January 2018, "research shows that agile organizations have a 70 percent chance of being in the top quartile of organizational health, the best indicator of long-term performance."[70]

A key element of Agile is the customer, as referenced in the four Agile values and 12 principles of Agile. Companies easily embrace the speed and flexibility of Agile, but they often forget the core reason why Agile exists: It's a way to create working software for customers who may have shifting needs and problems. It helps your company improve your overall customer experience and focus more on their needs. That's the true power of Agile.

**The 4 Values of Agile**[71]

- Individuals and interactions over processes and tools
- Working software over comprehensive documentation
- Customer collaboration over contract negotiation
- Responding to change over following a plan

**The 12 Principles of Agile**[72]

1. Our highest priority is to satisfy the customer through early and continuous delivery of valuable software.
2. Welcome changing requirements, even late in development. Agile processes harness change for the customer's competitive advantage.
3. Deliver working software frequently, from a couple of weeks to a couple of months, with a preference to the shorter timescale.
4. Business people and developers must work together daily throughout the project.
5. Build projects around motivated individuals. Give them the environment and support they need, and trust them to get the job done.
6. The most efficient and effective method of conveying information to and within a development team is face-to-face conversation.
7. Working software is the primary measure of progress.

8. Agile processes promote sustainable development. The sponsors, developers, and users should be able to maintain a constant pace indefinitely.
9. Continuous attention to technical excellence and good design enhances agility.
10. Simplicity—the art of maximizing the amount of work not done—is essential.
11. The best architectures, requirements, and designs emerge from self-organizing teams.
12. At regular intervals, the team reflects on how to become more effective, then tunes and adjusts its behavior accordingly.

### *Agile Can Take All Shapes and Sizes*

Although Agile is accepted as a modern best practice for development teams, each organization embraces Agile a little differently with slightly different results. The success of an Agile implementation rests in the consistency of how each individual member of a team interprets what Agile is, how it will help them, and what it can do for their business. The details about how Agile works within an organization can vary based on culture, but a sign of a successful implementation is the flexibility it provides the business and development team to meet customer needs.

I've worked with a number of teams that adopted Agile. The most successful implementations resulted from the technology team driving them and encouraging organizational acceptance. They experienced the direct benefits: reduced time pressure, ongoing improvement and innovation, reduced waste, and improved product quality. The business needed to change how it worked to develop a flexible product vision before starting an Agile development project. Rather than a thorough, fully-thought out vision that was highly (and needlessly) detailed, the business needed to provide a guiding vision where the entire team has room to contribute at all levels. The end result of every Agile implementation aligns the business and technology teams, allowing them to influence each other to determine what's needed to produce a great product. The developers aren't simply building what's requested. The business isn't dictating the final solution. Everyone is involved and included defining what the customer needs.

However, if the technology team isn't fully bought into the ideology and benefits of Agile, the implementation won't work as planned.

As an example, I was working with a client to help launch a product. We decided to leverage Agile methodologies to have the flexibility necessary to accommodate new customer requirements for our beta launch. This was an early-stage, SaaS startup with a small development team. We needed to quickly meet customer needs with new functionality while maintaining the beta by fixing bugs and enhancing existing features. The development team was adamant that they were leveraging Agile in their approaches, but it became clear that wasn't happening. They were open to daily SCRUM meetings and weekly demos regarding completed tasks for some transparency. They welcomed implementing more formal QA processes at all levels of development, from unit testing and code reviews to regression testing, to improve product quality. They appreciated receiving detailed stories to understand how the system should work. And prioritization kept them focused. But working in formal two-week iterations became a challenge. It felt as if there was a struggle between creating an end product versus making iterative progress with a few usable features.

They were driven to complete tasks to meet time lines. There is a difference. Agile was created for the business and development teams to have an opportunity to reswizzle priorities before an iteration to develop and release usable customer software features as needed. The developers could help brainstorm ways to meet customer needs quickly with the business. When a team works toward meeting a time line to complete a set of features, they view the complete delivery with all features that are pre-defined as the goal and achievement. When a team is looking at how they can release a set of features within an iteration (or two or three) for immediate customer use, they have a different mindset. They want to deliver what's possible as it is ready. If there are dependencies, then the team will communicate that it will require another iteration to complete the work, but the team is driven to continually deliver software for customers to use, continually improving features and functionality. For an Agile product, developing a basic, usable app and adding on what's necessary later is more valuable than waiting three to six months to deliver a monster app with potentially all bells and whistles pre-built (if the functionality even gets built), whether or not it is really needed. This disconnect between delivering a package of functionality versus iterative releases made product delivery challenging. And this is one of the main differences between Waterfall (packaged delivery) and Agile (iterative releases).

In this project, there was a perception that the startup was constantly changing its mind about the product. But that wasn't true. The top-five feature priorities were the same for over a year. We would switch our work prioritizations based on client requests. Changing priorities is not the same as changing the product. My client's customer was happy that we reprioritized work to meet its needs, but the development team had a different perspective.

Although the team wasn't fully accepting of Agile, they were impeccable at scoping and estimating the time development tasks would take to complete using their methods. So we implemented a compromise. We would submit stories and requirements; they would provide an estimate and complete the work. It was a hybrid of Waterfall and Agile, mostly Waterfall, but we were able to leverage the elements of Agile we needed to support our customer requirements, gain some visibility into the work, and provide the development firm the comfort of Waterfall that they needed to feel stable and complete projects. We launched a number of enhancements and new features using this approach. My client's customer was happy that they were getting a system that they could use and mirrored their offline process.

But development moved slowly. We later discovered that an ongoing challenge of this slow development turnaround time was due to a core architectural product issue, which wasn't revealed until a year later. In many ways, that was a symptom of the development firm not fully practicing Agile and embracing transparency. But this issue highlights another challenge of automated businesses in our new community ecosystem that's greater than not embracing Agile: the imperative for business partners to share value systems.

A disconnect of shared values in the company community of customers, employees, and partners can cause a series of endless misunderstandings across teams. In more traditional environments, as we'll see in examples for Lean Manufacturing and Sustainability, a company may not be concerned with how a partner conducted business and manufactured products as long as it was delivering on its agreements to the main company. In that case, the relationship isn't a partnership, but a traditional B2B customer relationship. In a partnership, companies share the benefits of the results. In a traditional B2B customer relationship, both companies maintain separate ecosystems, communities, and customers. What is delivered by the contracted, agreed upon date, and within the agreed budget matter. How that is done has no importance to the customer company. Or at least, that is the premise.

However, in the new automated world, the ecosystem of companies include customers and partners, where vendors are partners too. When a vendor is a partner, both companies are in a way sharing the same customers. A partner may deliver what the company requests, but the company's direct customers will be experiencing that product. In a way, the vendor partner is an extension of the company because they are producing the product or experience. It's like they are a type of extended employee. If the vendor partner has a different culture and value system than the main company, then the disconnect for employee treatment and product quality may be apparent. How can a company manage the disconnect without transparency? That's the problem. If a partner isn't willing to be transparent and an extension of a company, while maintaining its autonomy, then it has a very different role. It becomes a type of provider, not really part of the company's direct community. And this role over time becomes confusing, not just for the company, but the company's customers.

So how did my client's development company see their role in the ecosystem? I suspect they saw my client as a traditional B2B customer, not necessarily a partner. Through various conversations it became clear that *how* they developed the product was their business; they didn't believe that we needed to fully understand how it was developed. This made transparency challenging. However, I can't help but wonder that if we had a senior technical advisor available to ask the questions necessary to hold the development firm accountable if the project would have gone differently? But this point raises the issue of communication and expectations in the company community, a requirement of transparency. My client assumed that the development company would be a partner and exhibit the same transparency as an employee, exposing the good and bad of the technology decisions. But the development team saw their relationship differently: Their client was clearly a customer, needing to know only what was necessary.

Hopefully, their relationship changes in the future. There is promise because the development firm has adopted many Agile methodology behaviors, but until this last issue of transparency and their role in the company's community ecosystem is addressed, there will be ongoing challenges. Success for my client lies in the *how* something is made being just as important as the *what*. And their vendors need to be aligned and agree with that approach. Otherwise, such disconnects are destined to continue in the future.

## Agile's Manufacturing Counterpart: Lean (or Just-in-Time Manufacturing)

Lean methodology "maximizes **customer value** [emphasis in original] while minimizing waste. Simply, lean means creating more value for customers with fewer resources."[73]

Managers in Lean organizations are encouraged to look at an entire process, end-to-end, to gain a broad understanding of how a system can be optimized rather than identifying operational efficiencies at the department level. The Lean manager's goal is to design a process that allows the team to create a high-quality product that can be shipped quickly to customers. Only by looking at the entire flow can a manager better understand potential workflow blocks, discover waste, and identify underutilized talent. In some ways, this is similar to Porter's value chain outlined earlier. You need to look at all components of the chain to optimize processes for decreased costs or to get a better-valued product into customer hands. Looking at pieces doesn't bring revolutionary results.

In traditional assembly line work, individuals complete work that is task-based and repetitive, limited to a specific section of the line. Like their managers, they are focused on optimizing work in their area only. But in a Lean environment, workers have roles that often include multiple tasks in their section of the supply chain. This empowers them to understand the challenges and identify opportunities for reducing waste, improving workflow, and optimizing inventory management along their section of the supply chain, as well as its entirety. For example, rather than include eyelets to tie and lace a shoe, the worker may install the eyelets and the laces, and complete quality control tasks related to its installation. The operator could have ideas about how to optimize the process for any of these items. In a Lean system, everyone becomes responsible for quality control and process improvement because everyone is included working on the process.

Lean originated in Toyota in the 1930s, but some argue that it really started in Ford's end-to-end manufacturing process. Ford's assembly line was highly efficient, but they couldn't implement variety. This was the legendary reason why Ford only produced black cars; it was the only color they could support. Toyota had its own assembly line and by using the Lean approach as the Toyota Production System, it was able to produce product variety to meet customer needs.[74] It continued to optimize its processes over the years, developing best practices for improved product delivery to customers, including customizations. Other companies noticed and leveraged their system for their own purposes. Lean is now considered to be a fairly mainstream manufacturing approach and it has been integrated into Six Sigma to reduce waste, increase variation, and optimize workflow.[75]

Lean benefits many industries besides manufacturing. The book *The Lean Startup* showed entrepreneurs how applying

Lean methodologies and principles to their businesses could help them be hyper-efficient and streamlined. Lean has also been applied to software development to optimize the development process along with Kanban boards (a complementary and supporting tool for Lean that is also leveraged for Agile). Kanban "is a visual system for managing work as it moves through a process. Kanban visualizes both the process (the workflow) and the actual work passing through that process."[76] It was originally developed at Toyota in the 1940s by Taiichi Ohno to help manage the Lean manufacturing product lines. Supermarkets inspired him to create this approach through how they stocked their shelves. They provided the public with just enough product to meet demand, and the visual cue that they needed to restock was an empty shelf. To apply this idea to the workroom floor, he created a board divided into "To Do," "Doing," and "Done." When there are no cards in "Doing," a team member gets a card from the "To Do" list, moves it to "Doing," and starts the task. Once you complete the task, you put it into "Done." Ideally, you should always have a steady flow of cards coming into and out of "To Do" and "Done." If you have a backlog in "To Do," you have a flow problem. If you have too few items in "To Do," there is a backlog somewhere else (and eventually, you'll get too many items in your "To Do" area). Kanban is a great visualization tool to illustrate consistent or inconsistent workflow to improve flow and efficiency.

Today, this approach is leveraged by teams across industries to better understand project status and blocks. The digital product, Trello, is basically a digital version of a Kanban board.

Manufacturing companies, like Flex, use Lean to increasingly optimize workflow globally to have the right products available where customers need and want them. They now are promoting ideas like "sketch-to-scale," which brings new products to scalable, global markets quickly through prototyping, additive manufacturing, and real-time supply chain insights. They are also able to incorporate sustainability through these ideas as well to further meet customer needs.

Companies are delivering great customer experiences through the Lean Methodology because they are able to quickly and effectively deliver solutions to people's problems. By including a team to develop a workflow process, everyone can find better ways of working and producing goods. Teams know what's best because they are doing the work each day. By excluding them from the process, the value of their insights and contributions from in-depth, real-life experience and knowledge gets lost. This comes at a price and cost through future inefficiencies.

**The 7 Modern Tenets of a Lean System[77]**

There are seven tenets that frame how you should be approaching a Lean system within your team:

- Optimize the whole
- Eliminate waste
- Create knowledge
- Build quality in
- Deliver fast by managing flow
- Defer commitment
- Respect people

**5 Lean Principles**[78]

Often confused with the seven tenets, the five principles guide teams to practice the Lean methodology in their organization.

1. **Identify value.** What is the value that you are offering your customers? What do they need? How are they receiving it? This could be considered the problem your company solves.
2. **Map the Value Stream.** Maximize efficiencies and reduce waste by documenting the entire process. A process map helps everyone understand how a system works and makes it easier to identify and remove friction points and blockages.
3. **Create flow.** Discover intersecting points for waste or delays. The goal is to identify how you can streamline processes as much as possible without time gaps in production (people waiting for inventory, stock, or other goods to keep moving).
4. **Establish pull.** A customer's need includes a solution to their problem (the what) delivered in a timeframe (the when). In this step, determine how to get product to customers when they need it.
5. **Seek perfection.** Be the best team you can be through efficiency, an improved approach, and giving the most value to a customer.

### *Lean and Sustainability Solve Supply Chain Crises*

In the previous chapter, we reviewed how Patagonia addressed labor equality and sustainability through the supply chain, which resulted in providing meaning to customers. Patagonia worked with a partner to discover supply chain challenges based on subcontracted work and unethical, yet legal, employment activity southeast Asia. They tried to eliminate this and ultimately, support their brand. But they aren't the only company that struggles with inequalities in the supply chain. Companies like Nike, The Gap, H&M, and Zara experience this as well.

During the 1990s, companies like Nike and The Gap were frequently boycotted for operating sweatshops. The labor abuses included low pay (at times, wage theft), poor working conditions, abusive management, even forced abortions. Although hundreds would boycott their store, thousands continued to purchase from them. They felt pressure to change, but at the same time, not change because it ultimately didn't hurt their bottom line. However, Nike had a very different perspective.

Nike went from being a serial offender of poorly treating third-party manufacturing employees in the supply chain to recently maintaining their bronze supply chain standard across all manufacturers. There is more work to be done, although it took years just to get where they are now. It all started in 1996, when Jill Kerr Conway, a board member for Nike, argued that at least one director should be able to speak first-hand about the labor issues in the contract factories in Southeast Asia. The President of Nike agreed, and from 1997 until 2001, she regularly visited all of the factories.

What she noticed right away was that there was a clear communication problem between management and the workers. The workers spoke various dialects of Indonesian; management spoke Taiwanese. This caused friction because management literally didn't know how to communicate with their teams. Rather than discover the best way to communicate with their employees, the Taiwanese managers yelled single word commands, inadvertently creating a hostile and abusive work environment.

International Youth Foundation, an organization that supports the well-being of young people globally, persuaded Nike to create an NGO to survey the workers. It recruited women faculty from universities in various countries who spoke the workers' language and understood their cultures to do the research. This resulted in 67,000 anonymous interviews that provided insights for later management training.[79,80]

Meanwhile, Conway worked to make Nike accountable for its errors. In 1998, Nike CEO Phillip Knight acknowledged what was happening and that action was needed. He said: "The Nike product has become synonymous with slave wages, forced overtime, and arbitrary abuse . . .I truly believe the American consumer doesn't want to buy products made under abusive conditions."[81]

Conway, Knight, and the Nike board understood that American consumers didn't see these manufacturers as companies separate from Nike. To them, they were part of the Nike corporate ecosystem. If a third-party manufacturer was mistreating employees, then American and European customers perceived that Nike supported that practice as well.

As Nike was making improvements to the various manufacturing plants, it considered updating its operations approaches using more modern methodologies, like Lean manufacturing. Not only was Nike able to reduce waste and improve output, but it empowered workers to take responsibility for quality control and process improvement across their areas, ultimately increasing their value to the business. This process improvement decreased worker overtime, among other issues. Nike was able to identify problems in the manufacturing chain right away and fix them to produce savings in all areas.

Surprisingly, Nike noticed that employees in some countries were contributing more when they were using Lean methodologies.

> *Adopting even a single lean production line was associated with a labor compliance improvement of nearly a third of a letter grade, while a 100% lean factory saw an improvement of over half a letter grade. Overall, lean adoption reduced the probability of serious labor violations by 15 percent. The researchers also found a statistically uncertain but still positive effect on health, safety, and environmental compliance.*[82]

One reason this improved was that the managers were treating their employees better, valuing their opinions, and implementing their suggestions. Including the team's recommendations helped these production lines see an uptick in all of their measurements.

In 2005, Nike was the first company in its industry to demonstrate supply chain transparency by publishing a complete list of its contract factories.[83] It also issued a first version of a CSR report that detailed pay scales and working conditions in its factories and openly documented ongoing problems. Nike later published a Code of Conduct and Code Leadership Standards to protect worker rights and create safe working environments in these third-party factories. The Standards included a scoring and ranking system for factories (color-coded from red to gold) that assessed how each applied Lean methodologies, labor treatment, health and safety, energy and carbon, and sustainability. Environmental and human resource management performance was given equal weight as business metrics. By 2015, 86 percent of Nike's contract factories rated bronze or above.[84]

This may sound like a modest achievement, but some facts about Nike to understand the scope of their initiative:

- It has manufacturing contracts with more than 785 factories, across India, Vietnam, Philippines, and South America.[85]
- It has more than 1 million workers worldwide.[86]
- Nike manufacturers more than 500,000 unique products.[87]

Nike's management created a strong sense of community by listening to its suppliers, customers, and employees expressing their ideas and concerns. This allowed the company to grow (including the supply chain), to improve their reputation and brand, and to improve working conditions. Nike's implementation of Lean brought people together to make a better product and improve not just their working conditions, but their own lives.

## Design Thinking

We often underestimate the business benefits of design. It's often perceived to be a soft, squishy skillset. However, design and Design Thinking have had a profound impact on business results because it requires customers and employees to solve problems together.

> *When design principles are applied to strategy and innovation, the success rate for innovation dramatically improves. Design-led companies such as Apple, Coca-Cola, IBM, Nike, Procter & Gamble and Whirlpool have outperformed the S&P 500 over the past 10 years by an extraordinary 211%, according to a 2015 assessment by the Design Management Institute.*[88,89]

By placing people in the center of product development, marketing, and customer service, you aren't only creating a solution for their problem, but you are creating a more integrated customer experience that broadens a company's relationship with them. In a way, companies that implement Design Thinking encourage their customers to be more open about their problems. This allows employees to develop empathy and compassion for them, gaining insights about a potential solution while at the same time building customer and employee relationships. This culminates with a company developing a product or service designed specifically to solve those customer problems raised. The customers are able to test and provide feedback for the iterations and improvements to continue. This interactive process develops a conversation with a customer, which leads to a strong customer relationship.

Over time, the customers become an integral member of that company's community.

New products developed with this approach have the potential to shift how an industry works or it views itself, while inching a company closer to its corporate vision.

> *Recognizing organizations as collections of human beings who are motivated by varying perspectives and emotions, design thinking emphasizes engagement, dialogue, and learning. By involving customers and other stakeholders in the definition of the problem and the development of solutions, design thinking garners a broad commitment to change.*[90]

Not only does Design Thinking help you create a great product with customer insights, but it's a process that allows you to socialize proposed change through conversation and engagement. Customers and employees can respond to prototypes right away to provide feedback and suggest changes so everyone can quickly understand their impact. Similar to Lean, everyone is involved in the process to improve the company's solution or product.

Design Thinking isn't new. It originated in 1969 with the Nobel Prize Laureate Herbert Simon in the Science of the Artificial. It has become popular during the rise of automation because the output of Design Thinking is to create and redefine value rather than simply manage it. Over the years, companies focused on incremental changes that maximized existing processes and mapped them to the bottom-line, with the goal of increasing value. However, automation forced companies to find a way to respond to competitors that could produce radical innovations that changed an industry. Creativity may not have been valued in schools over the years, but it is something that companies needed to compete in this automated world. Design Thinking as a methodology filled the gap and provided the opportunity for companies to inspire such changes and redefine the value they offered customers.[91]

A great example that illustrates how Design Thinking works can be found in an Interaction Design Foundation article. One day, a truck didn't clear a bridge and got stuck. For days, people in the town were examining it to find a solution so it could clear the bridge. Finally, a young child asked why they didn't deflate the tires to fix the problem. By looking at the problem with new eyes and seeing the problem from a different perspective—a truck that needs to be lowered rather than pushed to emerge at the other side of the bridge—they discovered a new solution. That's Design Thinking.[92]

**The 5-Phase Design Thinking Model at the Hasso-Plattner Institute of Design at Stanford:**[93]

**Empathize.** Get to know your customer or user. Try to understand who they are psychologically and emotionally. And don't forget to determine the problem they want to solve and what they want your company's solution to achieve.

**Define.** Outline the problems and insights that your team has identified for these customers or users. If you can, summarize these issues in a statement that describes the value that the solution will bring them.

**Ideate.** The team generates ideas to solve the problem defined. A moderator could use different idea-generation methodologies to help the process. There should be lots of discussions, challenges, and collaboration by the team during this step.

**Prototype.** Start creating the solution. Produce a scaled-down product so people can experience the solution themselves, which will help you identify the best approach. "By the end of this stage, the design team will have a better idea of the constraints inherent to the product and the problems that are present, and have a clearer view of how real users would behave, think, and feel when interacting with the end product."[94]

**Test.** Redefine problems. Refine your understanding of the customers and users. The results from testing the prototype can be recycled into this iterative process to create better solutions.

This iterative methodology allows teams to constantly deepen their understanding of customers and users, more clearly identify their problems, and experiment with ideas and solutions for all to gain insights that could be reused.[95]

**The Four Principles of Design Thinking**[96]

- **The human rule:** No matter what the context, all design activity is social in nature, and any social innovation will bring us back to the "human-centric point of view."

- **The ambiguity rule:** Ambiguity is inevitable, and it cannot be removed or oversimplified. Experimenting at the limits of your knowledge and ability is crucial in being able to see things differently.
- **The redesign rule:** All design is redesign. While technology and social circumstances may change and evolve, basic human needs remain unchanged. We essentially only redesign the means of fulfilling these needs or reaching desired outcomes.
- **The tangibility rule:** Making ideas tangible in the form of prototypes enables designers to communicate them more effectively.

*Design Thinking in Customer Contact Centers*

Every call center targets fast response times. But at the same time, calls answered quickly by the wrong person could result in aggravated customers. They could get inaccurate information or the person could be transferred 10 or more times before finding the right person to answer a question. There are many best practices and tools you can use in your organization's action plan to direct calls. It's straightforward to get started using standards based on current best practices to understand the customers' expectations and adjust to complement your company's and team's culture. This is why in business there are no right or wrong answers. Depending on the people involved and the company brand and culture, a traditional or unorthodox approach could prove highly effective.

Years ago, I worked in a technical support center as a receptionist, ensuring the engineers answered the phones and customers got the help they needed. These engineers had a lot to do: help customers solve their problems, work with software engineers to get issues fixed, and general paperwork.

The phone was the communication medium of choice at the time. The World Wide Web was maybe two years old and few had access. We only got a few emails or faxes asking questions; most people called. The engineer's availability to answer calls was key to our success. Three engineers were scheduled to answer the phones at any given time, which was more than enough staffing based on typical call volumes. However, they were so focused to resolve customer problems that they would sometimes leave their posts for hours to talk to the developers. This wasn't a problem if one wandered away, or a second went away for a few minutes. But during a rush of calls, if there was only one engineer available for three to four hours, that soon became a disastrous customer experience.

One day, an engineer got 19 complex support calls during a four-hour shift while the other two engineers were fixing issues in their queue with developers. And yes, there was a huge argument that night about it among the staff.

It wasn't just the team dynamics that suffered. Customers who called and couldn't reach an engineer on the first try were forced to leave a message. At the time, leaving a message at a call center was the equivalent of submitting an email form with no confirmation message or email. These callers felt like they probably wouldn't get a response from anyone and would try calling the next day and sometimes in the next few hours. And they would make their opinions known.

I would often take customer phone messages and hear their frustration and the lack of hope in their voice. Many wanted to speak to an engineer right away. Some weren't happy if an issue took a while to resolve. They wanted to feel confident that we were addressing their needs.

A benefit of call centers is the immediate customer feedback you can get during a call experience. Many callers make it clear if your response or actions are satisfactory or not. It's easier to use this to your advantage (which is what we did).

Our department's goal was to answer about 90 percent of the calls upon first contact, fix problems in a specific time frame based on complexity and priority, and meet other industry standard metrics for a call center. We were doing okay, but we could have done better.

To fix this, we did some research with the team. I interviewed every engineer about their jobs to understand their perspective and their motivations for work. I wanted to learn how they wanted to work, their challenges and frustrations, and what made them happy with their jobs. We already knew that customers were frustrated because they couldn't talk to an engineer. We needed to hear the other side of the story.

After the interviews, I organized the results and recommendations, and distributed them to the team for review. Everyone had the opportunity to share their thoughts and feedback and validate that this change was in the right direction. After all, this was a way to help everyone on the team work better together. It was a collaborative effort.

Management, from the managers to the vice president, was included. I worked with my manager actively during this process to discover changes and implement the results. Everyone on the team was aligned throughout the process.

My managers and the team didn't want this document to be "rules." It sounded too formal. We decided to call it an "etiquette" instead. It was guidance as to how to work better together and give customers better service. No one was being forced to follow it; everyone was choosing to follow this to work better with the team.

After everyone agreed to the "etiquette," the metrics improved significantly and the team was happier. Customers felt relieved to hear an engineer on the phone. Some other great side effects:

- **Respect among team members increased.** No one left anyone alone on a shift, making them feel "punished." Everyone felt that their contributions and shift time were important.
- **There was greater collaboration** among the engineers, talking to each other more often.
- **There was a sense of stronger teamwork to achieve a new goal.** The team had a renewed passion to exceed expectations for metrics and set new standards.

And after a few more months, the team didn't just achieve the metric goals, they far exceeded them and set new records. Needless to say, this made customers even happier. You could hear it in their voices on the calls. This inspired the engineers to help more customers and offer ideas for improvements. And in the end, the team won an award for Best Complex Support.

There were a few reasons why this was so successful:

- **The team wanted the change.** I don't think this initiative would have worked if the team didn't want to work better together and achieve their numbers. They wouldn't have participated in the research or collaborated to create the etiquette, never mind follow it.
- **The team cared about the customers.** We had a few regular callers and people knew them well. The engineers cared that their customers were able to do a good job. If the team didn't care, this wouldn't have been successful.
- **When I say "the team," I include management.** If my managers and the VP didn't want this to improve too, this would have gone nowhere quickly. Their support helped make this change happen.
- **We got feedback directly from customers every call.** We took note if the customers sounded happy on the calls or not. We'd discuss what we could have done better to improve our processes. Luckily, we had a very short feedback loop with the nature of the business.

When I remember that effort, I originally thought I was helping the team answer more customer calls and do a better job, when in fact I was really helping the team improve the customer experience. In the end, it was the customers who benefitted from the team's work. They got better response time and service and a happier voice at the other end of the phone.

## Sustainability Improves Customer Experiences through Transparency

*Rather, "doing good" can have a direct impact on your company's ability to do well.*[97]

The *Oxford English Dictionary* defines sustainability as: "the quality of being sustainable—capable of being maintained or continued—at a certain level."[98] This leads us to an environmentally oriented definition, in which sustainability includes the models necessary for the human race and planet Earth to survive.[99] The UN Commissioner on Environment and Development defined sustainable development as "[meeting] the needs of the present without compromising the ability of future generations to meet their own needs."[100] In all cases, these definitions lead us to understand that today's business concern about the bottom line is insufficient. For a company to be successful, it needs to consider the impact of its decisions on all generations—today and in the future—socially, economically, and environmentally.

Not coincidentally, socially, economically, and environmentally represent the three sustainability pillars:

**Environmental:** Companies consider their material existence and use, which includes:

- How its activities impact the local environment, community, and government where it sells products and has offices or factories.
- Which resources it uses to create products including power and energy, materials, and chemicals.

- How a company handles and reduces waste—material, noise, odors.
- How a company addresses related energy and environmental uses like employee transportation, traffic, residential and retail growth.
- Other physical factors that impact stakeholder health and surroundings.

**Socially:** Companies consider the stakeholders who are impacted by company actions, which includes:

- Employee treatment and benefits (e.g., work hours, workload, training availability for future opportunities).
- Treatment of neighbors in the surrounding community (Does the company hear and address their concerns? Are changes made to improve the environment and conditions?).
- How customers are treated (warranties, guarantees, transparent processes, etc.).
- How suppliers and partners are treated (similar to employees or different).
- The treatment of other key stakeholders involved with the company.

**Economically:** what are the bottom-line cost of decisions? This could include lawsuits, environmental clean-up, taxes, and compensation for poor stakeholder treatment. Economic implications aren't limited to revenue and profits, but the ultimate impact of all factors on the bottom line over time.

**How are all three pillars related?** A company may generate a lot of revenue, but if employees work perpetual overtime and the company disrupts the community nearby with noise, waste, and smells, that company is creating cost. From a social perspective, the impact could include reduced productivity, a talent purge requiring the company to train new people, damaged reputations, and lawsuits. From an environmental perspective, the company may need to fund industrial clean-up (including noise pollution and debris), pay for excessive energy use, or assume costs regarding resources that a community can't continue to subsidize. A population influx with workers to support a company's sudden growth may attract more citizens than the local government facilities can handle, so additional schools, new roads, and homes would need to be built quickly. That may cost the local community money, which means increased taxes. These costs may sound inconsequential, but they have great impact on all involved. And to understand the impact of all factors, transparency is required by all parties to consider the best options for optimal results.

These three pillars consider the results of company processes from a different perspective, no longer limited to a revenue focus. If you work with sustainability in mind, your processes will achieve other success metrics—social and environmental—which will naturally impact your economic results, for the better. McKinsey's research noted how companies are already observing this in their operations:

> *[T]he share of respondents saying their companies' top reasons for addressing sustainability include improving operational*

*efficiency and lowering costs jumped 14 percentage points since last year, to 33 percent. This concern for costs replaces corporate reputation as the most frequently chosen reason; at 32 percent, reputation is the second most cited reason, followed by alignment with the company's business goals, mission, or values (31 percent) and new growth opportunities (27 percent), which climbed 10 percentage points since last year.*[101]

Companies are quickly realizing that when it comes to sustainability, it only benefits them to consider themselves members of a local community; and if it is a global corporation, it cannot escape being a citizen of the global ecosystem. A company's decisions impact every stakeholder around it in the same way a homeowner's decisions impact his or her neighbors. When a company understands its larger role and contributions within the communities, it can collaborate with them to create solutions. These solutions may be sustainable and create a sense of meaning for the community, but for the business, they are usually highly profitable.

Sustainability has a curious history, which started with the rise of automation and technology, which was perceived to be the driver of "progress." Dr. Jocubs Pisani wrote a paper that eloquently outlines the challenged history of sustainability. His views center around this quote:

*"Progress," it was realized, had provided justification for the reign of the free market, for colonial exploitation of non-Western societies, and for ravaging the biosphere. But progress, according to the critics of the concept, was nothing but an illusion. . .the application of the criteria for progress*

*would show that at no stage in world history had real human progress taken place.*[102]

After World War II, there was growing optimism about increasing the standards of living due to accessible technology, making everyone's lives easier. However, there was a significant downside to this "progress." Technological and corporate economic growth brought pollution as waste from machine processes in all forms: land, air, water. Corporations expanded globally to access cheaper labor and raw materials in a quest to reduce costs, opening factories in less industrialized areas. Over time, corporations took advantage of these local communities—their resources, their talent, their desire to "progress" and industrialize like other Western nations. Research in the 1960s and 1970s exposed that this business behavior was destroying the planet and, if left unchecked, would destroy human civilization. Humanity needed to change how we approached business globally.

Based on the business choices in the 1970s and 1980s, you have to wonder if businesses misunderstood the intentions of key business thinkers at the time. Many attribute the climate of corporate greed to Milton Friedman and his perception that a corporation was only responsible to increase its profits. But that perception is based on an incomplete quote. Milton Friedman actually stated:

> *There is one and only one social responsibility of business–to use its resources and engage in activities designed to increase its profits* ***so long as it stays within the rules of the game, which is to say, engages in open and free competition without deception or fraud.****[author emphasis]*[103]

Friedman, a Libertarian economist, was a supporter of ethical business, research and development for businesses to stay competitive, and corporations obeying laws that set market boundaries. He believed that the markets were the ultimate form of freedom because they supported individual choice. People could choose to purchase products that solved their problems best. However, when it came to environmental protections, he saw a clear role for government intervention. During an interview on Donahue in 1979, Friedman said:

> *[There] is a case for the government protecting third parties. . . The way to do it is to impose a tax on the cost of the pollutants emitted by a car and make an incentive for car manufacturers and for consumers to keep down the amount of pollution.*[104]

To him, the third parties, like citizens of other countries, that are getting punished or penalized due to pollution created poor economics. Not only did those populations not deserve that result, but the pollution impeded their own freedoms. In his perspective, a tax would impact the economics of owning a vehicle, making it undesirable for companies to produce cars with high emissions. Companies would want to avoid the tax; consumers would avoid paying the tax. In keeping with his views on the freedom of markets, this approach would allow the market to resolve the issue.

Considering this perspective, we could say that Friedman defined government's role as declaring which conditions had an adverse impact on society, or as defining the "greater good." Businesses would respond to that guidance by finding a way to follow the law which supported this "greater good."

The economic system he proposed—tax the outcomes you don't want—created a type of transparency that clearly communicated unacceptable behavior by companies or consumers. The companies that didn't observe those desired outcomes would eventually go out of business by being overtaxed and companies with behaviors that supported the common good would thrive, enjoying economic benefit.

Another business visionary, Peter Drucker, more openly supported sustainable ideas and the company's role to support the local community:

> *Leaders in every single institution and in every single sector. . .have two responsibilities. They are responsible and accountable for the performance of their institutions, and that requires them and their institutions to be concentrated, focused, limited. They are responsible also, however, for the community as a whole.*[105]

Unlike Friedman, who saw the government as a type of environmental regulator, Drucker openly stated that a business is an active part of a local community equally responsible for outcomes. To him, a company was responsible for its contributions, good and bad, in the larger ecosystem of government, community, and the market. All stakeholders worked together to create society. Some saw Drucker as an alternative father to CSR, not only because he wrote about responsible business as early as the 1950s,[106] but because he had visionary ideas that defined modern business. He foresaw the decline of the conglomerate in favor of smaller, specialized companies that contained knowledge workers. Companies would transition from hierarchical structures to become flat organizations, similar to orchestras.[107] In many ways, he predicted what a company in the information age would become and how it needs to behave in our challenged world. He consistently called for companies to be part of the community in order to succeed.

> "But the business enterprise is a creature of a society and an economy. If there is one thing we do know, it is that society and/or economy can put any business out of existence overnight—nothing is simpler."[108]
> —Peter Drucker, *Technology, Management and Society*

With this in mind, it shouldn't be surprising that Drucker understood the value of transparency in business and corporate social responsibility, or the sustainability movement. It is only through transparency that you can build trust and be held accountable to stakeholders. How do you know if a company and its employees' motivations and intentions are honorable without transparency? The true test of intention lies in actions. As the saying goes, "actions speak louder than words." It is only through actions that you can determine if the *how* and *why* of a company's activities are consistent with the company's claims, or their intent, to do good.

Looking back at the history of sustainability, without corporate transparency, less-developed countries had little reason to trust corporate motivations. Although Friedman, Drucker, and other business theorists saw businesses as a member of society, that perspective wasn't shared by many capitalists.

As Dr. Pisani wrote:

> *Less-developed countries were suspicious that sustainable development might be an ideology imposed by the wealthy industrialized countries to enforce stricter conditions and rules on aid to developing countries. There were fears that sustainable development would simply be employed to sustain the gap between developed and underdeveloped countries.*[109]

Sadly, this proved true. As stated in the section about Nike, corporate actions that demonstrated and supported this idea fueled the protests of the 1980s and 1990s against global companies that took advantage of citizens in these countries. Many less developed nations shared a quest for bringing Western "progress" to their countries and companies were more than willing to "help," although their intentions may have been questionable. Some of these countries didn't have employee or environmental protection laws in place, and there was the possibility to exploit this due to differing ethical values compared with Western values. We witnessed "sweatshops" in clothing manufacturing that Americans and Europeans didn't see since the early Industrial Revolution. Approaches like child labor, poor compensation, and dangerous working conditions extended to agriculture, mining (lithium and other minerals), and other industries. As we saw with Nike, the protests course-corrected some companies in how they treated third-party employees in other nations, but not others.

Through various methods and means, companies and countries could have collaborated to develop an approach for everyone to win. However, profits and the need to perpetuate the myth of progress got in the way. With the colonial aspect of "progress," you could imply that systemic white supremacy was driving this "progress" myth. This is especially true if we define white supremacy as a:

> *. . .political, economic and cultural system in which whites overwhelmingly control power and material resources, conscious and unconscious ideas of white superiority and entitlement are widespread, and relations of white dominance and non-white subordination are daily reenacted across a broad array of institutions and social settings.*[110]

This definition supports the idea of "progress" earlier defined by Dr. Pisani that the West propagated and which drove the world to adopt their model. He further wrote:

> *The concept of sustainable development was a compromise between growth and conservation. It was not ideologically neutral, because it was intended as an alternative for the zero-growth option and was therefore positively inclined towards the growth and modernization viewpoints.*[111]

Using this perspective and the historical context of sustainability, "progress," and globalization, sustainability was never designed to create transparency and trust between all parties. Instead, sustainability was constructed to benefit big business and their need for profits and growth (or cost reduction). It was up to the people inside businesses to change if they wanted to be a responsible citizen in the world.

As a response to the mounting global inequalities and subsequent protests, a number of companies shifted their best practices to consider how their company's actions impacted all stakeholders. One supporting movement is Conscious Capitalism. The term *Conscious Capitalism* was coined by the founder of Whole Foods, James Mackey, in his book by the same title. He outlined how Whole Foods addressed being a responsible "citizen" within the various communities it has businesses. It achieved this by participating in fair trade, paying fair wages and offering comparable benefits, encouraging employees to feel that they are part of the business (profit sharing and cooperative ownership), providing paths to management, selling customers goods that are healthy, and participating in the community, to name only a few activities. The book demonstrated through example what it meant to be conscious, or sustainable. What drives much of what's explained in *Conscious Capitalism* is how a conscious business can provide meaning for stakeholders: executives, the board employees, customers, and vendors.

Whole Foods delivered on many of its sustainable promises. But not all companies do. Although the intentions and motivations of socially responsible companies are in the right place, there is a need to validate if the company is delivering. Often, such claims become aspirational without an action plan in place to bring them to life.

Luckily, the organization B Lab created the Certified B Corp, a certification system for a conscious, socially responsible business. It's a way for companies to validate that they are practicing sustainability as outlined by B Lab's requirements rather than aspiring to make it happen using their own ideals.

There are five areas for assessment to be certified:

- **Workers:** This includes practices that make the workers feel that their contributions are valued and that they are part of a community.
- **Community:** This includes activities where the company includes the local and global community in its operations (employees, vendors) and participates in the community's best interest.
- **Environment:** The company is involved in the "fair treatment and meaningful involvement of all people"; they are a good global citizen using a fair share of resources and not damaging local community resources.
- **Governance:** A company's mission is driving the accountability of their company's success.
- **Customers:** This is a new area for B Corp Certification that addresses how companies should build trustworthy, honest, and transparent customer relationships.

The total score for the entire assessment is 200. To be a B Corp, you need to score at least 80 points. The average B Corp score is 95. This proves that this new thinking is not easy to implement and there is still valuable work to be done.[112]

The B Corp and other types of certification outline values that all participating companies must share and, through this process, establish transparency. People know the qualities, traits, and values a certified company must possess to be a member. To be certified, companies need to be open about who they are and how they operate. Very little is hidden.

In a way, customers provide another type of certification each time they purchase from your company. They want to be sure that your company is authentic. If your customers knew how you were producing your products, would they be comfortable with your approaches and decisions? This is how transparency makes companies accountable and keeps them honest. And this is why transparency is a necessary component to create a community. Companies that embrace methodologies like Agile, Lean, Design Thinking, and Sustainability typically have strong communities associated with them that also embrace transparency. You can't have a community if there are walls sheltering groups and how their contributions impact the bottom line. Everyone in the process needs to understand how their contributions make a difference to the company, the company community, and the world. Transparency and accountability are key elements necessary for people to collaborate successfully for the greater good, but the question remains: How do we measure them and their impact on the bottom line? Once we have a measurement system available to determine that connection, we'll move from the outcome-based progress model of driving to profits and technical capability to include an understanding of the impact of people in business.

**UN Sustainability Goals**

The modern notion of progress has created a great wealth gap between rich and poor that's not economically beneficial or sustainable globally. Ignoring the need to reduce this gap could result in civil unrest, hunger, and even death. The UN set a new direction for all nations to follow, focused on ideal outcomes. By focusing on the outcomes, we shift from blaming groups for the problems and focus on implementing solutions. This may allow us to address the pressing issues at hand, change how we achieve goals, and be more inclusive over the long-term. It is implied that cultural changes are necessary for us to achieve these goals globally.

The following lists the UN sustainable development goals, which addresses the needs of all nations across the globe. The main goal is to end poverty, but there are 16 other supporting goals that must be met in order for this to happen, including gender equality, improved infrastructure, and decreasing company footprints.[113]

GOAL 1: No Poverty
GOAL 2: Zero Hunger
GOAL 3: Good Health and Well-Being
GOAL 4: Quality Education
GOAL 5: Gender Equality
GOAL 6: Clean Water and Sanitation
GOAL 7: Affordable and Clean Energy
GOAL 8: Decent Work and Economic Growth
GOAL 9: Industry, Innovation and Infrastructure
GOAL 10: Reduced Inequality
GOAL 11: Sustainable Cities and Communities
GOAL 12: Responsible Consumption and Production
GOAL 13: Climate Action
GOAL 14: Life below Water
GOAL 15: Life on Land
GOAL 16: Peace and Justice Strong Institutions
GOAL 17: Partnerships to achieve the Goal

### *Missed Opportunities for Sustainability by Choosing Ease over Transparency*

As we know, many large global corporations, like Nike, work directly with factories around the world to manage their supply chain. This helps them to maintain control over the facilities and directly influence how they are managed. However, some don't. They will work with sourcers to place orders into factories to be produced. Sometimes these factories and plants don't meet the CSR standards established by these corporations and the corporations don't hold them accountable. But this happens often because sourcers have a different value system and view the relationship with an organization differently than the stakeholders and customers do.

For example, Li & Fung, a logistics management company, has 15,000 supplier factories in 40 countries, but it doesn't own or operate any of them. It coordinates the supply chain process, working with various supplier factories to deliver what's needed in time. It works with hundreds of companies to fill all of its factories with work. It prepares the factory, produces the work, and then moves onto the next project.[114]

Li & Fung does accomplish what's expected of a sourcer regarding supplier inspections and reporting. But its business doesn't support the type of commitment that Nike and Patagonia may have with regular work being assigned to specific suppliers. As reported in *Huffington Post,*

> *Li & Fung. . . [has] no guarantee that orders will be filled by the same factory twice, and audits are often carried out after the order has already been placed. And so clothing companies*

> *have no ability or incentive to fix what they find. It's like finding out the results of a restaurant health inspection after you've already eaten your meal.*[115]

Although most clothing companies now have sustainability standards that include manufacturing guidelines and employee satisfaction ratings, there is no way to support them if your factory and suppliers change for each shipment or product and your vendor isn't aligned. It's clear that Li & Fung doesn't share the same values as its corporate clothing company customers. It meets its customers' needs to get the clothing produced. The *how* of the process doesn't matter as long as the *what* and *when* and *how much* requirements are met. It continues to get outsourcing assignments because it meets those customers' needs. But it doesn't meet the perception of its customers' customer, which is that it is working as part of the company's larger ecosystem and community.

Walmart was responsible for producing 60 percent of its clothing at Tazreen. Tazreen was a clothing manufacturer in Bangladesh that had substandard working conditions and treated employees poorly. In 2012, the factory was engulfed in flames. Because the factory owners blocked the doors to prevent employees from leaving, the fire killed 113 people. The tragedy continued with the owners of the factory having political power and refused to be held accountable or compensate the families.[116] However, a year before the fire, Walmart inspected Tazreen and found it not meeting its standards. So how did Tazreen continue making clothes for Walmart? Walmart placed orders with other suppliers who sub-contracted with Tazreen. Eventually, Walmart did ban suppliers from using Tazreen, but as we know, the supply chain often includes vendors and sub-contractors who make decisions to get the job done. Again, for those suppliers, the *how* matters less than the *what* and *when* and *how much.* With that mindset, it's easy for an unacceptable vendor to be the vendor of choice again.

To save time, and ultimately cost, from researching and vetting their own vendors to include in their communities, such corporations paid the ultimate cost—including partners (who were like employees) who they didn't know and who didn't share common values with their community. The result was employee tragedy and a scandal. Lives were lost or damaged or irreparable from injuries or death. Sustainability requires all suppliers and vendors to become partners, extensions of the organization and the community. Not all companies do this practice, but there is a conflict of interest with the goals to get product delivered on time and within budget, and knowing how the vendors are working to meet standards and requirements for a humane workforce or responsibly sourced goods. This is changing by customers demanding to understand the details of *how* a product is constructed. To them, how a shirt is made is part of the customer experience of a shirt as much as the brand experience and what the shirt feels like to wear and touch.

## Why Understanding People's Motivation Matters with Automation

You can't achieve your business goals with any of these methodologies if everyone doesn't share similar motivations for why their business goals matter. Again, *how* an activity is done matters just as much as the *why* or *what* is being produced. And understanding people's motivations for *why* they make business decisions is key to success.

What motivates one person to be transparent and someone else not? What motivates a company or team to practice Sustainability or Design Thinking or Agile or Lean? What makes someone decide one idea is better than another? Decisions are not based on what you expect.

We often believe that business decisions are based on facts and figures. Companies offer a product that has the features customers want described with a clearly communicated value prop and persuasive messaging. And this is true to some degree, but in the end, we are people with feelings, emotions, motivations, and self-interest, who ultimately require meaning for our lives. We base our decisions on relationships and connections. This is a tall order to deliver. But it's what people experience every day.

There are three underlying reasons why people choose to complete any action in their lives:

- How they are feeling about the options they have (business decision or product)
- How they feel about their decision
- How they believe their decision will impact their lives and support or change their view of themselves

Antonio Damasio is a researcher and neuroscientist who discovered that people need feelings, and therefore emotions, to make decisions. In his famous case, "Elliott" had a problem. Although he was a formerly successful stockbroker, Elliott had a tragic frontal lobe tumor. After the tumor was removed, he couldn't hold onto his job, lost his marriage, and made some disastrous business and life decisions, turning his life into a tragic mess. After a few sessions, Damasio realized that Elliott's problem wasn't his intellect, but how he was (or actually wasn't) processing his feelings.

In one set of tests, the researchers showed Elliott photos of situations that would cause most people distress or great joy, but he showed no response. Then Damasio would hear his life story and realized that Elliott expressed no emotion about that either. Damasio made the connection between decisions and emotions when he noticed that Elliott could brainstorm a number of ideas, but he just couldn't make a decision. "'I began to think that the cold-bloodedness of Elliot's reasoning prevented him from assigning different values to different options,' Damasio wrote, 'and made his decision-making landscape hopelessly flat.'"[117]

After some research, Damasio realized that Elliott's problem was more closely related to feelings and emotions rather than rational logic. We all have "somatic markers," or feelings, to help us filter options and provide a shortcut for decision-making. These markers are based on memories of past experiences. So if you have had a lot of life experiences, you'll get a lot of feelings about people, situations, and circumstances and this will help you make a better decision. The physical memories will guide you so that you "feel good" about what you choose. An aspect of the experience—anything from a smell or similar action or experiencing a person with a similar personality—could spark such a memory.

In Damasio's example, sadly, Elliott didn't have anything like a somatic marker available to use. So he was overwhelmed by the options and therefore, didn't make any choices.

Damasio's theory validates the paradox of choice as outlined by Barry Schwartz: It's hard to make a decision when you are overwhelmed with many valid options. Schwartz outlined in his book an example of consumers being presented 26 jelly flavors at a mall to sample. The salesperson was more effective when he offered only eight to be sampled rather than all 26. But Damasio takes this one step further claiming that the desire to "feel good" and feelings related to memories guide decisions. To sum it up, the number of options available to choose from is only one factor that influences decision-making. The other factor that simplifies the decision-making process comes from somatic markers, or feelings.

From another perspective, Damasio's explanation sounds alarmingly similar to the definition of intuition. When I first learned about Damasio's perspective, I shared it with a friend who was a strong believer in intuition. Needless to say, I ruined her perspective of spiritual experiences by reducing it to biology and somatic markers based on memories of past experiences rather than spiritual meaning. But I found Damasio's theory refreshing and almost relieved that we rely so much on feelings and emotions to make a decision.

We are always looking to feel good. We often base our decisions on the quest to achieve this, using "logic" to support our feelings. We can use the example of relationships. Let's say you have a good friend and feel good around him or her. Let's say you meet someone similar to him or her. Your body remembers these feelings with your friend and that's what intuition is: your body talking to you through its feelings, which becomes emotions. And that helps guide you to make a decision to talk to this person, or not. This knowledge is especially useful for us in marketing.

By creating a feeling in our customer experiences, we can tap into these somatic markers and memories to help people associate a past feeling with a solution. If we keep the feeling pleasant, then these experiences will be associated with pleasant thoughts. And who doesn't want to constantly feel great all the time? If you combine this with self-interest, you can better understand what is driving your customers, partners, and even employees emotionally.

What are individuals getting out of customer experiences and interactions beyond an object or information in a customer experience? The reward could be validating a perspective of themselves, which makes them feel good. That's why some people choose to read certain magazines; they may genuinely like the articles or just owning the magazine may reinforce a worldview that makes them feel comfortable. It could be that the product triggers feelings associated with a past memory that's comforting. What do these people see as a reward for purchasing beyond your product? What is truly in it for them—their ego, their selves? That's the self-interest.

And that's what you need to consider for each stakeholder in your company, too.

We could apply Damasio's work in the context of why executives choose to follow Sustainability practices. Or Design Thinking. Or Agile. Or Lean. Some reasons may be related to the bottom line. But some reasons may be related to how "modern" the managers and executives will appear by adopting these new approaches, how much money they will save, or how innovative they will be by creating a product that will increase revenue. Or they may value how they compare with their friends. Or how they are perceived by their customers because they will enable a great experience. Research is needed for a concrete answer, but you can see the point.

When it comes to motivations and decisions in business, feelings and emotions can take center stage. Rather than simply analyzing facts, people may use facts to support emotions and personal motivations around decisions. In the end, people decide which action to take based on what will make them feel good about themselves and their self-image, how the decision validates the option they selected, and how they see this decision changing (or not changing) their lives.

This is why people in your company community are key to a successful action plan. Implementing a process that makes everyone feel included and successful will make them feel good, ultimately make them more productive, improve their self-image, and in the end, increase your bottom line.

## Conclusion

I have worked on a number of products/projects as an experience strategist and project/product manager. Through these experiences, I have found that you can have the most amazing product concept or idea, but if you don't have a plan to make it real, complete with marketing exposure and revenue goals to guide promotional tactics, and the right team, it won't happen.

Sometimes people believe that if you build it they will come, but that's not true. An analogy I use frequently in this book: If a tree falls in the forest and no one is there to see it, did it fall? And that is true for your product. Marketing and sales support the revenue- and relationship-related KPIs. Manufacturing supports product production KPIs. You need a high-level visionary road map to know your ultimate, end goal and create granular, near-term plans that move you toward that final destination. Without including your customers in your business, how can you solve their problems, help them live a better life, or sell a product to them?

You may want to build a customer-employee community, but you have a business to run. You need to balance including customers in your community to receive their feedback and integrating them into your organization to create new solutions with maintaining productivity to continue operations. By starting small, asking customers for their feedback starts customer conversations that will lead to more interactions and great customer experiences.

It's through these type of small steps and near-term plans that we can create effective and tangible customer experiences that complement the product being produced today to see immediate results. Plans that include customers—people—will always change with the market and shifting business priorities. Messaging will need to be adjusted from time to time as customer needs change, industry trends appear, and you determine the type of relationship you want to achieve with them. But people—customers and employees—are the constant in these interactions that build relationships.

Action plans are necessary, but it's people who make them effective. You need transparency to build trust, share ideas, work through communication issues, and clarify motivations. There is no single "correct" way to accomplish any goal except to make sure everyone in your company's community is included and working towards the same definition of success with the same motivations. The new process methodologies—Agile, Lean, Design Thinking, Sustainability—focus on people and meeting their needs first. These approaches have proven not to just treat employees better and engage customers, but they are more profitable. This should remind us that in business, the *how* is always just as important as the *why* and the *what*.

CHAPTER 5

# People: The Community, Making The Vision a Reality

There are various layers inside each company that impact work style, efficiency, and collaboration, from employees to teams. Each has its own benefits and challenges.

When I think about organizations and an individual's impact, I'm reminded of the story *The Princess and the Pea* by Hans Christian Anderson. As a refresher, a prince searched the countryside for his princess bride with no success. One rainy night, a princess arrived at the door. The king and queen let her stay the night and set up her bed: 20 mattresses and featherbeds with a small pea buried beneath. They believed that a true princess—a true leader—would be sensitive enough to notice a single pea, a tiny imperfection buried far away under the many beds.

The next morning, the princess claimed that she couldn't sleep and that something was in the bed. From one perspective, you could say that this meant that she was so delicate that she felt the tiniest of problems. But from another perspective, you could say that her heightened sensitivity helped her notice the smallest of problems buried in between the beds. Someone who is sensitive enough to identify a problem so small and removed from themselves is an effective leader with high empathy and compassion. Leaders understand that success is a result of happy, comfortable people. They also understand that unhappiness is contagious like a disease: When one person is unhappy, many others assume this trait, becoming unhappy too. If the princess could identify that something was wrong with the mattresses, you could imply that she was sensitive enough to identify unhappiness in the kingdom, even amongst those far removed from her social class. She had a hypersensitivity to discomfort and unhappiness.

In this new business environment in which customers are included in a company's community with employees, it's easier than ever for employee unhappiness to spread to customers. And if this happens often enough, the community will decay, relationships will deteriorate, and your company's revenue will ultimately decline.

Leaders do more than make business goals happen. They guide people to build effective communities. And to build an effective community, you need to be sensitive to what's going well and what's going wrong. Leaders sometimes remove themselves from the day-to-day operations of a team or organization to be "more strategic," but when they do this, they are removing themselves from the core of the business.

A business is like a pond. Drop a pebble into the pond and you see the ripple effect throughout the glass-like top surface. In a business, all of your employees are like the pond surface and experience the impact of that pebble. This often happens with a disgruntled employee, who will often act in ways that negatively impact other team members. Those impacted will then negatively impact others—and the wave continues. A great leader who is part of the pond will notice this happening, feel this disruption, and understands how this could impact the organization. He or she could stop it before the ripple reaches the customers. But in today's world, in which customers and employees interact directly, the ripple can happen in an instant, so leaders need to be one step ahead to prevent that from happening.

*The Princess and the Pea* reminds us that individuals impact a team, which can impact a division, which can impact the organization and leadership. And if we include customers within the employee community, it's even more important to understand how employees are feeling about their jobs, their colleagues, their team, and their lives so we can lead functional teams and ensure that our teams are building great customer relationships. By understanding how customers are feeling before, after, and during their experiences with a company plus employee job perception, you can see the how the relationship between both groups impacts the company. One unhappy employee could destroy a number of customer relationships very quickly through direct or indirect interaction.

Here are some examples of how each layer impacts the employee and customer dynamic:

**Individual employees** may have a difficult time working with a customer if they are wrestling with personal work challenges. This is why employee happiness is so important. Without it, you could risk an employee speaking negatively about the company, or not providing great service out of revenge or similar motivations—all resulting in a sub-par and generally unsatisfying customer experience.

**Teams** may not produce their best work if the members aren't motivated, aligned through consistent goals, or well compensated. Team members will compare their experiences with each other and if they perceive biased treatment, then they may respond by working less or competing internally. Internal competition doesn't sound like a horrible idea at first. But on deeper inspection, if each team member is competing to be the star rather than collaborating as a team to produce the best work, you have a dysfunctional team. The "every person for themselves" mentality isn't productive.

**Divisions/departments/organizations** may have a difficult time working with a customer if there are cultural challenges among teams. Inconsistent goals across teams could cause internal politics, infighting for resources, or competition based on false beliefs of which team is most valuable. (They all are, but when teams don't have shared goals, a perceived hierarchy is formed based on which team seems to have easier goals to achieve. That team appears to be "favored." And this creates internal competition.)

Employees provide the talent that makes a company successful. Next to customers, they are the core of your business and drive your operations, including all customer

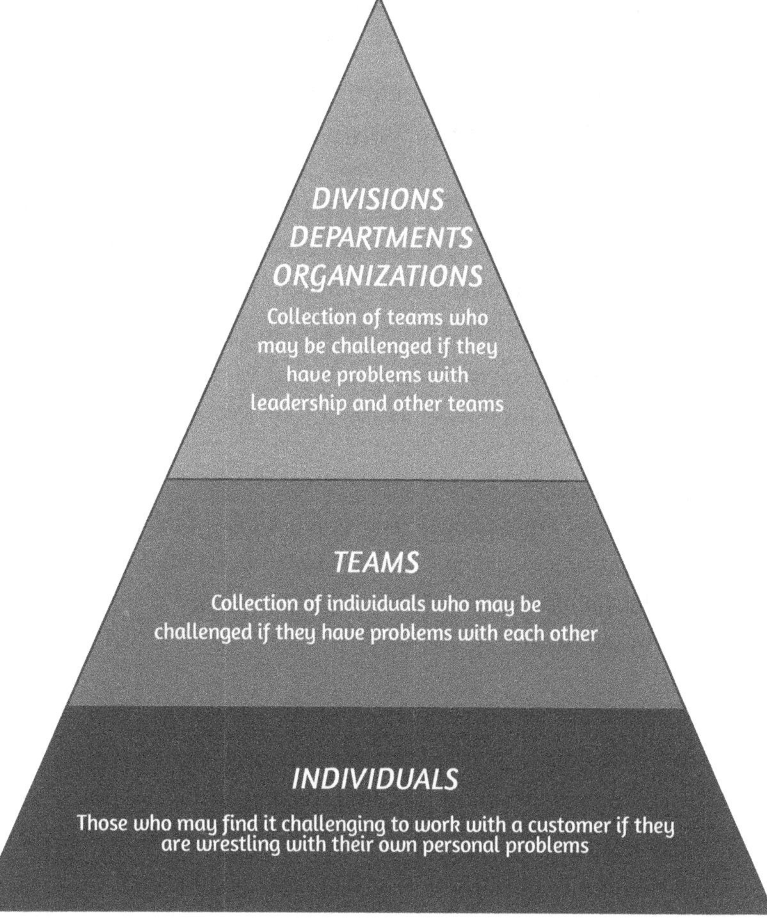

DIVISIONS
DEPARTMENTS
ORGANIZATIONS
Collection of teams who may be challenged if they have problems with leadership and other teams
TEAMS
Collection of individuals who may be challenged if they have problems with each other
INDIVIDUALS
Those who may find it challenging to work with a customer if they are wrestling with their own personal problems


*Figure 6: Employee and Customer Challenges in an Organization*

experiences. Leaders like Richard Branson and Gary Vaynerchuk strongly hold this perspective and have been outspoken about it on many occasions. Employees are more than key assets to a company. They design processes and create the automation systems that complement and further streamline the company's existing operations. They also create the solutions (products and services) for customers. Without them, you wouldn't have a business nor customers.

## The Power of Employees: Interpersonal Relationships and the Value Employees Provide

Employees and their relationships with their colleagues contribute to a company's success. Every employee wants to contribute value, which is key to building an organization. If an employee doesn't feel they are providing value, it is likely that the employee won't feel connected to their peers, never mind being able to connect to a customer through empathy or compassion.

> *"Individual commitment to a group effort—that is what makes a team work a company work, a society work, a civilization work."*[118]
>
> —Vince Lombardi

The value employees and teams create goes beyond revenue-building to building relationships with each other and customers. We may see employees as the people who do the work, but what if we saw them as part of the larger organization's community that included customers?

In that case, every employee becomes a representative of the company who is able to build a relationship with a customer or prospect. That perspective change shifts the conversation regarding how employees are treated and compensated, and expands their roles:

- Employees would need to keep in mind how they talk about the company and have some type of PR training.
- Employees would look at customers and prospects through the eyes of a business development or sales professional trying to see how they could provide more value.
- Employees would become customer service professionals and discover new ways to better serve customers.

In some ways, each employee almost becomes the CEO for their role. They are building a microbusiness to create a great customer relationship. This stretches employees to go well beyond their functional role to provide greater value, and create a culture where employees are empowered and included in the business as a peer, even with those who are senior to them.

Empowered employees allow flat organization structures and self-managed teams to exist. If every employee is the CEO of their role, understands the company vision and brand, and develops an action plan to achieve it, and if managers serve their team by removing blocks and helping their employees achieve their goals, then you create an organization that more closely resembles a collection of smaller entrepreneurial organizations than a top-down, managed hierarchy.

It may sound like chaotic individualism run amok, but if everyone who is a CEO of their role collaborates, they are all assuming leadership for what they do. This means that they will take greater ownership and be more accountable for their recommended plans, activities, and results. This also allows this team to be empowered to build a better team and business. Naturally, such a team will want to share their own fulfilling work experience with others and encourage them to be part of it.

Employees are sharing their work experiences already today through social media and in their relationships. Employees who love their jobs let their network know when there is an opening in their companies and encourage their friends to apply; employees who don't like their employers keep quiet. Employees who love their jobs share their employer's successes and feel that they are part of it, as if the success is their own; employees who don't connect with a company or their role this way won't share the success. When employees share their experience in your company with others, they are also connecting to customers and prospects to extend your company's customer experience and brand. The employees see it as an extension of themselves and their role, and they embrace the corporate vision, becoming part of the company's community. That is where employees add the most value.

How can you enable your employees to provide that value? The following traits indicate you are on the right path:

- **Your team likes and respects each other,** and sees the value each team member provides.

- **Defined roles and responsibilities clarify how everyone can provide value.** This creates room for your team to thrive.
- **Proper staffing allows employees to contribute effectively.** They can then provide the most value without competition or trying to cover gaps.
- **Each team member buys into your vision.**

We'll explore each of these in more detail in the following sections.

### *Your Team Likes and Respects Each Other*

Leaders often assume that their teams like and respect each other, but sometimes that's not true.

Here are some questions to help you determine the relationship health of your team:

- Does your team choose to hang out with each other after work occasionally?
- Do they do activities with each other without a company-sanctioned activity?
- Does your team occasionally eat lunch with each other (rather than everyone being on their own all the time)?
- Do you hear laughter often?
- Does your team help each other solve problems?

On teams in which colleagues like and respect each other, the answer to all of these questions is *yes*. If you answered *no* to any question, you may want to find ways to improve team dynamics and encourage relationships.

When we want to improve efficiency on a team, we often discuss how to optimize workflow and processes. That's the obvious answer. But another way to improve efficiency is to improve employee relationships.[119] We know that employees are vital to a company's successful operations and to bring them to life. But sometimes we forget that *how* the employees interact with each other through their work styles and relationships reflects the company's culture and communicates the brand.

An element that should be present in every company's culture is respect. Without respect, you can't experience empathy and feel compassion—the basis for successful team relationships and dynamics. If you don't respect someone's opinion, even if you disagree, how can you have a working relationship with that person?

Sadly, in many workplaces, disagreement is seen as a sign of disrespect when in fact disagreement is a way for the team to improve. Isn't it better if the team finds fault with a project or idea before a customer or key stakeholder sees it? How your team works through disagreement indicates the health of your team's culture. Do they have a logical, calm conversation sticking to the facts, building consensus? Is it an impassioned debate in which the team wants to come to the best bottom-line recommendation? Or do they call each other names with no constructive discussion? (Hopefully, they don't do that. That is disrespect.)

Not understanding the difference between disrespect and disagreement is a challenge for many organizations. The chart on pages 204-205, Feeling Pity to Compassion, outlines a way to understand how disrespect, pity, and contempt is the opposite of respect and compassion and how this could impact your organization.

If your team members are demonstrating pity, contempt, and sympathy toward each other, you may have an empathy problem. How can you build empathy and compassion with your customers if you can't even build it on your employee teams?

We sometimes don't realize that pity to compassion is a sliding scale. With pity, you feel a type of contempt. You believe that someone got themselves into their unfortunate situation and probably couldn't help themselves get out of it, even if they wanted to. If you feel sympathy, you feel bad for someone for getting into that situation, but you aren't up to the task to help them solve their problem. If you feel empathy, you can feel someone else's feelings and understand their emotions. There isn't really a desire to help; the focus is on understanding. If you feel compassion, you don't care how someone got into that situation, but you can understand how they are feeling objectively and want to help them solve their problems.

It makes you wonder if we should instead be focused on compassion rather than empathy.

This is why it may be compassionate to disagree with someone in a respectful way. You want to solve the problem at hand with them. However, if you don't care to solve the problem and want to be right, you may be feeling pity and contempt, which signals disrespect for the other employee. You don't believe that their perspective, although different, could be just as valid as your own. That thinking subconsciously dismisses a colleague's view as being less than yours. The

# FEELING PITY TO COMPASSION

| QUALITIES | PITY | SYMPATHY |
|---|---|---|
| Thoughts while feeling the emotion | "That's sad." | "I'm sorry you are sad and going through a difficult time." |
| How sadness is experienced | Includes condescension and contempt. | Shifts to reflecting on life. |
| Connection between Person A and Person B | None. Don't see anything shared in common. | Little shared in common. Limited connection. |
| How Person A views Person B | Objectifies him or her. | There is a detached perspective. |
| How Person A feels about Person B | Feels subtle contempt for him or her. | Respects him or her. |
| How Person A believes that Person B got into his/her situation. | It was self-inflicted (consciously or sub-consciously). | A situation happened and the result was this current experience. |
| Does the Person A believe Person B can solve his/her problems? | Nope. Not really. | Sure. He or she will find a way to solve the problem. |

| EMPATHY | COMPASSION |
|---|---|
| "I can feel your sadness and understand why you feel that way." | "I can feel your sadness, understand it, and want to help you fix it." |
| Simply understood. | Understood and a motivation to find a solution emerges. |
| Shared experiences. | Shared experiences. Know a solution is possible. |
| There is a connection. | Humanizes everyone involved. |
| Respects and accepts him or her as he or she is today. | Loves him or her. |
| Understandable decisions were made, and he or she is where he or she is now. | It doesn't really matter how anyone got here; we need to fix it. |
| Full confidence he or she will find a way to solve the problem. | Yes. Let's collaborate to solve the problem. |

desire to help someone resolve a problem, compassion, is a sign of respect and goodwill. This is always present in a healthy work environment.

> We sometimes forget that we work with our team members for at least eight hours each day; we should enjoy their company enough to join them for a cup of coffee or tea.

Signs that your team needs to improve their relationships with each other include:

- **Your team blames each other for problems.** Blame is the main signal of interpersonal relationship challenges on a team. If there is a problem and the discussion becomes accusatory, focused on personal failings rather than discussing solutions and processes, you have a blame problem that should be resolved quickly.

- **Your employees seem frustrated.** Employee frustration demonstrated through high conflict and problematic team situations is often related to blame. This is a signal that your employees may not be collaborating well. If your team seems frustrated, don't blame them for their emotions and tell them to "choose to feel better." Frustration is a sign that the team has encountered a problem that they can't solve without leadership's involvement—or they would find a way to solve it. There may be larger team or organization problems that need to be solved. Some example cases:

    - It's not clear who from the organization needs to be included on a project to complete it.

  - Roadblocks keep surfacing between teams that need resolution.
  - Team members may be in the wrong role. Either they don't enjoy what they are doing, they aren't using their best skillsets, or they are in a role that they don't have the skillset to do and need training. In all cases, they aren't effective and need to be in a role in which they can be effective and contribute to the team.
  - A team member may not be getting the respect they deserve and you have a bullying problem.
  - Not all team members are held accountable to the same standard. This inequality will create factions to justify the manager's preferences.

- **You notice your team expressing contempt and sympathy for each other rather than empathy or compassion.** People are objectifying each other. Generally, people feel contempt and sympathy for those with whom they don't connect or respect, and that is the result of objectification. Sometimes this trend starts in leadership, management, and HR when employees are referred to as "resources," as if people are like a computer or desk. This label is the first step of objectifying what people offer a team. If that language is used in a team, the team members may only see each other as offering value through skillsets; the perception of the humanity in their contributions is lost. Here's how you can change this perception:
  - **Use the word *talent* to stop the employee objectification.** (Only people provide talent.)

- **Value is not in *what* the employee contributed, but *how* they solved the problem.** Anyone can produce a deliverable; not everyone can produce something useful that was well done or a document that made the team feel that all of their contributions were included along the way. Everyone contributes differently. *How* someone contributes should be celebrated. That represents their true value.
- **Celebrate everyone equally.** Having favorites establishes competition. Not having favorites encourages equality. Focus on how everyone contributes different value; value the individual and *how* they work. We can't replicate what we offer a team as an individual. However, we can try to replicate work to get attention and be a favorite.
- **Assign roles based on what people do best, not on what they should be doing.** Encourage detail-oriented employees to proofread or complete final reviews before distributing reports. Let strategic visionaries dream where the company should be in five years. Inspire analytical types to review metrics and provide insights. Basically, have everyone on your team work where they excel. Balance what people like to do with where they do great work. That produces the best team and helps people respect—not compete with—each other.

### *Defined Roles and Responsibilities Clarify How Everyone Can Provide Value*

Defined roles and responsibilities help team members understand how they can effectively contribute to an organization. Most employees are looking for ways to add value, and if managers and leaders aren't defining roles, employees may define their own. This often results in conflicts with what the team or larger organization needs. Too many employees may independently decide to work on similar projects while some projects may have no one covering them. This opens the team to competition and power battles, especially if their compensation and reward plans encourage it.

Defining roles has another result: By defining roles, you can help a team stay focused to achieve a company's goal and make a team more effective. Roles make it easier for a team to collaborate and add value, positioning them as complementary colleagues working toward a goal rather than competitors trying to win.

We may downplay roles as restrictive, forcing employees to "stay in their lanes" and reducing creativity or contribution, but they do exactly the opposite. Roles create room for people to add value and contribute, providing guidelines and boundaries. Through well-defined roles employees can be successful because they clearly know what's expected of them.

A benefit of roles and responsibilities lies in how your team members interpret them when discovering opportunities in your organization. Your team may partner to work on an initiative that could radically change how the company operates. Together, they may see a larger initiative that could save tremendous money and decide to achieve that goal. If each team member is the CEO of their role, they will know the details of their job focus and what could be done to improve results. That knowledge paired with other team members who are also CEOs of their role can create a business case for savings or increased revenue. That's a very powerful team of self-motivated leaders.

The call for employees to act like a CEO or company owner isn't new and is based on helping employees see how their contributions impact the bottom line. For years, the employee mindset based success on following directions and doing what you are told. In the current business world, employees are finding creative ways to contribute value to the business—and what better way to contribute value than to help drive bottom-line results either as savings or earnings? But what if this view were expanded for employees to improve the customer experience and encourage employees to not only improve the bottom line, but keep customers engaged and solve their problems?

The best way to do this is to find a way to hold employees accountable and reward them appropriately. When I managed a division's website for a large IT company, my team was held accountable for three areas: revenue (through lead generation capabilities), customer engagement, and communicating customer solutions. Being held accountable for contributing to the bottom line was nerve-wracking. I often asked the VP of marketing, "But what if we don't make it? We don't have direct control over the lead revenue we generate." And he replied that he set goals that the team would definitely achieve. He had more confidence in my team and me than I did. After a huge gulp, the team and I went to work. The team included writers and developers, and we were all accountable to improve site traffic, drive leads, and ensure that the site was communicating appropriate solution messages. If the site wasn't performing as we wanted, we made improvements, each taking responsibility to contribute to achieve these goals. For example, the developer on our team found a way for us to get a site redesign for free by leveraging work from another team. Needless to say, we all jumped on board, reworked our content, and transitioned to the new design. The team took ownership; we were all CEOs of our job, invested in the success of the site.

And the results we achieved supported this idea. From the site, we generated more than $30M in lead revenue per year. A slow quarter was $600K in leads. We even took it upon ourselves to reach out to sales and business development teams in the regions to ensure that leads became sales. Our defined roles helped us contribute in dramatic yet constructive ways to make us a powerhouse team.

With the rise of automation and the inclusion of customers into your company ecosystem, the idea of the hero employee died while team collaboration rose. No one can single-handedly drive success in an organization anymore. Automation has simplified doing the work, but *how* the work happens touches more roles and is more complicated than it was years ago. Individuals can make contributions and influence team members to change how they work and perceive tasks, but teams make those huge shifts in your organization to change output, perception about work, and what it means to achieve a goal.

By customers becoming part of your company's ecosystem, they become part of your community. Everyone now interacts with the customer more directly, to the point that the customer could be considered a distant team member. Customers don't have roles and responsibilities or receive compensation like your employees do, but they do provide contributions and feedback to improve the organization. Their role should be limited, but at the same time, as part of the community, they have a vested interest in your company achieving its goals. You need to define a customer role and how to best work with them so they can add value to your company beyond paying for your product.

Some suggestions for their role could be membership on a customer advisory committee, providing a forum for them to support other customers using a product or solution, or providing a way for them to submit product feedback and ideas for improvements.

**What if this isn't happening in your organization?**

- **Imbalanced power causes power struggles on the team.** People are focused on competing for rewards rather than achieving a goal. Some who have similar roles may be in a better position to succeed. This will create a power struggle—as well as a vacuum for the work that is not assigned or being completed.

- **Frustration.** Your team may be flailing, trying to complete work, or just checking out, refusing to contribute because it's not clear how they are contributing value to achieve the end goal.

- **Increased competition rather than collaboration.** If the team is competing for a reward, it won't focus on collaborating to achieve a goal. There needs to be an incentive for team members to collaborate until they are used to working together and it becomes a habit.

- **Not including customers in your work**. If you don't know your boundaries in your role, how can you possibly include customers in your work to get feedback? Clear roles help you extend the idea of team to customers because you know how everyone contributes and where they can contribute best. **No roles implies no clear path to success**.

### *An Example: Roles, Collaboration, and Business Development?*

When I worked at a global IT company with more than 300,000 employees, I learned quickly that you can't achieve any goal alone in an environment that large; you always need to collaborate with others to get anything done. What was most important in that environment was understanding how different people in the organization could help you. You didn't only have to have a solid understanding of your own job, but you had to understand all of your colleagues' jobs and how you could best work with them to get almost anything done.

Networking became part of my job. I had to understand how to partner with teams and colleagues to complete a task.

Some find this challenging and difficult because it's a lot to remember each day. I find it exhilarating because it's business development with individuals, not just businesses.

The key to success with networking was understanding everyone's roles, boundaries, and interests.

- What was that person's role in the team? The organization? How did that role fit into the bigger picture?
- What was everyone's interest in seeing the project succeed? What were they getting out of it?
- Where could people truly help? Where did their help stop and someone else's help begin?

But there was a catch: You couldn't push your agenda on someone else. You had to be open to their perspective based on their knowledge of that area of the organization and accept their feedback into your project. Initiatives that leveraged everyone's feedback succeeded. Those that did not, failed. Miserably.

When all employees on a team are the CEOs of their jobs and roles, gathering open and honest feedback is easier. And that makes it easier to collaborate.

In that IT company, I discovered that when the team came to consensus to complete a project, we had amazing results. The customers loved what we did. When we didn't get along, that came through in the customer experience. Either the project didn't happen and was abandoned along the way or the experience was fractured because not everyone agreed with the approach and our contributions weren't aligned. The customer could see the output of the disagreement in their experience.

**What if this isn't happening in your organization?**

- **Roadblocks galore!** If you can't get everyone's input and come to consensus on a plan, problems will arise at the last minute and your project won't launch. The problem isn't usually people withholding information. The problem is that people don't trust you enough to share these issues from the start. For whatever reason, there is no relationship established for them to feel comfortable enough to speak freely and provide critical feedback. If they do give that feedback and it is dismissed, why bother? People want to feel heard, and they only feel heard if they trust you.
- **You don't really understand how the organization operates.** If you don't network and you don't listen to the guidance your team or network gives you, you have no idea how the organization works and how to get anything done. This is why some executives in large companies get frustrated when they issue a command and nothing happens. Many of these executives have *no* idea how their organization really works, who really does which function on which team, who really pays for such an initiative, and other types of questions. They choose not to ask and don't listen to their teams. If they did, they would discover that some tasks that they may think are quick to complete are actually quite tedious and vice versa. The most successful executives I worked with knew exactly how everything worked in their organization. They may not have known the specific details of someone's job, but they did know

the general steps involved to complete a task and who could help make something happen. And they personally knew the people who did the work, which is always key. Relationships make change happen.

- **You don't really understand the culture of your organization.** How employees voice their concerns says a lot about the culture of a company. Some will talk one-on-one; some will give bad news with their manager not present; some are open about all issues all the time; some will use different language in front of their managers versus when they are alone. This makes a difference when building a relationship with a colleague to create a better team. If you don't understand these nuances, you may be inadvertently ratting out your teammate to their manager or exposing a problem that, for whatever reason, can't be exposed. Process-wise this may be necessary, but to develop relationships to get work done and maintain a positive community, this isn't the best approach. There are other ways to achieve a similar goal.

*Proper Staffing Allows Employees to Contribute Effectively*

How an organization staffs its team communicates their value system. Employee compensation, seniority, placement in the organization hierarchy, temporary versus permanent status, and job requirements and qualifications provide employees signals about a company's culture and value system. Staffing decisions also signal how you value an employee's contributions and where you see them fit into the team. This information during the hiring process informs employees about their level of responsibility, the amount of power they have to make decisions, and how their role is perceived in the team and the larger organization.

Rather than speak in generalities, here's how some specific situations could be interpreted by employees and teams:

| SITUATION | EMPLOYEE PERCEPTION | TEAM PERCEPTION | CUSTOMER EXPERIENCE IMPACT |
| --- | --- | --- | --- |
| **Overworked employee(s)** | Doesn't feel valued—as a person, in the role, or for his or her contributions. | Same as employee.<br>Team may witness this and start to consider how the company views all of their jobs. | Customer may notice the employee attitudes and feel that the company doesn't care about the employees—or them. However, some customers may not notice the nuance between how the company treats customers and its policies. And they probably don't care, nor should they.<br>The bottom line: The company doesn't care enough to create a great experience for the employees or their customers, which is their business community. |
| **Temporary roles** | Doesn't believe they are required long-term.<br>May be part of a pilot program or new product.<br>May anticipate signals for how to transition to a permanent role. | Same as employee.<br>It may be difficult for the team to take a temporary worker seriously because they don't have formal "ownership." | If a customer can sense that the employees aren't invested in their jobs, then the customers may not be invested in the company's products.<br>The customer may also perceive temporary roles as if the company isn't stable. Why not make it permanent? |

| SITUATION | EMPLOYEE PERCEPTION | TEAM PERCEPTION | CUSTOMER EXPERIENCE IMPACT |
|---|---|---|---|
| **Permanent roles** | Company finds the role necessary.<br>A sense of safety and value to the company implied in this role. | Same as employee.<br>These roles are taken seriously in the organization. | The customer perceives the company as making good staffing choices and as being stable. |
| **Individual overqualified for the role** | Frustrated in the role.<br>Constantly looking for a way to contribute value that the employee believes they should be contributing (special projects, etc.).<br>Will always search for a promotion or way to get ahead. | Unclear motives for hiring manager or organization.<br>Suspect that the company has big plans for this employee.<br>Suspect that the company was looking for a "bargain deal." | The customer may wonder why the company hired someone so senior for the role and eventually support him or her to get promoted, even if it means being subversive to the team. |
| **Individual underqualified for the role** | Confusion about why they were hired in the first place and what the company expects them to contribute. | Believes that the company doesn't value the role. | The customer may wonder how the company chooses to hire employees and question the company's ability to find talent and their legitimacy. |

Of course, there are more examples than what's included here, but this should help you understand how your actions as a hiring manager impact your organization and employee community beyond filling a role. The team would most certainly discuss how their dynamics will shift with the new employee and team member based on the expected contribution by the person who will fill the role. Depending on the significance of this person's role, not only will the team dynamics change, but the project the person is working on could shift to be more or less effective. Depending on the person's role, even the company's culture and brand could be impacted.

A new team member is another form of communication that impacts the customer experience depending on that person's role, and the impact on the team and customers in the larger company community.

Your hiring choices have an impact on your company's customer experience reaching as far as how customers perceive these employees. If customers notice that the employees are stressed, they may interpret that as the employees being overworked, as the way the company operates, or that the culture embraces stressed out people. Customers may perceive that the employees don't take their roles seriously because they are temporary and wonder if the company will be around for a while (why not hire permanent people?) or wonder why the company doesn't take the role seriously to hire full-time staff or not respect that team enough to staff it properly. Customers probably won't do an in-depth analysis of your hiring decisions and how they impact them, nor should they need to do that. But they may recollect their experience with these employees and wonder why it is so poor. They may create their own stories to provide satisfactory reasons. Sadly, those reasons will most likely blame their poor employee experience on company policy rather than the hiring practices or individual personalities.

**What if proper staffing isn't happening in your organization?**

- **Employees won't feel that their contributions are valued.** If you design a team so there isn't enough support to complete tasks, your team may feel that the company doesn't care. Companies will fund what they want to see accomplished. If a team isn't properly funded, the team will wonder if their work matters to the organization. And if the team includes temporary employees, they will wonder about the longevity of the project.

- **If individuals don't feel valued, then the teams may suspect that they aren't valued either or have questions about the company's values.** Employees on your teams will make assumptions about their role if they are not feeling secure and valued.
- **Employees and customers may make assumptions about a company and its future plans that are not true.** Rumors start because people have insufficient information to understand why an event is happening so they create a story that makes sense to them based on their own perspective. Be mindful of the roles you have in your organization so that they reflect how your organization truly works.

### *Each Team Member Buys into Your Vision*

We often underestimate the power of individual team members and the impact they can have on a team and inside a company when they aren't bought into a vision. If each team member provides value to the team, and at least one team member doesn't understand a vision and its impact, then there is a severe risk that the team won't be able to achieve its goals. Discord and toxic ideas spread easily through an organization. But to managers, it's often not clear how quickly this can happen or how permanent the damage can be.[120]

We could consider related research to understand how ideas spread in an organization. Stephen Dimmock and William Gerken completed ethics research about the impact of financial advisors who conduct misconduct. As stated in the *Harvard Business Review (HBR),*

> *[They] found that financial advisors are 37% more likely to commit misconduct if they encounter a new co-worker with a history of misconduct. This result implies that misconduct has a social multiplier of 1.59—meaning that, on average, each case of misconduct results in an additional 0.59 cases of misconduct through peer effects.*[121]

To fully understand the impact of this situation, we need to understand what is meant by "peer effects," which is defined as workers who learn behaviors or social norms from each other. We learn about company behaviors and processes this way. However, it can be alarming to realize that company culture and behavior are learned in the same way as misconduct: through peers. Misconduct seems to be passed more easily, especially if you work closely with someone. As the *HBR* article concluded:

> *Within this restricted sample, we found strong evidence of peer effects just like in the main sample. These results show that, independent of any effects from managers, employee behavior is affected by the actions of peer co-workers. . . . Thus, similar individuals, who likely interact more, have stronger effects on each other's behaviors.*[122]

We could say that learning misconduct in a company is similar to learning a company's or team's culture, including the vision and mission. Therefore, learning to ignore a company's culture, its vision, and its mission is similar to learning misconduct. I'm not proposing that violating ethics rules and misconduct is comparable to not following a vision or not ignoring a company's brand values and culture. Those are very different ideas. What I *am* proposing is a parallel between how team members can be susceptible to corruption if they see another team member setting that example in the same way as a team member seeing a colleague not following a manager's or company's vision or cultural expectations.

To take this one step further, following corporate policies or rules is similar to observing and fulfilling the corporate vision and values. Both are types of rules or guidelines. Both involve thinking about the greater good versus personal gain. Employees overly motivated by personal gain and challenged by authority and rules may find it difficult to be aligned with any company vision. If an activity as legally severe as misconduct can be transferred to someone else in a team and culture, an activity less severe like not following a vision most certainly can, too, with similar impacts to the team.

### *Teams and Addition through Subtraction*

A friend and colleague would frequently use the sports expression "addition by way of subtraction" to describe the situation by which you remove a problematic team member to improve your team culture and results. To her, if a team member isn't adding value and instead adds problems to the team, it may be time for the individual to find a different team.

I have experienced this with teams on many occasions and have been involved in conversations discussing the impact of a team member departing or being invited to leave. Sometimes, the result was a sigh of relief and business carried on more easily without the person on the team. In one instance, a writer was adding more revisions than necessary to each piece she wrote and was not completing her work on time. We were worried about the impact of her leaving because that work would be divided among the remaining members of the team. However, after discussion, we realized that in some ways she wasn't adding the value we thought she was adding and we could easily re-absorb that work. She wasn't always listening to the subject matter experts, which caused excessive revisions. In some cases, she simply wrote copy that didn't communicate the product, solution value, or benefit. It created a poor customer experience and the team needed to compensate by rewriting during the editing process or we would give up and allow the copy to stay on the site as-is. She wasted the subject matter experts' time, our time, and her time, as well as budget money. In the end, her work didn't help us achieve our goals, never mind the company vision. We determined that her loss wasn't going to be as difficult as we thought.

From the example, you can see that with one individual not aligned with your team's vision, mission, and goals, your team can easily work toward the wrong goals and create a less-than-adequate customer experience that doesn't reflect the company's brand or values. The impact is infectious, detrimental, and, ultimately, unnecessary.

**What if a leader doesn't address this?**

- **There will be unclear expectations, conflicting goals, and little to no collaboration on the team.** A team could implode if there is no alignment with a leader's vision. Everyone would establish their own goals for their own personal gain. This would result in missing corporate objectives.

- **Team members who poison the team may leave a bad taste in people's mouths.** This won't impact only the immediate team, but everyone working with that individual. The spread across an organization could be far greater than anticipated—and possibly reach an entire company, depending on the employee's role. Although customers may not know that this is happening, they will sense something is wrong through the fractured customer experiences.

- **You are encouraging an environment that invites interpersonal conflict in your team and beyond.** Lying. Personal motivations. Alliances for personal gain and not to achieve team goals. Nothing good comes from allowing someone to maintain their own vision and not be aligned to the company's goals.

## Impacts of Company Culture

A company's culture is defined by its brand values, how it defines success, its goals, and how these elements are implemented by the leadership. There is a lot of room for creativity in how a culture grows and evolves.

*Company Politics: Cultural or Not?*

We often say a company's culture is political, but politics is a symptom of cultural discord, not interpersonal challenges or a reflection of cultural values. Here are some situations in which politics arise:

- Inconsistently executed brand values
- A misunderstanding among teams of a company's mission, vision, and brand
- Conflicting perception regarding how success should be rewarded
- Unclear roles and responsibilities among teams (often duplications and overlap)

When we focus on creating a brand, identifying brand values, and developing a corporate culture, we often forget that there are baseline culture "types" defined according to the organizational culture assessment instrument (OCAI). This is a "validated survey method to assess current and preferred organizational cultures. The OCAI is based on Quinn and Cameron's *Competing Values Framework Model,* which has been used by over 12,000 companies worldwide."[123]

The OCAI identifies four core cultures:

- **Clan culture**—focus on collaboration and teamwork (flexible and internally focused)
- **Adhocracy culture**—focus on energy and creativity (flexible and externally focused)
- **Market culture**—focus on competition and achieving concrete results (stable and externally focused)
- **Hierarchy culture**—focus on structure and control (stable and internally focused)

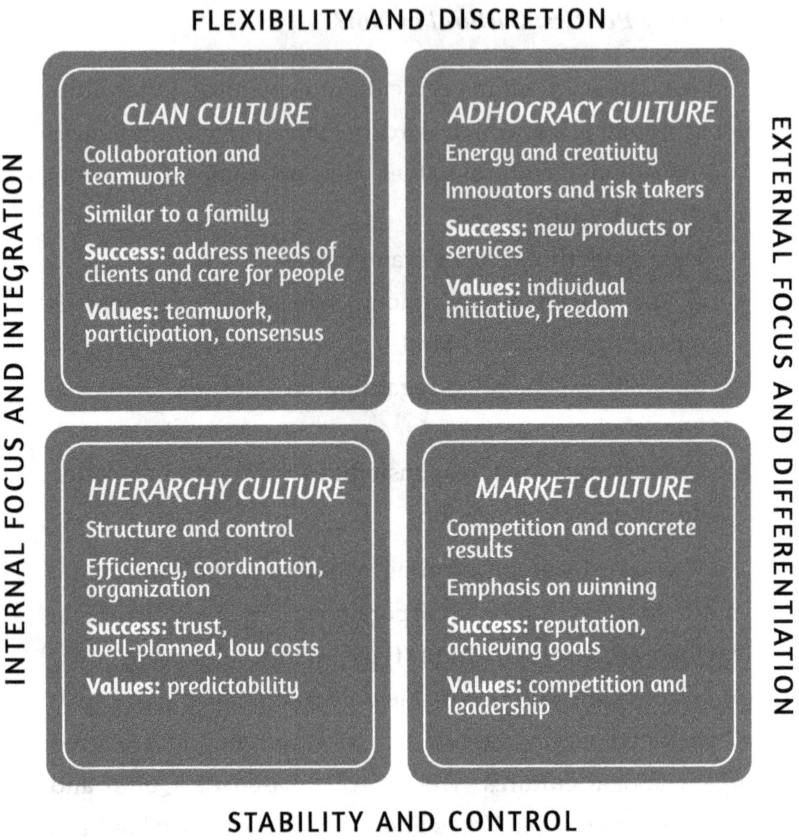

*Figure 7: OCAI Quadrant Diagram*[125]

All companies fit into one of the four culture types. A company may exhibit traits that combine two of the types, but that is rare; usually there is one dominant type that describes a company's core culture. "The four parameters of the framework include internal focus and integration vs. external focus and differentiation, and stability and control vs. flexibility and discretion."[124]

The culture your company has may impact how you implement a customer experience. A clan culture may create experiences that support customer collaborations. Adhocracy may encourage customer creativity. Market cultures may create experiences that help customers achieve specific results, from specific bottom-line results or key metrics. Hierarchical cultures may focus on creating digital processes and streamlining experiences. We don't realize that our company's culture, which is a reflection of our company's brand, impacts how we interact with customers. Although a customer experience is an extension of a company's brand, it is also an extension of a company's culture. Does this mean that there are four basic ways to interact with a customer? In a way, yes. Company cultures will favor approaches for interacting with customers and messaging their solutions. But the complexities of a brand's expression can be found in how it is executed, in the values expressed, and in the communication approach used.

## Accountability: The Agreement Experience

Another factor that impacts a company's culture and its expression through a customer experience is accountability.

Stephen Darwall, a contemporary moral philosopher who develops deontological themes like respect and accountability, described what it means when we are accountable to another person:

> *[W]e put ourselves in their hands, give them a special standing to hold us answerable, and make ourselves*

*vulnerable, through projective empathy, to their feelings and attitudes, not just as the latter's targets, but as feelings we can bring home to ourselves and share.*[126]

There is a movement for companies to be more transparent, but that may be challenging for a hierarchical culture or a company in a security- or finance-related industry to achieve. However, transparency is a key mindset required for building trust, creating a great customer experience, and developing accountability. So how can a company overcome this if transparency is not naturally part of its composition or values?

***What Is Accountability and Why Does it Matter in Leadership?***

Accountability runs deeper than responsibility. Being responsible means that you will personally complete an activity. Being accountable means that you are responsible for achieving a specific outcome. Typically accountability is associated with the ultimate decision-maker and authority for an organization, but anyone in a team could be held responsible to achieve an outcome. This is why accountability is closely related to leadership. Leaders are focused on achieving specific results (or outcomes). The individuals responsible for activities may or may not succeed contributing to the result, but that's not necessarily their job. Their job is to get to the work done. Leaders are empowered to achieve a successful outcome in the best way possible, including changing the course of action and activities if the original action plan isn't effective.

Accountability means that you will achieve what you say you'll achieve—and take responsibility if you don't. It's not about the work done. It's about achieving a goal.

Being accountable also means that you are responsible for upholding an agreement. Employees may be responsible for upholding agreements with customers in their day-to-day work, but the company and its leadership are ultimately responsible for these customer agreements, even if a customer is already part of the company community. No matter how close a customer is to the company (even if they are perceived to be "family"), how involved they are in company activities, or how they provide input, that is not an excuse to take a customer for granted. Each customer interaction is an unexpected gift. But this means that a customer has accountability too. Although a customer owes your company nothing, that doesn't mean that customers can't be held accountable for its success or failure. A customer is just as accountable for a company's success as its employees and leadership because they are members of the company ecosystem and community. They aren't *responsible* to directly provide the input or take action (it is the job of employees to gather that information), but they are minimally *accountable* to provide feedback to the company upon request. They also provide input and feedback through their actions, digital footprint, expressed preferences, and direct comments. This feedback is vital to keep a company in business and understand who its customers are.

However, for a company to expect customer accountability, it needs to be held accountable by customers to meet their expectations as well. To me, there are five customer expectations for a company that will help build trust and encourage engagement:

- **The customer expects that the company cares to build a product that will solve their problems.** A company needs to be vulnerable and open to listening to what the customer needs and expects from their solution. Companies can't assume that they know exactly what their customer wants. They don't. They don't live their lives and they don't know what they think, even if they feel they are empathetic to their customers' challenges. Research is required to understand them. Such research can include metrics and statistics collected from their digital footprint. In business today, customers expect that companies will do this on their own. And companies that don't won't be able to connect with their customers to create an experience that builds trust, encourages engagement, and creates this environment of accountability.

- **The customer expects that the company cares to get to know them.** Every interaction is an opportunity for the company to get to know the customer. Customers today know that companies gather data about them and are comfortable with that, even if the company is slightly intrusive regarding privacy issues. If that information gathered will create a better product and experience for customers, they generally accept and approve of it. However, this comes with an implied agreement that a company will also protect their data. We may think that customers are clueless about the use or misuse of their data in business, but that's not true. Most people understand and are sensitive to hacking issues in their digital lives and the implication of identity theft. However, they also understand that companies track their purchases and know how good of a customer they are. So customers today expect that this information is taken into consideration during every customer experience. If not, a customer may be disappointed by assuming that the company "knew" who they were and didn't provide any indication of that. Some example of customers assuming that a company knows who they are include:

- Customers calling a company on their cell phone and the company validating who the customer is (not asking who they are).
- A company merchandising products to you based on past purchases and browsing history.
- A company not asking you why you don't have cable at home because you gave the same reasons the previous 49 calls.

- **The customer expects the company to be able to solve their problems.** Customers often don't know how to describe their challenges and how to solve their problems by identifying requirements. And they shouldn't need to do that; that's not their job. The company has professional researchers who can guide them through the requirements gathering process and find ways to help the customer best. However, for requirement-gathering activities and for research, the customer needs to be available to participate and provide those insights. Customers generally want to participate and be part of the company's community and this activity is a great way to do that. Most customers don't know how to create a solution for their problem in the way a company and its employees can. Requirements gathering events with customers can be inclusive, engaging, and fun! They have a great time sharing their thoughts and ideas.

- **When a customer purchases a product, they expect it to work as advertised.** That is part of the agreement they make with the company when they purchase it: The product works as promised and meets the marketing promises it made. That's what sets customer expectations. Products and solutions should work as the customers expect it to work.

- **If the product doesn't work as expected, the customer expects the company to fix it.** This is also part of the unspoken agreement made during the purchase, or an explicit agreement in a warranty or guarantee. A customer often doesn't care how the company fixes it or how many people it contacts or calls to do it. The process is less important than the action.

To be fully accountable, a company needs to build a two-way communication channel with the customer to accept feedback and insights, which will help establish an emotional connection. This can start by tracking a customer's digital footprint using metrics from a product, marketing, or support. If a customer is able to use this company's product to solve a problem that is important to them, that person may write review content with more information that extends their relationship with that company and may create a deeper connection or relationship with the company or its readers. Purchasing a product cements the relationship through a type of commitment. A feedback loop with the customer or prospect provides the company with direct insight for how its product can help them better strengthen their connection. Activities that support this process include surveys, support calls, feedback emails, or even comments on social media. That's one way that a company can be held accountable—and be vulnerable. The company can then understand what's working well and what needs improvement. They are open to critique. Even if the company doesn't have all of the answers, that's okay. They understand the customer's needs so they can solve them in the future.

A transparency mindset is important among employees to reduce blame and improve communications.[127] Encouraging employees to work more openly with each other, focused on what needs to be done and why it needs to happen, will help them be more productive. When a team is focused on who is doing what in a specific way, they are not as effective or innovative as simply making sure that the feature is built. Focusing on *who, what,* and *how* when a team is executing a plan subconsciously limits the number of available solutions to a problem because it is focused on considering only the approaches that include those parameters. Focusing on the *why* for a project redirects your team's focus to achieve a business goal rather than complete a task and allows them to freely determine which activities will achieve that.

This idea can extend to customers. Customers want to understand that key features are being implemented or their issues are being fixed. They are less concerned about who is doing the work or how they are doing it or what exactly is being done. They simply want it done. This is why customers may seem to have more creative ideas. They are not limited by organization structures that may dictate which team is responsible for completing a task with a specific approach. They just want their work done to achieve their own goals.

Without customers included in the process to be held accountable to voice their concerns and needs, a company can't be held accountable to deliver a valuable solution. A dependency between a customer and the company needs to exist in order for the company to be successful. If one side drops its accountability, then the company is doomed for failure.

### *Case Study: Holding Telecom Accountable*

All of the major telecommunication companies have had PR disasters due to their lack of customer communications and/or poor customer service departments. Comcast, AT&T, Sprint, and Verizon have had their fair share of dramas in the past 20 years. Comcast had a customer service agent who treated a call to end service as if he were trying to save a relationship from a breakup. Even the customer claimed during that call that the way the agent was handling it was a demonstration of the exact reason why he was ending service.[128] Then there are the AT&T outages, especially one in the fall of 2018 when Internet service was down for all of North Texas and a number of other regions across the US. AT&T originally claimed that a fire caused by lightning striking a switching center started the outage, but later retracted that story. It's unknown what exactly caused the outage. What made matters worse was that AT&T provided no updates to consumers or businesses, nor refunds for replacement services.[129] Just as the widespread outage started, AT&T had such poor internal communication that customer service had no idea there was an outage. These agents either performed diagnostics for callers or told customers that the outage would last for 24 to 48 hours.

These telecom companies don't fail in the traditional sense because there often aren't many other options for customers to switch service, or the available options are equivalent. But their reputations and customer trust levels have been irreparably damaged. In 2018 in the UK, 75 percent of 500 telecom executives surveyed claimed that downtime has caused them to suffer reputational damage.[130] You could say that this is purely a UK perception, but 38 percent of US adults rated telecommunications customer service departments/ representatives as the worst in America.[131,132] Add to that customer service PR disasters and your company can only survive if you are the only option in town. Fortunately for many telecoms, this is true. However, in these cases, if a customer no longer trusts your company and you have a negative reputation, you have a lot of work to do just to have a neutral experience with customers.

According to the peak-end rule, people remember an experience as the average of the most intense part of the experience and what happens at the end. In the case of Comcast, that individual customer had so many poor experiences, and the end just added to the list, making his memory of Comcast the worst. For the AT&T outage in North Dallas, people remember the lies and that the Internet returned online with no announcement, so they remember a neutral, yet aggravating, event. If a telecom wants to improve the experience and be extra memorable, it needs to focus on making the most recent experience the best ever to balance the other experiences.

Another way to improve customer experiences would be for the telecom companies to hold themselves accountable for their issues. Instead of doing nothing or aggravating a situation, if a telecom acknowledged how it contributed to a problem, it may build some trust. And if telecoms created solutions to solve customer problems, they may be better supported.

As an example, AT&T had a video solution through UVerse that rivaled Netflix, Hulu, and Amazon Prime combined (until they removed some key programming channels). Unfortunately, few were aware it existed. Imagine if they bundled that service with their Internet service rather than just cable. They would have entered the Internet TV market and offered a great solution for all. But they continued to be focused on selling cable separately—not media access. They solved the wrong customer problem and, in the process, missed an opportunity to win not only customers, but a customer memory of a great experience and simpler media access. Rather than connecting with customers to build a relationship, understand their needs, and provide them what they want, the telecoms continue to sell what they want, how they want. They don't acknowledge the customer. Amazingly such telecoms are puzzled when customers still don't trust them or have a poor relationship with them.

## Corporate-Level KPIs Selected to Define Success Consistently across the Company

The selection of KPIs to indicate success has a profound impact on a company's culture. It sends a signal to the employees and customers that communicates the company's values. Some companies may value lead generation and the revenue funnel above all other metrics. Or they may value product adoption. Or repeat buyers. As Tony Robbins says, "What you focus on is what you get."[133] So, it logically follows, what you track and measure in your business are what you value and experience in your company as a result. This is why all teams should maintain complementary KPIs within a company.

If all teams are proving how they contribute to the bottom line directly through at least one metric and one team isn't supporting that metric, you have demonstrated that one team is held to a different standard and has a separate mission than the others. It's as if you have very separate companies inside a company with different goals. This will create controversy in your organization and destroy any unity you previously had. Such a discrepancy is often the basis for company politics.

Teams will wonder why they are held to a different standard or why one team gets off scot-free from being accountable to a more difficult goal. In fact, if all the teams are working toward the same goal, that brings them together into a tighter relationship rather than achieving separate yet isolated and divergent goals. Camaraderie is built through a shared mission.

But there are deeper challenges when each team has different KPIs:

- How do you create a unified customer experience if one part of the organization is focused on achieving a very different result than the others?
- How do you prevent a customer from seeing this disconnect that becomes obvious in your organization's operations and messaging?
- How do you create unity when your company is desperately broken?

Your experience externally to customers will become just as disjointed as what's happening internally with the politics unless your teams all leverage consistent KPIs. There's no way around it.

For example, let's say your company has a KPI for revenue generation for your product teams, but your branding team's success is measured by net promoter scores (NPS). Those are different forms of measurements. Revenue is tracked directly through campaigns, forms, and funnels. Net promoter score is tracked through a simple question: Would a customer recommend someone to purchase your product? It's an informative measurement and provides great insight; however, one KPI is much easier to improve and less accountable than the other. What's challenging about NPS is that it's not as committal or direct as a purchase and doesn't tie as neatly to your bottom line. Someone could have neutral feelings about your company and say that *yes*, they would refer someone to your company. Any survey operates under the premise that responders are honest, which may or may not be true depending on subject matter. Revenue always proves to be a very committal, defined metric. Someone needs to be so committed to a product that they purchase it. And this purchase can be directly related to people liking the product. If they purchase it, don't return it, and leave a good review, you could say that the product or service is a success.

In many ways, one could argue that the team measured by NPS has a perceived easier goal to achieve than the one measured by revenue. It would be more equivalent if it was a measurement of brand loyalty across the board, but the actions and energy involved for a team to achieve a concrete revenue number in no way compares to achieving a good NPS score.

## How a Culture Responds to Change

Although there are four cultural types described in the OCAI, the perception that teams have of automation and new technologies impacts how companies embrace change and innovation, especially in their customer experiences. A few key drivers for automation's acceptance in an organization's culture include its industry, trends, the need for automation to support profitability, and the openness of employees toward new ideas. These may be directly related to a company's culture, the company's community culture, or an individual's belief or value system. There are many factors why people accept or reject automation and technology, especially in customer experiences.

In the end, two main factors can drive teams to build great customer experiences in a company: curiosity (researching and understanding, identifying problems and situations) and creativity (brainstorming and producing or creating solutions). Together, these traits can innovate customer experiences in any company.

## Curiosity: Identifying Problems and Situations

Although *Harvard Business Review* highlighted a study about curiosity and its treatment at the workplace, the study of curiosity is nothing new.[134] A few years ago, I met Lynn Borton, who has a radio talk show titled *Choose to be Curious*. She is an expert in curiosity, or, as I see it, the craft of learning how to ask *why*? She also asks other questions, but her primary focus in her work is to understand people's perspectives and motivations.

Curiosity is an effective mindset because, by its nature, when you practice curiosity you are suppressing judgment. You are interested in learning why something exists as it does and discovering the motivation behind people's actions. This is why curiosity is a key element of listening and understanding others. By accepting information at face value, you can ask more questions to gain a deeper understanding and ultimately gain insights into the root cause of the issue, as well as people's motivations for beliefs, perceptions, and actions. There is no assessment about an insight being right or wrong. What you are learning is just a fact or a truth for that individual or team. By gathering additional metrics and data, or facts, you can gain additional insights to create a deeper understanding. By withholding judgment, you are able to explore more possibilities because personal bias isn't inadvertently shutting down options or alternatives that may seem unorthodox.

Company cultures that embrace curiosity are able to innovate because they are willing to explore ideas that may counter the general convention of possibility. Such teams don't dismiss ideas until they have experimented and found them improbable or unlikely to implement because they will result in few gains, are too costly, or both. This enables teams to contradict previous assumptions and understandings they may have about their business, industry, product, or customers. They may be more open to notice data anomalies and explore their significance than a company that rejects curiosity. This openness is the key to listening to your customers and understanding their motivations, needs, and desires. They can often share information that contradicts your understanding of them and their world.

In the end, curious companies have an easier time being open to new interpretations of existing knowledge and to experiment, explore ideas, and ask customers questions to gain new insights. The end goals of curiosity are fact-finding and understanding, which may confirm biases or disrupt convention. It provides the groundwork for the next step for creating great experiences: creativity.[135,136,137]

> "What we know from science is that our greatest regrets don't come from trying and failing, but from not approaching at all. That inaction bothers us more."[138]
>
> —Todd Kashdan

## Creativity: Solving Problems

> *Creativity is characterized by the ability to perceive the world in new ways, to find hidden patterns, to make connections between seemingly unrelated phenomena, and to generate solutions. Creativity involves two processes: thinking, then producing.*[139,140]
>
> —Linda Naiman

Creativity allows a team to create new realities through operations, processes, brand, product, and, ultimately, customer experiences.

But creativity doesn't exist on its own. Without its partner—curiosity—creativity quickly becomes personal expression, or art, rather than a way to solve people's problems. Creativity and curiosity go hand-in-hand. You can't be creative without being curious. And you can't be curious without being creative.

Creativity allows you to use the knowledge gained through curiosity and the process of discovering people's needs to approach a solution in a new way, breaking free of traditional thinking to see new possibilities. Curiosity encourages one to explore anomalies and understand what's unique and different. It provides the spark to know which questions to ask next when trying to understand existing systems. By using creativity and curiosity together, you may be more open to see problems that others may not believe exist today, see possibilities for a better future, and provide a solution with knowledge that many may have never considered.

Sadly, creativity has gotten a bad reputation and hasn't always been welcomed in business settings. We sometimes hear the word *creativity* and think about paste, safety scissors, crayons, and finger paints, thinking that it is something for children or hobbyists. We are taught in business school that real professionals work with numbers and facts, following playbooks and guidelines.

But there is an opposite extreme to creativity: Some businesspeople worship at creativity's altar and give it too much freedom in an organization. Deliverables, time lines, and tasks become secondary to inspiration. The accomplishment of a team becomes creativity itself—not a product, solution, or tangible result. Sadly, creativity alone doesn't guarantee paying customers.

Creativity leveraged in the right way in business gives you the courage to ask curious questions that can help you create new customer experiences that engage people emotionally. It also allows you to see your industry, trends, and company in a way that challenges the status quo. That new perspective may provide the insights you need to consider a different solution to your problem, one that is most likely more effective than what you are doing today.

### *Case Study: Small, Local Printer Hits Big with Curiosity and Creativity*

I worked with a small, local print company in the Bay Area to improve its digital user experience. The company specialized in printing club flyers and other digitally printed materials. Its customers liked its low prices and that they could drive by the printer to pick up their order, saving on shipping and turnaround times. They also liked that the company offered an online tool to place an order and manage the artwork.

I first started the project by doing some research. I did a competitive audit to understand the digital print space and then did some customer research. I called a handful of customers to get a better understanding of how they used the online store. The calls revealed a number of insights, but the two key takeaways from the exercise were:

- **Customers loved this printing company.** The system at the time was problematic, but that didn't stop customers from placing an order. Customers willingly developed intricate workarounds to get the system to do what they wanted. They made the solution work so they could work with this company.

- **Two factors influenced a customer to make an order: total turnaround time from placing an order to delivery and the cost.** Customers would spend time researching cost and time options, and clicking arrows back and forth on the browser for what seemed an infinite amount of time until they got the ideal price and time combination. This was a tedious task that they did out of necessity to find the best price to get what they wanted when they wanted it.

Knowing that the customers loved the printer that much informed me that any improvement would increase revenue substantially and encourage customers to love the company even more. So we decided to take an approach to help customers better understand the relationship between cost and turnaround time.

There were two factors for cost and time:

- Turnaround time for producing the print job
- Shipping time

By allowing users to calculate their time and cost options on the shopping cart, users were able to find the best comparable price for their needs. We also allowed users to update the quantity requested, just in case. It was a risk to be so transparent with customers, but at the same time, they were already figuring out this information on their own by using the browser buttons. This was the feature that customers truly wanted, and it was later adopted by other online, digital print companies. This printer increased sales on the first day this was launched, and it decreased the time users spent determining the best price for their print project.

By being curious about what drove customers to choose this printer, understanding what really drove their purchase decisions, and having the creativity to develop a new approach that was more transparent for the customer, the printer was able to simplify the customer purchase experience. This led to the printer increasing its revenues and expanding its digital footprint while influencing significant change in the industry.

## Conclusion

Employees are the cornerstone of any company; they do the work to make revenue happen. However, what if the company's policies make it hard for its people to do that? Or make it hard for the employees to connect with the customers because they are using tape, paste, and spittle to make broken processes in an organization work?

That's often what happens in organizations.

I have worked with many companies who have these problems with their teams, making automation projects difficult to implement. Top-level KPIs influence how budgets are managed, which also influence employee perspectives on how they do their jobs. Discrepancies in the KPIs may cause conflict between teams or challenging hiring practices that get employees and customers to question the company's motives. Team members may not be bought into the company vision or goals and that thinking could spread across the organization. There could be power struggles with perceived favorites. Poorly defined roles could exacerbate existing team conflict. Company and team culture have tremendous impact on productivity and performance, although it is often underestimated.

One approach to correcting challenging corporate policy is to let it simply fail. Sometimes that's the only way to highlight problems in order to make a change. Another option is to identify the issues that arise from automation and to develop a better way to achieve the goals.

When employees are tied up in corporate drama, they can't do their job and connect with customers and consider their needs effectively. They are too concerned about issues regarding their boss, results, other nonsense, and keeping their jobs. When you remove these issues from an employee's day-to-day life, you have empowered them to take their job to the next level and become the CEO of their position. Then your team can more easily network inside the organization because no one needs to worry about political conflicts, and they have the time to develop relationships that will enable everyone to succeed. How a company's culture is defined by KPIs, brand, action plans, and management determines an employee's success. If these are not aligned across the organization, your employees will find it challenging to collaborate and your customers will experience disconnects at every touchpoint with your company. If your employees can easily collaborate, they will create experiences that customers can connect to emotionally so they feel that they are part of the company's community. Curiosity and creativity will emerge as values and practices to find non-traditional solutions to company problems. Over time, you can then involve customers more in the business, making them accountable members of not just your team, but the company community.

CHAPTER 6

# Customers

Customers have generally been an elusive group for large, multi-national companies that don't have a way to directly interact with them. They were traditionally seen as "the other"—distant stakeholders who provided a company with revenue, who weren't always understood. Companies focused on creating products rather than solutions further defined this chasm, allowing the presence of customers to create an "us/them" rather than a "we" dynamic. The customer stakeholder needed to be pacified so the company could succeed and collect more revenue. From my experience, companies like this were characterized by "updated" annual personas, rarely based on research but instead on marketers' perceptions of whom they wanted to target. It was less of a persona and more of a target market definition based on business requirements. Or there were no personas available at all; the target included people with specific job titles in a specific industry who may or may not have purchase power in their organizations.

It wasn't until I worked with a SaaS company with a strong consulting team that I noticed that customers inspired companies to produce a better product to meet their needs. And if one customer had a problem, many others had similar problems, exhibited in slightly different ways. The company, in this case, was focused on creating solutions to customer problems, making adjustments as needed to its product to meet those needs. Customer success was central to that company's success.

## What's Old Is New Again

We keep hearing about the "new way" companies are developing solutions rather than just products. As I noted earlier, I'm not sure that is entirely true. Companies have always created products that solve customer problems. However, the "new way" acknowledges that companies haven't always included a direct feedback loop with customers. The middlemen insulated them and their business practices from customer feedback and interaction. A company can't create a product that solves a problem (and most products do solve problems) without any customer input or feedback.

Customer experiences have always been important. Companies always were interested in:

- How customers used the product (for what purposes and to solve which problems).

- If customers recommended the product or company to other people.
- Customer purchase patterns.
- Customer complaints. (If you don't know what's broken, how can you fix it?)

We like to believe that what we do today is new and innovative, but it always seems that what's old is new again. The same is true with companies including customer feedback and input in their product and marketing research efforts. Customers have always been part of product development and marketing, since early trading. Merchants and vendors always wanted to sell a few items and ask for feedback to determine if others would be interested in buying more. Merchants would gain knowledge about market conditions and competitors globally through trade. In the 19th century, as vendors and merchants went beyond their local markets to national and global distribution, they needed a more sophisticated way to understand what customers wanted and to market their products. They would contact local media to understand trends and concerns, and place ads in local magazines and newspapers. This was the birth of advertising and market research. To understand if the ads were reaching the best target audience and measure advertising effectiveness, Daniel Starch developed a research method in the 1920s. It may sound intuitively obvious, but he theorized that advertising needed to be experienced in order to be considered effective. He and his associates interviewed people on the street, asking if they read specific publications and remembered specific ads. Leveraging similar thinking to determine advertising effectiveness, George Gallup developed "aided recall," in which participants were prompted to see if they remembered an ad. As media channels expanded to radio and later TV, these methods gained popularity.

Another key figure emerged in market research in the 1940s: Ernest Dichter, who developed motivational research, a precursor to ethnographic research. Dichter believed if an advertiser "figured out the personality of a product, they would understand how to market it."[141] It's still an approach focused on the company and product, but as you can see, the focus of this type of research continues to narrow into understanding the customer and his needs.

As telephones and TV became more popular, so did quantitative research. It was easier to get input from customers and research what it meant to be a customer experiencing a product—including feelings about using it. It seemed that understanding how people felt about products mattered most. That's why during the 1970s, focus groups emerged as the preferred qualitative research method.

With the adoption of the Internet, research got even more granular. Almost overnight, a plethora of data was available about every customer regarding their Internet activity; every click, tap, and selection could be recorded. Researchers know that people often say one thing and do something very different, and the Internet allowed researchers to observe user activity and determine if people's claims were consistent with their behaviors.

The rise of computing, software, the Internet, and mobile devices allowed computers to be accessible to everyone, which meant that software had to be usable by everyone without having pre-existing computing knowledge. Tapping and selecting became the optimal user experience; speech and voice were introduced as the future of interaction design. Typing was (and still is) quickly becoming a skill of the past. Usability was no longer a way to avoid training costs or to provide "nice" features to customers. It was a requirement to enter the market with a successful product. Mobile apps no longer required previous knowledge of any software to get started. Customers expected that they could successfully complete transactions on these apps without any training. Intuitive, or being familiar, was the user experience approach many apps required.

Sometimes in product development, we like to think that making an app or tool easy to use is altruistic. But easy-to-use products that don't require training or support are the products that are more easily accepted by the customers. This makes building a relationship with customers easier and may encourage them to buy a company's product. The value that the product brings to them is clearer if less time is required to install and be trained on how to use it. And the more useful and easier a product is to use, the more likely a customer will encourage others to buy it. This has been proven true again and again. This is how viral products are born.

Sales and marketing have traditionally been slightly manipulative in their motives for the sale. It is hard not to try to get that first transaction. But what happens after that? The most successful companies connect with the customer to build a relationship beyond the single sale. Customers are more loyal to you when they buy into your vision and ideas, not just your product. The best way for companies to get customers to buy into their vision and ideas is to build a relationship with them and encourage them to experience multiple sides of your company with your employees. This is why you need a variety of conversations to engage your customers. Show them different aspects of a problem, the solution, different applicable uses, and the results they could expect to see from the solution you create.

## Employees vs. Customers

Employees accepted an invitation to join an organization (a company) to actively make a difference in an industry or the world; customers bought into the organization's solutions and vision for a better world and to help solve their own, personal problem. They are part of the larger company team to create a solution. If customers are part of the larger company team, that means that the relationship between them and employees should be transparent. Both sides, employees and customers, should be held accountable with collaboration, open and honest communication, and a sense of service.

Customer experiences provide that and encourage customers to participate in the business.

Customers shouldn't be expected to share the commitment to a company that employees do. Customers are loyal to many different companies because they solve the different problems that they may have. Employees are also customers of other companies. These multiple relationships give us insights into what it means to be an employee *and* a customer, so we almost become a professional at both. We can compare and contrast these experiences across different companies, further discovering what works best for a company or brand.

Let's say a family owns a Ford Expedition and a Toyota Corolla. Most likely, they shared some similar experiences with both brands and car models. They may shop at Whole Foods and Albertsons food markets along with a local farm stand. They may also purchase Oreo cookies or the store-brand version of the cookies and notice the difference in not just cost, but packaging, taste, how they break, and how they feel. The parents in these families may work at Verizon and AT&T telecoms, having the same job. They may discuss how their companies address problems differently and respond to customer questions and challenges. They may see how the brand influences not just customer treatment, but how they do their jobs every day.

We experience brands all day, either as an employee or a customer. Our varied experience helps us learn what works and what doesn't. Toyota may have a phenomenal warranty whereas Ford offers more accessible parts. Or Whole Foods has a greater selection of food for a vegan, but Albertsons has a larger general selection and better prices daily.

In the previous chapter, I outlined the customer expectations of a company. This list outlines what customers see companies as being accountable to deliver. But this idea works the other way, too: A customer should be accountable to help a company.

What should a company expect of a customer, besides purchasing a product?

- **Provide open and honest feedback about products and operations.** Customers must provide this feedback so the company can improve. If a company doesn't understand the challenges and problems of its product, it can't adequately help customers solve their problems. There needs to be some type of feedback loop available for success.

- **Pay a fair price for the product.** Sometimes customers want to pay close to nothing for a quality product. This isn't fair to the company—or the customer. Expecting products to be free isn't helpful for a company to continue being in business. And it doesn't help a customer. People tend to value what they pay for regarding products and services. So if they value and prioritize your goods, they should pay something.

- **Choose whether they purchase or not.** High-pressure sales doesn't help anyone. It also doesn't help how people see your company. The decision to purchase needs to be with the customer. They could be encouraged to purchase during the relationship-building process in the buyer's journey, but ultimately a customer decides if they want to purchase a product or not.

- **Be an honest champion.** This can't be stressed enough. In a world in which companies push multiple messages at customers, we listen to our peers. And if a peer is giving you information that isn't true, that doesn't help you or the company. People need to share their experiences honestly. It helps everyone in the process.

**The Complementary Roles of the Employee and Customer**

| EMPLOYEE | CUSTOMER |
|---|---|
| Create the product | Use the product and provide feedback |
| Identify customer needs | Provide input and insights about how a product is used |
| Create a quality product | Provide input and insight into what a quality product is |
| Provide guidance on a structure or process for communication | Provide information and feedback |

## Research: Part of a Dialogue Whereby Sometimes You Need to Read Between the Lines

*Some people say, "Give the customers what they want." But that's not my approach. Our job is to figure out what they're going to want before they do. I think Henry Ford once said, "If I'd asked customers what they wanted, they would have told me, 'A faster horse!'" People don't know what they want until you show it to them. That's why I never rely on market research. Our task is to read things that are not yet on the page.*[142]

—Steve Jobs

Jobs and Ford had a point. You can't just ask customers what they want and give it to them. Many design researchers will observe people in their homes, workplaces, cars, and more to understand how they do what they do and what issues they are experiencing. From there, designers, analysts, and engineers determine how the problems identified could be solved through a product or service. But the researchers are observing problems that many customers don't see or recognize. They are living their lives and grow accustomed to the inconveniences they are experiencing, interpreting it as part of life. It's the designers, analysts, and engineers that are identifying the challenges and creating improvements.

Years ago, I attended a design research class offered by the Design Management Institute. Two researchers from Philips presented a case study about how they eventually created the HUE LED lights. The researchers visited a number of people in their homes to observe their lives—what they did, the challenges they faced, what worked and didn't work for them. After conducting some interviews, the researchers found that many people wanted to change the mood of their homes, which included changing the color of their walls. Some were prohibited from painting their walls due to rental agreements requiring white walls or avoided doing it simply because of the amount of time involved to paint an apartment (which includes the time to rearrange and store furniture during the process). That's when the researchers and designers realized that they could create a light that could shine different colors on the walls and give the room a different mood. This product did amazingly well in the market, and there are now many products similar to this available.

Cultural anthropology encourages fieldwork that includes onsite visits. These visits may appear to be intrusive, but over time participants grow accustomed to the outside observer and starts to reveal insights about their daily life.[143] This produces ethnographies, which can provide profound perspectives about customers that couldn't be discovered from other types of research or data and helps bridge data gaps found from digital sources.

## Product Adoption through the Familiar

Jef Raskin, one of the most talented user interface designers ever, believed that there was no such thing as intuitive functionality or products. People relate to interfaces by connecting with what is familiar to them. They tend to use products and objects that they already understand, like a light switch. As babies, we watch our parents use them. So when we are toddlers, we understand how they work. This thinking impacts how we receive an innovation. This is why in product development, we leverage familiar paradigms and patterns, like shopping carts. If the product feels familiar, it will be perceived as intuitive. And if the product is perceived as intuitive and it solves a customer's problem, then it will be well received. Raskin shared his thoughts on this:

> *Even where my proposals are seen as significant improvements, they are often rejected nonetheless on the grounds that they are not intuitive. It is a classic "catch 22." The client wants something that is significantly superior to the competition. But if superior, it cannot be the same, so it must be different (typically the greater the improvement, the*

*greater the difference). Therefore it cannot be intuitive, that is, familiar. What the client usually wants is an interface with at most marginal differences that, somehow, makes a major improvement. This can be achieved only on the rare occasions where the original interface has some major flaw that is remedied by a minor fix.*[144]

—Jef Raskin, Intuitive Equals Familiar

This leads me to one of my favorite stories about latches versus doorknobs. My uncle told me that one of the major differences between Germany and the US was the use of latches rather than doorknobs. It was confusing for him to understand how to lock a latch so, of course, he had a stressful experience locking doors in Germany. I thought he was being silly until a German friend of mine shared a story of when she was an exchange student, new in the US, and wanted to take a bath in her new host home. She had no idea how to lock a doorknob. Needless to say, it was not a relaxing bath.

So what does this have to do with products, adoption, and customers?

Let's consider a development like the computer. It was a product that resembled a typewriter with challenging adoption. Most consumers didn't understand why they needed it in their homes. They noticed immediate uses, like budgeting, typing letters, and engaging with entertainment through games. Those uses seemed helpful, but they were not compelling enough to spend thousands of dollars to have one in their own homes. If it looked like a typewriter or word processor, then why not buy one of those instead? Or get a computer for work or school if the use was more applicable there? Typing to play a game wasn't very intuitive, especially with games already on the market like Atari's Pong, which used a television screen and a joystick-type of controller.

Entertainment provided an early use case for a modified version of a home computer. Atari's home console games, later eclipsed by Nintendo, filled a need for TV entertainment that didn't involve watching a show. And it was easily adopted because you didn't need a special monitor to play those games. A television would suffice. With the rise of the Internet, devices like the Xbox, PlayStation, and Wii had computing capabilities for group gaming, communications, media (videos and music), and shopping. Beyond those use cases, there weren't many reasons for incorporating computing at home. Maybe online shopping, but most people would do that at work. (Shh! Don't tell the boss!)

Smartphone adoption was easier because people readily understood texting as an alternative to talking and it was easy to understand the convenient relationship between the phone and a personal organizer. Products like the Apple Newton and hand-held personal organizers like the Palm Pilot already introduced such ideas. The main iPhone innovation by Apple and Steve Jobs provided access to a wide collection of apps (including a camera, calculator, maps, and more), movies, and music combined with the communications functionality of a phone filled a need that people didn't know they had. It made computing accessible and broadened its use beyond business, entertainment, and communication to integrate into daily life more than a personal organizer. It became a convenient computing device available on the go. And its expanded use was a natural progression of using the personal organizer metaphor on a phone to adopt all functionality that exists on a computer. Who knew that we would be so reliant on map apps for directions or decide to use our cameras to document our lives on social media? Then again, the apps used familiar metaphors and leveraged the convenience of a mobile phone, easily accessible in your pocket.

Mobile computing and apps not only provided users with great benefit, but companies benefitted from all of the data they could gather while customers used the phone apps, including where and how they used them, how long they were operating, and more.

When it comes to digital products, we understand how someone interacts with products from discovery through support, but what happens when the user isn't online? What is that user doing? How do they live? Is there another way to support the user that we aren't considering because we don't know and don't have that data?

Designing great customer experiences require understanding the complete customer—their life online and offline. As stated earlier regarding customer research, sometimes understanding the offline experience can give you the inspiration you need to improve your customer experience, moving your company into a new market or position. However, there are other methods to understand your customer offline: the customer journey and the customer relationship lifecycle.

## Make Every Interaction an Opportunity to Get to Know the Customer

Customer journeys emerged as a great tool for us to learn how customers make decisions, what motivates them, and how they gain insights and complete transactions. We often reference customer journeys when we look at purchase paths or other company transaction flows. However, I'm not sure customer journeys are the only way to understand how a customer builds a *relationship* with a company and the strategy companies use for creating that.

Today, much of the relationship-building with customers happens through salespeople, social media, and customer service or support. We look at the communications in such processes as persuasive yet they sometimes represent a siloed experience. Often we isolate activities based on departments, so sales will work to sell the product and marketing will communicate how the product can help. These groups provide separate customer messages that may complement or contradict the efforts of the user experience team to create a product. These communications activities are largely people-based, undocumented, and hard to automate—or are they? We understand the events and transactions required to convert a customer to a sale. But what is truly necessary to develop a relationship with a customer? I'm not sure we discuss that in business today. We discuss how to make a sale and how to get a customer to make a second purchase to formally "convert," but that's not necessarily the same as getting a customer to develop a relationship with your company, whether they purchase or not. Conversations about the goals of social media and loyalty programs are the closest we come to this.

If we look at revenue as the result of a great customer relationship, we could shift our focus to discover how a customer builds a relationship with a company and how this relationship should be considered just as important, if not more important, than how a customer completes a transaction. Not everyone who has a relationship with a company will be a customer, but ironically such individuals could become your greatest promoters and influencers. How could this be used to your company's advantage?

## A Customer Journey, a Customer Relationship Lifecycle, or Both?

We have defined a journey as a way to map a transaction or conversion process for a prospect/customer and provide an understanding of motivations, decision factors, influencers, and time lines. There are two main ways to use a journey:

- **The general path that most customers use when making a decision:** a tool to understand who those customers are and what they do in the decision-making process
- **The path a customer takes to complete a transaction with your company:** a tool to understand how you strategically work with customers and influence them along the way

Both are necessary. When you start creating marketing programs, products, and sales strategies, you need to understand how people make decisions in your industry. From there, you can create programs for your own company and over time study how these programs together help a prospective customer make a decision, convert, and continue developing a relationship with your company.

But there is a strategic step missing in the creation of customer experiences: understanding how to build a relationship with this customer. It looks beyond individual, facilitated transactions, to build trust and a deeper connection that will last years and possibly influence others to purchase too.

To illustrate my point, consider what you do when you plan a dinner party. We could consider a dinner party to be like a product you sell or a transaction event. It's most definitely a step to build a better relationship with others.

Let's say you decide to invite a diverse group of people to your house for dinner. Your goal for the night is for everyone to leave feeling happy, celebrated, and connected. You know that you first need to organize the evening, invite guests, convince them to attend, plan and cook the meal, decorate your house, and follow up afterward to ensure that everyone had a great time. You may research other dinner parties for food or decoration ideas and other entertainment experiences, like hiring live performance artists or planning games, to inspire your party. You could say that this research is helping you define the general customer journey for your product (the dinner party event).

A great dinner party is an orchestrated experience that leaves you feeling a specific, yet intended, emotion. It can be casual or formal, which invites different communication styles, conversation topics, food and decoration choices, entertainment options, and invitation options. No matter which approach or style you choose for your dinner party, your intended result is connection—to ensure that everyone connects with each other, that they feel that they belong to the group, and that they are part of something bigger than themselves. After most dinner parties, hosts want all guests to feel celebrated, not just the guest of honor or themselves. In fact, many hosts want to be slightly invisible since the event is their gift to the participants. At a disastrous dinner party, people feel excluded, isolated, or outright rejected. This could happen from disrespect by the guests, a controversial conversation topic, or a general mishap or accident. But most of the people at the dinner party should stay friends afterward, or minimally become acquaintances.

To get started planning a dinner party, most of us complete a pre-step activity: We know who we are inviting. Consider all of the possibilities. We often do this for dinner parties subconsciously when we invite our friends. There may be friends who cannot be introduced or in the same room because their personalities are too extreme, and arguments would follow. Or we may decide that a diverse group of friends require entertainment and games to divert their attention from a conflicting conversation or, worse, dead silence. Nevertheless, some questions we may ask ourselves when planning the guest list include:

**Who are they?**

- What are their personalities like?
- What do they do for fun? For work?
- What are their families like?
- What interests do they have in common? Where are they different? Do their interests clash?

**What are their motivations in life?**

- Are they always looking for deeper or closer connections with others?
- Do they love to meet new people? Are they looking to meet people like them? Or do they have a diverse circle?
- Do they go to dinner parties just for the great meal and liquor? Or are they looking for a general adventure?
- Are they looking to feel safe?

**What is their current friendship situation with you?**

- Are they close friends or casual acquaintances with whom you want to be closer friends?
- Where did you meet them?
- Do they know each other?

**What do they need from this party and your friendship?**

- Greater connection?
- Fun and entertainment?
- A place to go for the evening?
- Something else?

**What do they consider to be a great night out?**

- Do they enjoy the company of others and expanding their social circle?
- Do they seek out great entertainment and celebration?
- How about excellent conversation that broadens their horizons?
- Something else?

**How do they value a fun night out?**

- Is cost or payment a factor?
- Are they always looking at pictures and memories of the past?
- Are they focused on building relationships?
- Something else?

After considering who is coming to the event and who they are, you would then need to decide how to run this event to improve your relationship with them. Following are some considerations to make during the planning process:

**Understand their role in their lives.** Who are they and what is their life like, especially when it comes to socialization?

- Sometimes married couples need both to agree to attend an event. Is this the case? Or is this person the sole decision-maker in his or her own life and can attend alone?
- Is work important to them and are there hard considerations regarding work hours?
- Does this person experience a lot of life surprises? Suddenly sick children or adults? Car troubles?
- Busy people may prefer parties to get caught up with a large number of people quickly in one meeting. Is this person like that?
- Are they generally introverted or extraverted? An extravert will definitely attend no matter what. An introvert may be reluctant if it is a large group or it will be a loud event.
- Something else?

**Understand their personal motivations to attend parties.** Why do they choose to attend to go to events?

- They are always excited to meet new people or visit people they haven't seen in a while.
- Generally, they want to have fun and adventure and seek unique experiences.
- They're not likely to sit at home one more lonely night.
- They like to taste new foods.
- Something else?

**What are the factors to get to *yes*?** These are the details that could get to the *yes* or *no* decision.

- Dietary decisions
- Easy location and transportation
- Timing and conflicts with other commitments
- Something else?

**Based on the factors to get to a *yes dec*ision, what information does this person need?** This uses the answers to the previous question to start creating an action plan.

- Understand the menu or just know that you have their back regarding the menu. This is based on the respect and trust someone has in you, your decisions, and your relationship with them.
- Potentially a schedule of the evening in case the person needs to run out for a personal emergency or work commitments.

- Detailed parking information or information about public transportation nearby.
- Other information that would build trust, inform the guest, and get him or her to *yes*.

**Why would someone *not* come and how would they try to get out of it?** We don't like to consider why someone may not come to our parties, but it can happen. Understanding the reasons behind a *no* would help you plan an evening no one would forget. You would be identifying the various personal challenges and determining ways to overcome those adversities. And you'll be creating an event that includes everyone's preferences.

- Food being served. They may have allergies or be vegan, and if you are offering no options for them, they have an easy exit.
- Activities like games are something they don't like to do, and hearing that you may have them would discourage them from attending.
- There will be people who they don't like attending and no way to avoid them. If it is a small dinner party and there are a few people attending whom this person doesn't like, they may bail at the last minute.
- This person may know no one there and is too shy to meet new people. For some, going into an environment in which they know no one is terrifying. For some, it is exhilarating. You need to balance this knowledge with the personalities of whom you are inviting.

- There may be children in the guest's household who would get sick, have events, or have something else happening. Offering childcare or a child-friendly environment could get these people to yes.
- If you are hosting a formal event, hopefully your attendees have formal attire. If not, this could be a factor for someone not to come (and not admit to you that he or she can't afford to purchase a gown or tuxedo).

**What's a successful evening to you?** How do you define a successful night? That's your measurement of the event being a great night or a disaster.

- Everyone is talking and laughing. That's usually a sign of everyone having a great time.
- Eating all of the food. This shows that people didn't leave hungry and enjoyed themselves.
- Compliments to the host. This is always a great indicator of a great time. Hearing no feedback about an event is nerve-wracking. Did they say nothing because they had a terrible time? Or because they had so much fun that they forgot?

**What are your activities?** This is the step where you take everything you considered earlier and create an action plan—or at least start to plan the event schedule strategically so you can have actions in place.

**What about the next time? Will there be a next time?** You may want to consider next steps after the party. Will this be an annual event? Or is it a one-shot evening? Do you plan to engage with these friends again? What's the story you want to provide to people after the event occurs, and how do you expect to encourage it to happen again?

By not addressing the strategy for your dinner experience and considering the event from the perspective of those involved, from the invitation process to deciding to attend to the refreshments and the day after, there is a lot of room to create a poor experience. You could have mismatched styles and themes, or offer a casual invitation to a formal dinner, or invite a group without complementary interests, or pair dishes that clash on the palette such as a heavy dessert with a heavy meal, or use decorations that clash with the food color or season (like holly sprigs in the summer if you want to create a midsummer night's dream theme). Other unfortunate consequences include inviting a vegan to a roast beef dinner, holding an outdoor summer barbecue for a group of 80 year-olds who hate the heat, or inviting children to a formal evening party. You need to see the bigger picture and end result of the party, or journey. What do you want to achieve with the relationship and experience?

And we can't forget to consider the experience for someone leaving midstream. Anyone could drop from the process at any time. What would that mean for the rest of the party, their relationships, or your relationship to them? Will some be offended if others don't attend? Someone could say no to the invitation, leave the dinner early, or just not show up.

That's what the customer relationship lifecycle provides: a strategic viewpoint to make better decisions before your detailed plan.

## Why the Customer Relationship Lifecycle for Businesses?

The customer relationship lifecycle is a way to look at how you interact with customers in a circle rather than in a straight line. It uses the same elements of a journey, but when you think about an experience in a circle, you shift your perception to see a customer experience as ongoing, not a process with an end goal. And that prompts you to consider an experience in a different way.

- What do you need to consider if someone decides to refill the product?
- What if the product breaks? How does choosing a replacement work?
- What if the service is unsuccessful in providing meaningful results for the customer? What can the customer do as recourse?
- How about alumni situations? Or VIP programs? Or loyalty programs? They are starting a different type of relationship with your organization or school.

By considering the relationship with your customer, you consider the interactions you design in context of how the relationship could progress and improve. From this, you could also understand what is needed for someone to make various decisions along the journey.

It also helps to consider what happens when someone jumps into the middle of the journey. This happens all the time in business. You would need to provide the right information to these people to catch them up so they can make the decisions necessary. Or someone may jump out of the buying process and not progress further. Such a diagram and approach could help you better understand what's happening, see that neither action is negative, and understand how to leverage such a relationship better for the customer and the business.

### *The Case for the Customer Relationship Lifecycle*

Each time I worked on customer journeys, mainly buyer journeys, we mostly discussed the purchase event. But a customer relationship isn't limited to any single transaction or purchase. For example, let's say we want to create a journey for a student choosing a college to attend and understand what influences that decision and encourages that student to graduate. The journey for a college student doesn't stop at graduation. Post-graduation, that student has a different relationship with the college; he or she is now an alum. One could argue that the path for alumni involvement would require a different customer journey. However, in many ways this isn't a separate journey, but a new phase of a relationship with the university that is based on his or her experience during the previous phase (the experience at the college or university as a student). If the connection between the school and student was close while a student was an undergraduate, logically, the connection should deepen in the next stage of the journey. But what would influence someone to see it that way? That's where a journey doesn't necessarily work. A journey is linear with a start and endpoint. It could include a point for loyalty. But loyalty isn't a step or activity; it is a relationship state. So technically, in this case, the alumni journey would require a new path, even though technically it's not a new journey but a different type of relationship. It's part of the lifecycle of the relationship with the student, now an alum. It's just a different, and hopefully deeper, connection.

This type of relationship isn't unique to colleges and universities. This also happens with not-for-profit organizations, companies, and other groups. Sometimes the deeper connection to a company occurs when the individual becomes an employee or a salesperson. Within Mary Kay and other multi-level-marketing organizations, the conversion path starts with becoming a customer and eventually becoming a salesperson. Those aren't different journeys. It's the same journey, deepening the connection and relationship to the business.

Years ago, I worked with a professional organization to help revise its brand communications. When I asked the president if the conversion moment was becoming a member, he quickly corrected me to say *no*. It's when a person becomes a volunteer. To that organization, direct involvement was the ultimate engagement because it represented a deeper relationship with the organization.

Professionals may feel more comfortable with linear journeys, with a start and end to the process. It seems like a simpler way to understand how a process works. But relationship-building isn't really a process. In such an approach, we can lose an understanding of how the relationship formed. Relationships aren't linear. They change and evolve, moving toward deeper or more shallow connections. If you look at customer interactions based on purchase or conversion actions rather than how to create a relationship, you may be missing the point. A relationship isn't the result of activities. A relationship and its phases are a result of motivations, feelings, emotions, and, most of all, experiences.

### *Why I Support This Approach*

While working on buyers' journeys years ago, I realized pretty quickly that we had a problem: What happens when the user buys and installs the product? What if we made all of these promises during the marketing and sales process, only to find out that our product didn't deliver as we thought in marketing? No one really knew the answer, and we didn't really discuss it. Marketing wanted to meet the targets for marketing-generated revenue, sales wanted to close deals, and executives wanted to increase the bottom line. Sure, everyone wanted the customer to be happy, but marketing was so focused on creating a buyer journey that what happened post-purchase with the customer regarding their concerns was nowhere to be found in this equation. Customer service was barely considered, even though they quarterback and clean up most customer issues and challenges. Our mission was to convert someone into a lead to make that purchase transaction.

I was baffled. To me, we weren't in the business to sell products; we needed to sell solutions to customer problems. Through the grapevine, I heard that there were salespeople who sold the product to customers who believed that it was

**Comparing the Customer Journey and Customer Relationship Lifecycle**

| JOURNEY | LIFECYCLE |
|---|---|
| • Always has a beginning and an end | • Enter into a cycle / process that has no beginning or end; infinite |
| • Transactional | • Driven by relationships and conversations |
| • Single, repeatable path | • Path doesn't end; always moving and is dynamic<br>• Path may change for each audience |
| • Usually is a path to purchase or to complete another activity; a type of conversation experience<br>• Doesn't always consider usage or post-purchase activities<br>• Understands the factors behind a transaction | • Includes product use and support<br>• More experience-driven<br>• Creates a connection not just facilitating a transaction |
| • Focus on driving a user to an end result (often purchase) | • Focus on end-to-end; moving from being a prospect to customer (then repeat for refills / repairs) |
| • Step-driven process | • No real steps; could go backward or forward |
| • Doesn't go backward; usually is forward only | • Could move anywhere in the lifecycle |

the right solution for them, but these customers later returned it. These customers may have assumed from advertising, marketing, customer stories, and product reviews that the product solved their problems, and of course, the salesperson didn't disagree so he could earn his commission and achieve his goals. However, through this interaction, it became clear that there was something wrong with the sales process. Sales wasn't consciously helping customers solve their problems, and customers weren't able to use self-service tools to find a solution to their problems. They understood what the product did, but they didn't fully understand the problem that the product solved. Somehow that communication got missed during the customer journey, most likely because they jumped to the solution part of the journey right away. The solution was known in the industry as being top of the line, so it's not surprising that someone would assume that such a product would solve their problems and they would think they needed it. We are taught in our culture that the best is the best for everyone. That's why everyone wants the top-of-the-line product. But the cultural fallacy is that. Just because a product is top-of-the-line and costs the most doesn't mean that it is right for you.

This highlights how people aren't linear in how they make decisions. Sometimes, people jump into the middle of the purchase process—signing up for a demo or trial product when they just aren't ready—and that should be okay. As we know, customers don't think in terms of problems and solutions. They may jump to find a solution for a poorly defined problem because this particular solution is the hot trend right now or, as mentioned, it's the top-of-the-line solution so the customer falsely expects that it should do what they need. Some customers don't even think they have a problem to solve. Sometimes they are attracted to a solution because they believe they need it, even if the solution may not be for them (because it doesn't solve their true problem).

Each time a customer goes to renew a contract or purchase a replacement part, get a repair, or get support, they may be reconsidering their purchase and buy something different. What is a company's strategy to keep a customer using its product and happy with their purchase? "Lock-in" strategies work at first, but is that approach really a way to keep customers? It's equivalent to holding a customer hostage to keep the relationship. And what type of happiness do you expect your customer will have? Is it contentment? Or maybe excitement? We rarely talk about that. The focus is typically how to keep them buying from our companies.

Journey maps optimize a specific experience, usually purchasing, but it could be another process. In this case of the lifecycle, we are looking to optimize the relationship with a customer by reviewing the outcome and the strategy. The activities that the customers experience in this process represents the actual customer experience itself. The lifecycle is a strategic view of the relationship and activities that can be leveraged to complement a journey.

To build a relationship, the purchase or conversion point is not always the end goal; the end goal is developing a great customer relationship that lasts for years.

So how do you achieve this?

The irony is that we often don't talk about it. We talk about how to get more leads and more customers or how to create a great experience. But *why* are we doing all of this? The *why* is that we want our companies to have "friends," or influencers, and more customers. And to do that, we need to think about these people differently than in reference to leads and revenue. We need to see them as people while we build communities and relationships.

Sales and support understand this completely, but sadly, they are often the teams left out of the journey creation process. However, if we want to create a relationship lifecycle, we need to include them.

From my perspective, the journey is one expression and communication of the larger customer relationship. Before we create journeys, we need to understand our customer's thinking and motivation when they develop a relationship with our company. But how do we do this?

**The customer relationship lifecycle:** providing strategic insights in how to engage with customers best, not to complete a transaction, but to have a collaborative relationship with them.

### *How to Use a Customer Relationship Lifecycle Framework*

With customers more involved and engaged with our companies, we need a new way to understand how to build relationships with them. The following graphic summarizes a model, which includes a four-phase lifecycle, similar to a typical customer journey, outlining the high-level phases of the relationship. However, there are eight steps to use the framework to understand your customers and discover their needs, motivations, and goals in their own lives. In many ways, this is like the dinner party example discussed earlier in the chapter. It's a generalized version that you could use for any product or experience.

The four phases of the customer experience lifecycle:

- **Pre-purchase:** This is a very early stage of the buyer's journey, when customers are first identifying their problem and discovering solutions. Often, customers don't identify a problem clearly on their own. They do this by investigating solutions and reverse-engineering the problem they have. This phase includes a lot of discovery, learning, and *a-ha* moments for the customer, who will identify their challenges through customer stories that describe similar challenges that they are having.

## CUSTOMER RELATIONSHIP LIFECYCLE

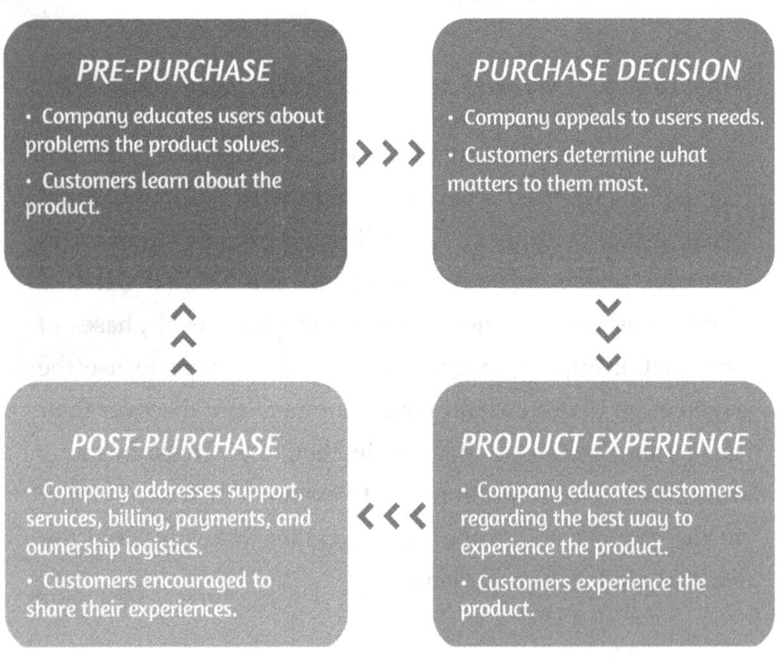


*Figure 8: The Customer Relationship Lifecycle*

- **Purchase decision**: By this stage, customers have realized that they have a problem and need a solution. Often at this step they will research competitor solutions and understand the market landscape. They are looking to find the right solution for their problem.
- **Product experience:** The product needs to solve the problem. And the experience of the product needs to meet certain customer expectations regarding value and worth.
- **Post-purchase:** This stage includes warranties, guarantees, pricing, and support. These are all experience factors that could make a difference from a customer referring your company and product to someone else, buying a refill or replacement (which is often similar to going through the entire lifecycle again), or dropping out of the relationship. This is also when customers write reviews and use the product actively.

Keep in mind that a customer can enter the relationship at any time, fall out of it at any time, or remain in a step forever.

**Why only four steps and not six or eight?** Four keeps the process simple enough to consider how a customer experiences deciding to work with a company. The evaluation process restarts with refills, repurchase, or a deeper relationship decision, such as participating in a loyalty program (that could be a type of new product). Loyalty, engagement, and becoming a fan reflect a deeper relationship state that happens post-purchase, while the customer continues to use the product. I wouldn't consider it a separate process step; it's another lifecycle iteration that represents building a deeper bond and relationship state between the company and customer. The steps reflect key decision points to develop any relationship; the number of times a customer rotates around the lifecycle represents the depth and strength of the connection, or the state of the relationship. If a customer purchases a widget and uses it regularly, he goes through the lifecycle once. If a customer is invited to be in your company's VIP program, he goes through another lifecycle iteration to evaluate if he wants that type of relationship and build a stronger bond. That second iteration should include activities to build a closer customer relationship and greater support for the brand.

That's why I find it fascinating to understand how customers are motivated to take the next step. What information does a person need to realize that he or she has a problem? What facts or feelings will help a customer realize that your solution is right for them? What type of support mechanisms need to be established so the customer feels comfortable making the purchase? How can the product experience continue consistently through the purchase and support experiences?

Before you create a journey, you can use this framework to help develop a general strategy for interacting with customers to build a relationship with them. What do you want to achieve at each step? What are customers thinking during that step? How are they motivated? By looking at the complete picture, you can consider how each group will respond in each step of the process.

Included after each iteration description is an example to better understand how to apply this process to your company. One of my favorite household cooking gadgets is the vegetable spiralizer to make zucchini noodles. There are a number of companies that make various versions of this tool, but for illustrating the process, we'll create a fictitious company called Healthy Prep. Its main product is the "Go-round Spiralizer," a battery-powered spiralizing gadget that includes up to five shape graters. Healthy Prep also sells a no-scar grater and spaghetti squash spork.

- **Mission:** Provide people fun ways to prepare vegetables.
- **Distribution:** Online and through Amazon
- **Cost:** You can buy it online for $40 retail.
- **Product Awareness and Marketing:** Online ads, social media, late-night infomercials, and demos at fairs and events
- **How it works:** Put your carrot, zucchini, or other tube-shaped vegetable into the "Go-round Spiralizer" and it will automatically be cut into 1 of 5 available fun shapes. It's like a coffee grinder for vegetables.
- **Support & service:** If you have a problem, you can call an 800 number or visit the website to get a replacement. It has a one-year product guarantee and warranty.

The company discovered that by transforming vegetables into fun shapes, children are more willing to each their vegetables. And with the tool being automatic (battery-powered), good for use up to 1,000 uses, dishwasher-safe and easy to clean, you can use it regularly to get your kids to finally eat vegetables—and like them.

The target market includes parents of picky eaters. Most of these parents are busy juggling work, parenthood, and other family and community roles. This individual doesn't have a lot of time to prepare meals, invest in researching intricate recipes, or discover new food ideas. However, to get a picky eater to like vegetables, you need a lot of creativity to present them in a new way. The parents' motivations are for their child to eat nutritious meals, to feel good about their choices, and to feel like successful parents. They don't want to spend a lot of time achieving these goals, so it helps that the spiralizer is easy to clean and store.

What does success look like for parents:

- Their child eats veggies without complaints.
- Parents can easily create new dishes that the family loves.
- New dishes are simple to make and don't require a lot of cleanup.

***Note that this is an imaginary product with an imaginary customer.*** You may have a target customer for your own product that is researched and documented. I can't stress enough the value of persona research to understand your customers. You can use the lifecycle to discover what you need to understand about your customers, which could inform what your persona research should include. However, great customer personas are based on actual research using actual people. It's difficult to be successful when creating a great experience without this knowledge.

Again, this version of the customer relationship lifecycle itself has four steps, but there are eight iterations that you can use to help you look at your customer a little differently. *You would ideally complete this process for each persona you have for your company.*

## HOW TO USE THE CUSTOMER RELATIONSHIP LIFECYCLE

***STEP 1:***
Map your customer's role.
*What do they do?*

***STEP 2:***
Determine motivations.
*Why would they want it?*

***STEP 3:***
Determine decision factors.
*What would make them say yes?*

***STEP 4:***
Determine considerations.
*What do they think about?*

***STEP 5:***
Determine exit points.
*Why would someone NOT want it?*

***STEP 6:***
Determine success measurements.
*How do we define success?*

***STEP 7:***
Plan supporting activities.
*What to do to get someone to buy?*

***STEP 8:***
Address refills or repairs.
*Why would someone keep the product?*

*Figure 9: Using the Customer Relationship Lifecycle*

**Step 1: Map your customer's role.**

Map your customer's role throughout the process. Are they the buyer, a stakeholder, or an influencer, or do they have no voice? Consider their activities when using the product, benefitting from the product, purchasing the product, or maintaining the product.

Understanding how someone interacts with your company will help you gain insights and an understanding of the type of relationship you could have with that customer.

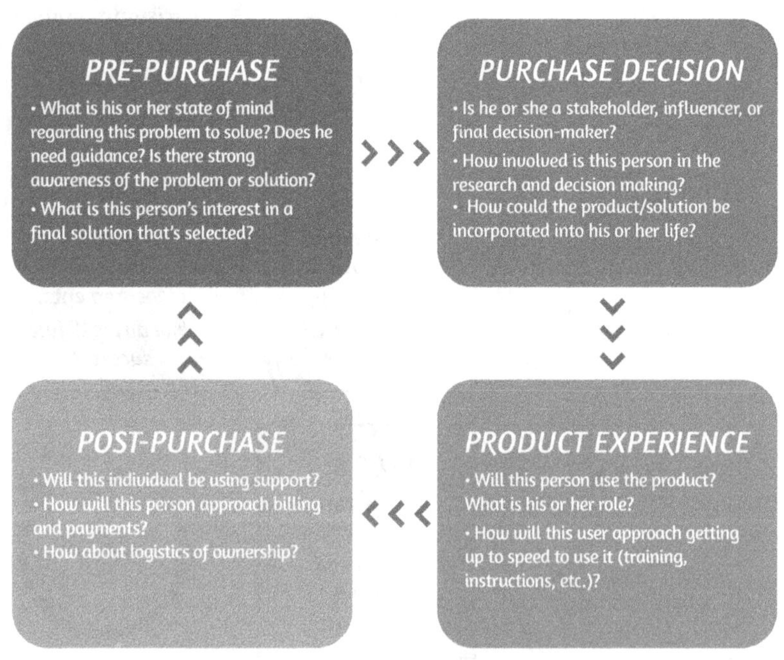


*Figure 10: Sample Questions to Map Your Customer's Role*

Note that each role will get its own lifecycle—and ultimately, a separate journey. You can understand a customer based on how they interact with you, and use this knowledge about them to create the right experience that will resonate with him or her.

Following is an example of how you could complete this chart for the target parent customer for the "Go-round Spiralizer" by leveraging a persona research report. For each step, you could include:

- A description of the role this person will play in the decision making process and insights into how someone in this role makes a decision,
- Considerations about what they may be thinking regarding the product/solution, the problem it solves, and expectations about the price point, and
- What they may expect or want this solution to be.

This is a first pass at considering who these people are and what they think about throughout the process. It's a way to peer into their minds to understand them and their needs.

# BUYER OF GO-ROUND: PARENTS

### PRE-PURCHASE

- Knows that his or her child won't eat veggies and has to find a way for him to do that. This is an ongoing problem.
- Doesn't consciously look for a solution or have time to do that; it's not top of mind. But if a solution comes along, all the better.
- Will ask friends for advice and help.

### PURCHASE DECISION

- This person is the decision-maker who is casually researching options.
- Decision was made based on feedback from friends/family (direct or social media).
- Price is a factor. Product should be inexpensive and well-made.
- Wants something easy to use that is simple and not complicated.

### PRODUCT EXPERIENCE

- Wants a product that is familiar and easy to use (will return otherwise).
- Doesn't expect complicated instructions.
- Doesn't expect complicated assembly.

### POST-PURCHASE

- Doesn't want to contact support or customer service.
- Doesn't want to have to invest in maintenance, repairs, or replacements for at least 3-5 years.
- Product is easily cleaned.
- Possibly replace after a couple of years if the product is inexpensive.

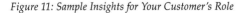

*Figure 11: Sample Insights for Your Customer's Role*

**Step 2: Determine motivations.**

When we look at the customer relationship lifecycle, we need to consider a customer's motivations as they move from one step to the next. What are they thinking about? How could that thought work in their best interest? What is someone's motivation to take action? What's in it for them?

The goal of this step is to understand the types of motivations that may influence someone to purchase and use the product regularly.

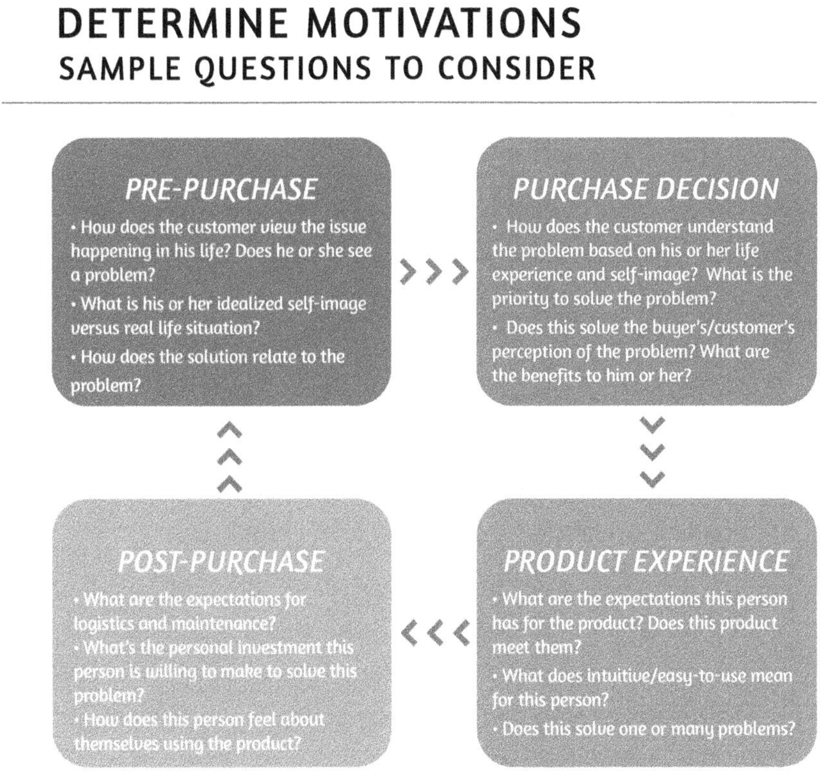

## DETERMINE MOTIVATIONS
### SAMPLE QUESTIONS TO CONSIDER

*PRE-PURCHASE*

- How does the customer view the issue happening in his life? Does he or she see a problem?
- What is his or her idealized self-image versus real life situation?
- How does the solution relate to the problem?

> > >

*PURCHASE DECISION*

- How does the customer understand the problem based on his or her life experience and self-image? What is the priority to solve the problem?
- Does this solve the buyer's/customer's perception of the problem? What are the benefits to him or her?

*PRODUCT EXPERIENCE*

- What are the expectations this person has for the product? Does this product meet them?
- What does intuitive/easy-to-use mean for this person?
- Does this solve one or many problems?

< < <

*POST-PURCHASE*

- What are the expectations for logistics and maintenance?
- What's the personal investment this person is willing to make to solve this problem?
- How does this person feel about themselves using the product?

*Figure 12: Sample Questions to Determine Customer Motivations*

To use this step, you'll need to consider the target parent customer of the "Go-round Spiralizer" as people with feelings and emotions. Consider their life beyond having the role of being a buyer of your product. Some questions to answer in this step:

- Consider how this individual sees himself or herself as a person: in society, in the family, among friends, at work, etc. How could this solution benefit his or her self-image in those places? How would that motivate him or her along the process?
- What are the solution benefits to them—monetarily, emotionally, physically?
- What are the thoughts and feelings that will motivate him or her to choose this solution?
- What is the impact of other people's influence directly on the decision or indirectly through his or her perception of the person owning this solution?
- How does the person want to be perceived by others: as part of the group, as an innovator—or does this even matter?
- Is the solution for a single situation/problem? Or is it versatile, covering multiple scenarios/problems?

The key discovery you need to make in this step: Which pain point in their life is so severe that they would adopt a new approach to make their life easier?

This is not easy to discover. You need to first understand both the person's current and idealized self-image. Then you need to use that information to discover the thoughts and feelings that will motivate someone to make a decision to move past the current image and achieve that idealized self-image. In this example, we could say that every parent craves to be perceived as a good parent and see his or her child happy and healthy. This is true across all segments—for a parent in society, in their family, with friends, and at work. Being perceived as a good parent is a key motivator for someone to purchase this specific solution, but is that alone compelling enough to drive someone to buy the tool? In this case, you may want to explore additional motivations, realities, or beliefs that are associated with his or her current self-image. For example:

- They want a simpler life because they have too much to do each day. They don't want to have to spend all day to make healthy food that their kids will eat. That's one more thing to do.
- They aren't a professional chef. They don't want a complex tool to use that requires intense learning to master. And they want dinner to be exciting every day without a bunch of training–can this support that?
- They have limited time and budget. They can't hire someone to clean up after them so they don't want something difficult to clean or maintain.

From these motivations, you can identify the thoughts and feelings, individually or together, that will guide a parent to make a decision and prioritize solving this problem.

You may be curious why you want to consider a customer's motivations before understanding the types of information that they need to make a decision. If people make decisions based on meaning, feelings, emotions, and self-interest, you need to understand their general life motivations before determining which types of information will validate that. In this case, if a person wants to be perceived as a great parent, how does he or she think? What types of decisions support that thinking? If you create an experience using facts first, you will be contemplating the types of information that someone will logically need to support a decision. This won't allow you to see the person as an emotional person with many types of lives; you'll only see the facts that will make someone buy. That's important, but people use facts to support their choices. This is why many companies create too much content. They consider what will logically engage people, not what will emotionally engage people. Ideally, you want to emotionally engage people first and later support those feelings with facts. This step helps orient your thinking to do that.

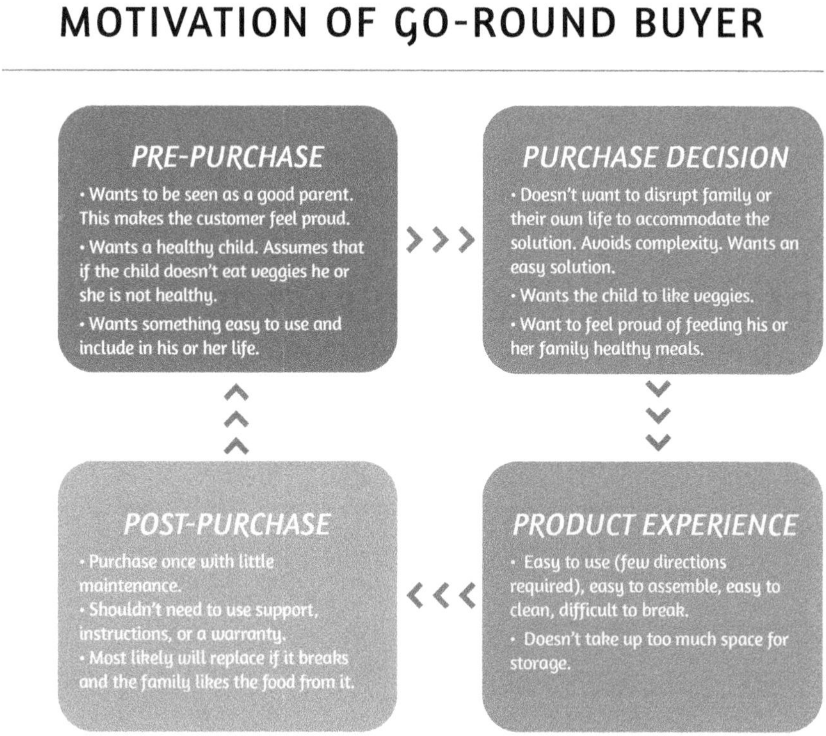

# MOTIVATION OF GO-ROUND BUYER

## *PRE-PURCHASE*

- Wants to be seen as a good parent. This makes the customer feel proud.
- Wants a healthy child. Assumes that if the child doesn't eat veggies he or she is not healthy.
- Wants something easy to use and include in his or her life.

>>>

## *PURCHASE DECISION*

- Doesn't want to disrupt family or their own life to accommodate the solution. Avoids complexity. Wants an easy solution.
- Wants the child to like veggies.
- Want to feel proud of feeding his or her family healthy meals.

## *PRODUCT EXPERIENCE*

- Easy to use (few directions required), easy to assemble, easy to clean, difficult to break.
- Doesn't take up too much space for storage.

<<<

## *POST-PURCHASE*

- Purchase once with little maintenance.
- Shouldn't need to use support, instructions, or a warranty.
- Most likely will replace if it breaks and the family likes the food from it.

*Figure 13: Sample Insights for Customer Motivations*

**Step 3: Determine decision factors.**

What actions or information drives someone to take the next step? What helps him or her make a decision? In this step, consider what someone needs to do as an activity or what he or she needs to consider before moving to the next step.

## DETERMINE DECISION FACTORS

### SAMPLE QUESTIONS TO CONSIDER

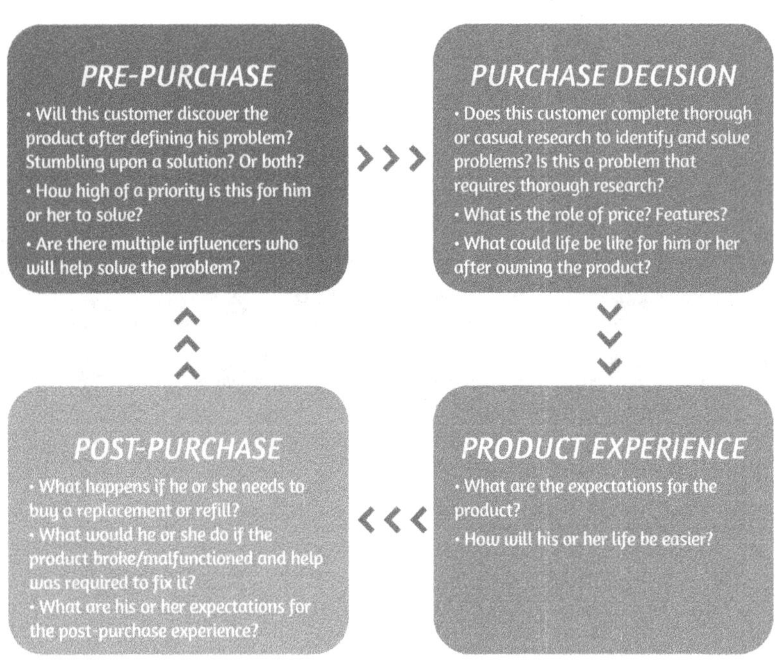


*Figure 14: Sample Questions for Decision Factors*

This step outlines the realizations that the prospect or customer must make to move to the next step in the process or possibly leap a step. In this case, we need to consider what the parent needs to realize in order to purchase. These realizations include shifts in beliefs, developed curiosity, and acceptance of new convictions. Some considerations:

- **Logistics:** price, product maintenance, product support and service
- **Acknowledge challenges:** Help the prospect and customer discover the problem they are experiencing and determine how that is challenging them today.
- **Prioritization of the problem to solve:** How badly does the prospect or customer need to solve their problem? Is it an urgent problem to fix? Something that they just discovered? Can they see their problem in a way so it's more urgent?
- **Inspiration and hope:** encourage the prospect and customer to envision what life could be like after using the product. Help them see a new future and consider how that new future will feel.

One approach to get people to make a decision is to get them to envision their life in a new way and see a new possibility. Sometimes, you can achieve this through customer stories by encouraging existing customers to share their realizations after using the solution and explain to others why they selected it. This usually outlines the problems that they had, why this was the best solution for them (compared to others), and how it helped them. It helps a customer connect to a company by seeing themselves in that customer. This is why customer quotes and testimonials are so powerful.

To understand better how your customer may be thinking during this step, listen to some customer testimonials as part of your research. If you combine this with your customer motivations, you'll get a better sense of who your customers are as people and what they need to believe, think, and feel about choosing your solution to help them with their problem.

## GO-ROUND BUYER DECISIONS/ INSIGHTS

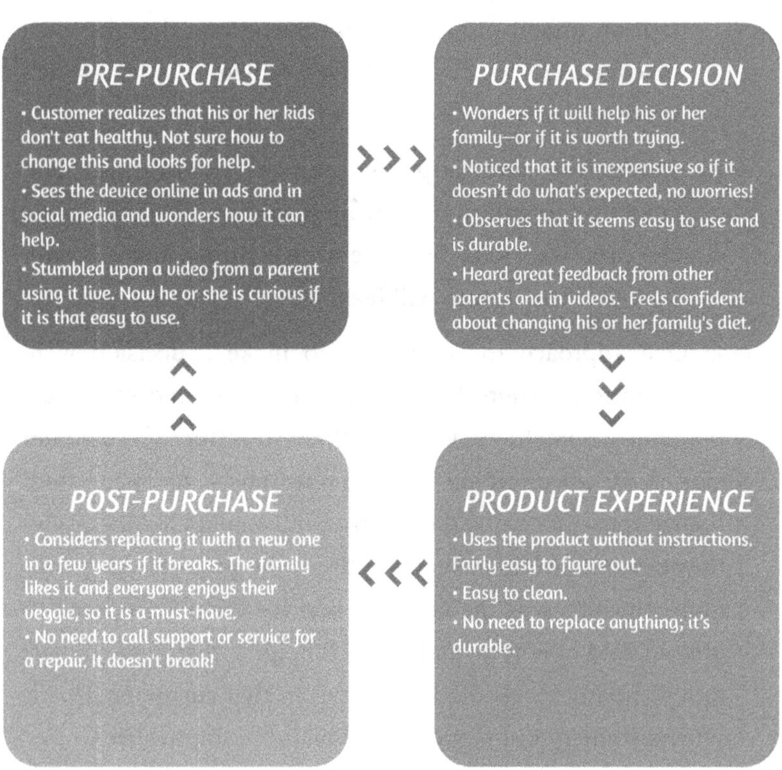


*Figure 15: Sample Insights for Decision Factors*

**Step 4: Determine considerations.**

What *information* do prospects/customers need to make decisions based on your understanding of their motivations? Now that you have a better understanding of what prospects/customers may be thinking at each step, you can identify what information will help them make a decision in your favor.

## DETERMINE CONSIDERATIONS

### SAMPLE QUESTIONS TO CONSIDER

*Figure 16: Sample Questions for Considerations*

Unlike the previous steps that are more focused on customer psychology and the emotions involved in decision-making, this step explores the concrete thoughts customers may have when making a purchase decision. This step answers: What facts and information do people need to decide to purchase this product? What will help them feel like they made a great decision?

We are taught that we use facts to make a decision that we feel good about when in fact we often feel good about an option through somatic markers based on situational familiarity and use facts to justify our feelings. That's why we don't consider facts to support a decision until this step. For example, let's say the spiralizer has enough speed and power to cut through four zucchinis in fewer than three minutes. That is amazing performance and great information, but is that information that will sell your product? It is information that supports how easy it is to use and how it makes cooking dinner faster and simpler, but as a standalone fact, does it inspire people to feel that they need it in their life? Probably not.

A better fact that may help a parent choose this spiralizer may come from the result of a survey of kids who eat meals made with the spiralizer versus those who haven't experienced it to discover which group enjoyed their vegetables at dinner more. If the group who experienced the spiralizer did, that's a better fact to use because it can support the parent's purchase decision. Who doesn't want to make eating vegetables fun?

In this step, consider which information is key for customers to know about your product and which information will support a story that connects to them emotionally. Product facts and achievements are powerful, but they alone don't solve someone's problem.

This is a great topic to include in your persona research. What you may have thought was a compelling fact or point of information about your product or solution really isn't. Often, people aren't actively looking for a solution to their

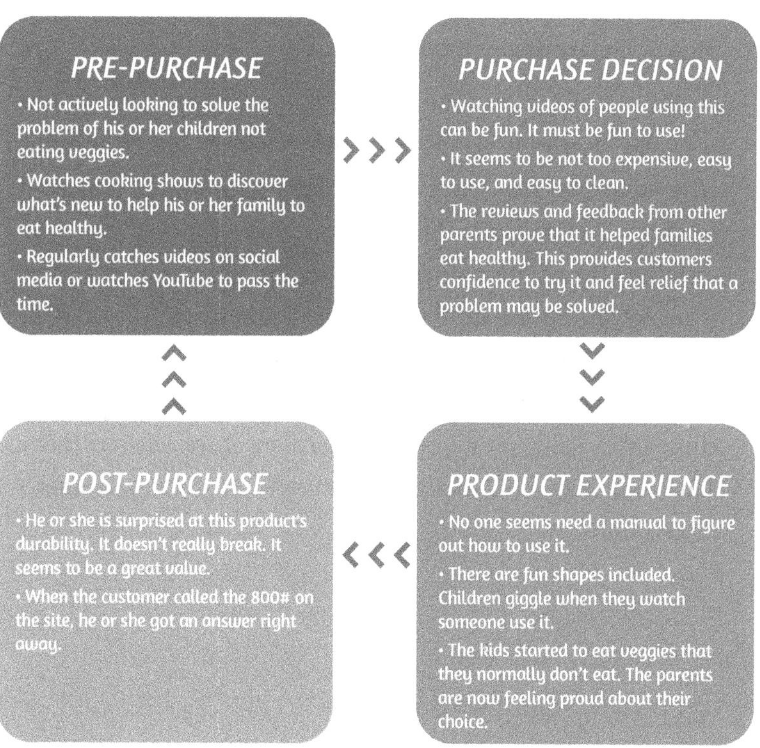

GO-ROUND BUYER CONSIDERATIONS
PRE-PURCHASE
• Not actively looking to solve the problem of his or her children not eating veggies.
• Watches cooking shows to discover what's new to help his or her family to eat healthy.
• Regularly catches videos on social media or watches YouTube to pass the time.
PURCHASE DECISION
• Watching videos of people using this can be fun. It must be fun to use!
• It seems to be not too expensive, easy to use, and easy to clean.
• The reviews and feedback from other parents prove that it helped families eat healthy. This provides customers confidence to try it and feel relief that a problem may be solved.
PRODUCT EXPERIENCE
• No one seems need a manual to figure out how to use it.
• There are fun shapes included. Children giggle when they watch someone use it.
• The kids started to eat veggies that they normally don't eat. The parents are now feeling proud about their choice.
POST-PURCHASE
• He or she is surprised at this product's durability. It doesn't really break. It seems to be a great value.
• When the customer called the 800# on the site, he or she got an answer right away.


*Figure 17: Sample Insights for Considerations*

problem because they often haven't clearly identified it. This could be a challenge for you—or an opportunity. These spiralizer customers browse for ideas and then get inspired or motivated to make a decision. Use this to your advantage. In this case, the customer may stumble upon your product in social media or hear about it from a friend or work colleague. Price may not be as much of a concern as maintenance, ease of use, or even access to ideas for how to use it. It's key is to know what problem you are solving for the customer, how solving that problem makes them feel, and how it supports the ideal image the customer has of himself.

**Step 5: Determine exit points.**

People exit a relationship with a company for various reasons. Consider some of those reasons and determine why someone may leave your company or stop using your product. The considerations during this step may give you insights into additional customer motivations and what they want so you can create experiences and messaging to save the relationship—and the sale!

Here you can understand why someone may exit your company's sales process—and discover ways to stop them. This will help you expand your view of your customer's motivations.

# DETERMINE EXIT POINTS

*Figure 18: Sample Exit Points*

This is my favorite step because it provides the most powerful insights about prospects and customers. We often try to find ways to convince people to purchase a solution or product. But if you consider why someone would say *no* to your solution early in your process, you may gain perspectives about the challenges your solution faces in the market. The issues around customers rejecting your solution may not lie in the solution itself, but in how your customers may view your solution, the problem you are solving, or even

# CUSTOMER REASONS TO EXIT

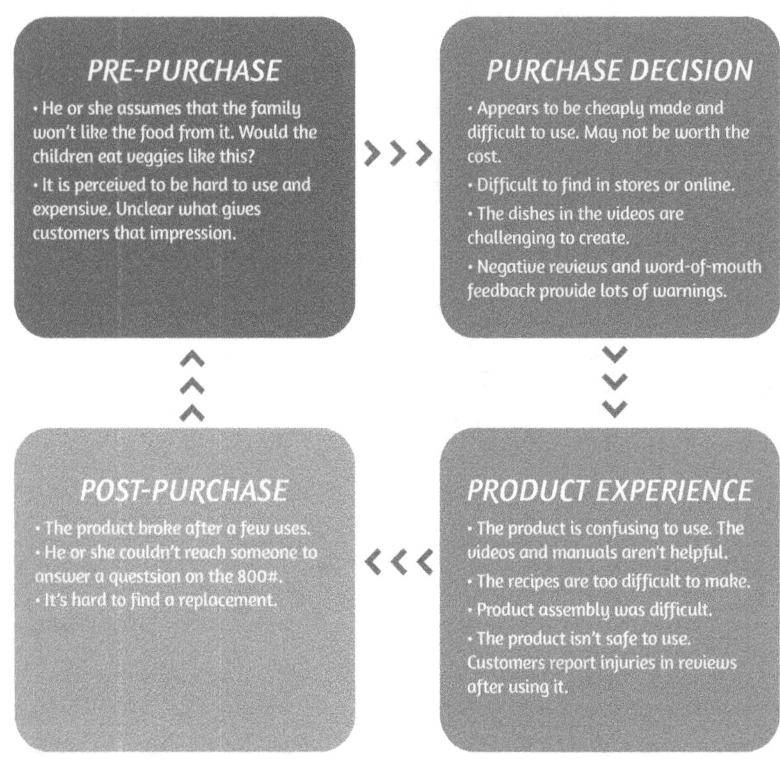


*Figure 19: Sample Insights for Exit Points*

how they see their problem. It may also lie in other factors about product perception and the customer's prioritization of the problem in their own life, or something else happening in their family's lives.

If you consider the objections that you may encounter when developing a relationship with a prospect or customer, you can develop a strategy to work around it. And in the process, you will most likely uncover the winning product strategy.

**Step 6: Determine success measurements**

Before defining what you want to do to appeal to your audience, how do you define success? This is very important to consider early in the process of creating a customer experience because it helps a company determine what it wants to achieve with this relationship. What metrics does the company value and define as successful? The outcome of this step is to decide which metrics will inform your company that your action plan is working.

## DETERMINE SUCCESS MEASUREMENTS

### SAMPLE QUESTIONS TO CONSIDER

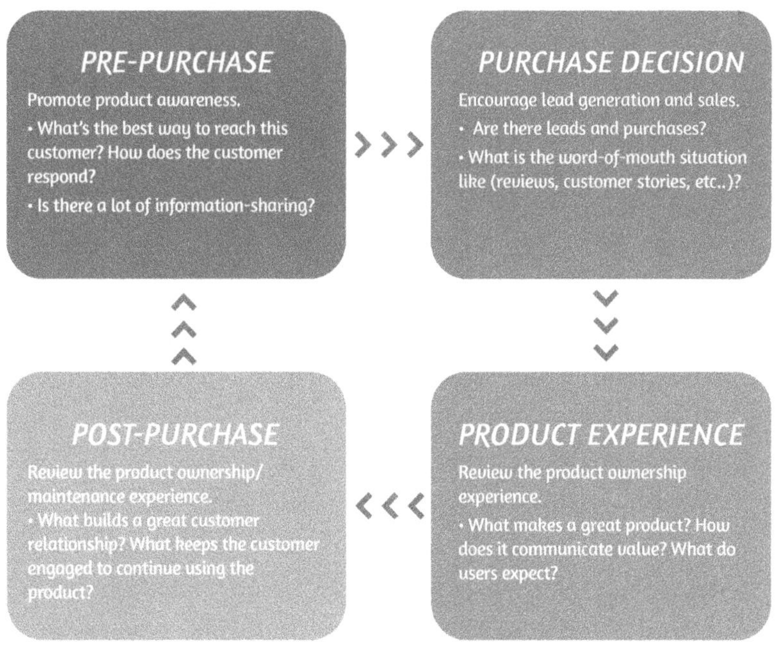


*Figure 20: Success Measurement Considerations*

# IDEAS TO MEASURE SUCCESS

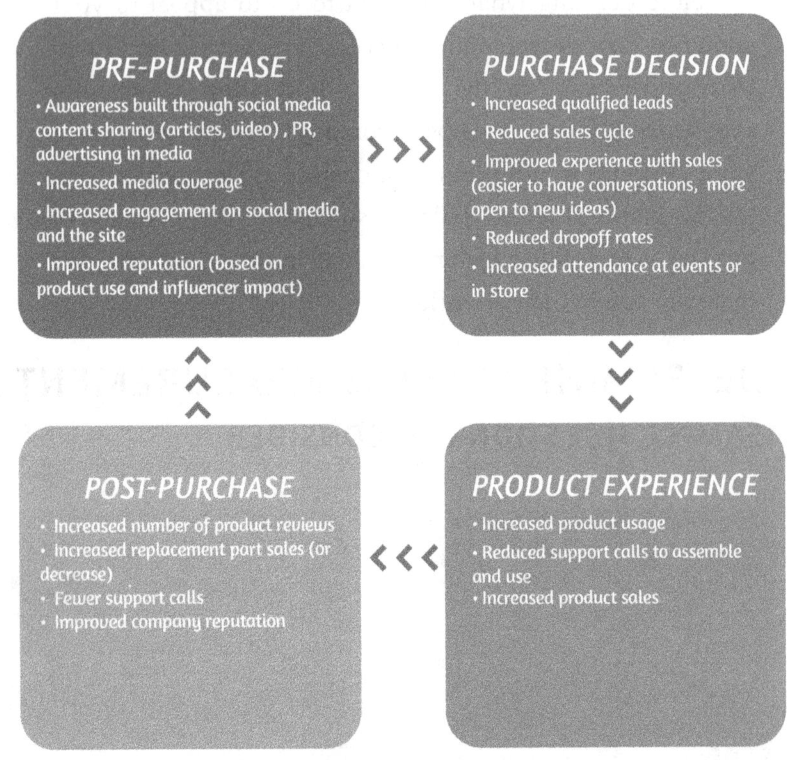


*Figure 21: Success Measurement Ideas*

Sometimes we wait until we have completed designing a program to determine which metrics determine success. However, identifying what success looks like can guide us to clearly understand which elements are required in creating customer experiences that result in better connected customer relationships. This example includes more traditional definitions of success, but you could extend this to include the popularity of hashtags (to be more easily found), supporting high engagement, or great product reviews that confirm claims, which supports accountability.

# DEFINING SUCCESS FOR THE GO-ROUND PARENT

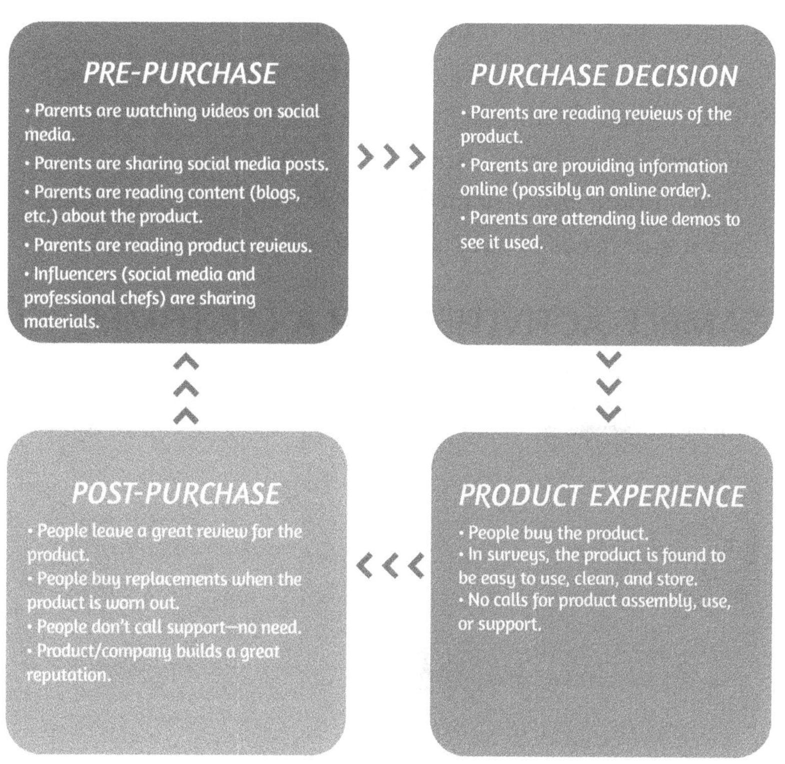


*Figure 22: Success Measurements*

**Step 7: Plan supporting activities.**

Leverage the work completed during the previous steps to identify journeys or activities to further engage with customers and build a relationship. Consider the previous steps as requirement gathering sessions for this step and use those requirements to create an action plan. What's most fun about this step is that it encourages you to brainstorm ways to communicate with prospects/customers based on what you know about them. You can be as creative as you like to capture their attention and engage them.

At this step, you can start to create ideas and list activities that support the insights you developed during this process to create a customer experience solution. The output here could include different methods to purchase the product, key features it needs to have, and what types of communications

SAMPLE ACTIVITIES FOR A CUSTOMER

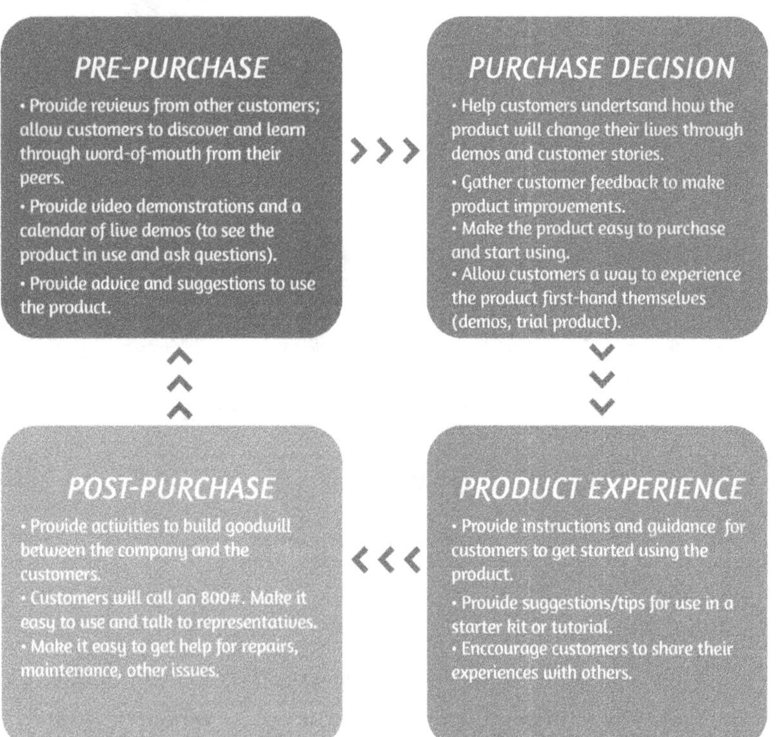


*Figure 23: Sample Customer Activities*

you need created in different media so people can understand what you are selling. You may interview existing customers, leverage product reviews, or find third parties to review and compare your product. There are many ways to solve the problems you identified in steps 1—5 and support how you will measure success as defined in step 6. This is when the plan creation process begins at a macro level so you can see how the activities in each area can influence others to build a customer relationship.

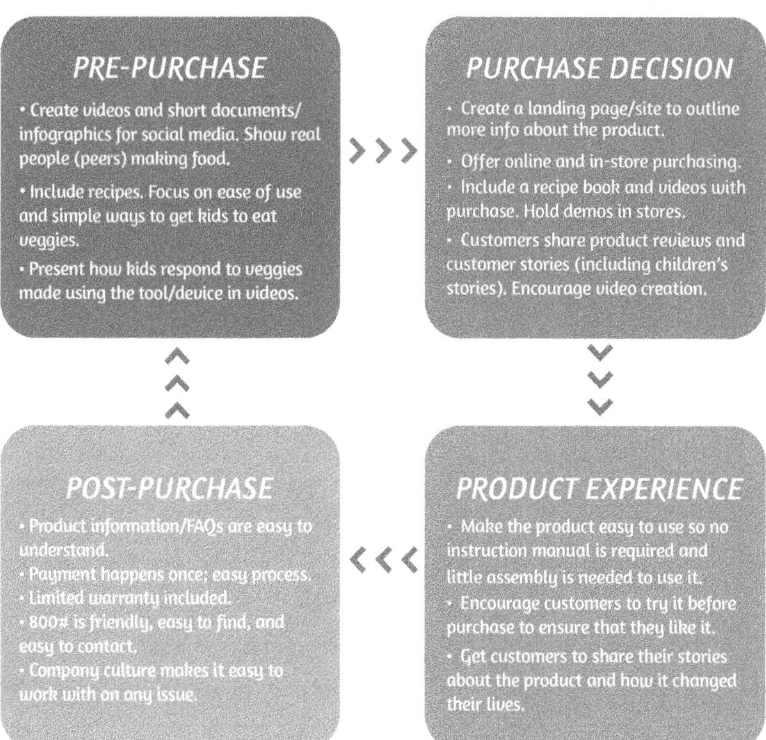

GO-ROUND CUSTOMER SAMPLE ACTIVITIES
PRE-PURCHASE
• Create videos and short documents/ infographics for social media. Show real people (peers) making food.
• Include recipes. Focus on ease of use and simple ways to get kids to eat veggies.
• Present how kids respond to veggies made using the tool/device in videos.
PURCHASE DECISION
• Create a landing page/site to outline more info about the product.
• Offer online and in-store purchasing.
• Include a recipe book and videos with purchase. Hold demos in stores.
• Customers share product reviews and customer stories (including children's stories). Encourage video creation.
PRODUCT EXPERIENCE
• Make the product easy to use so no instruction manual is required and little assembly is needed to use it.
• Encourage customers to try it before purchase to ensure that they like it.
• Get customers to share their stories about the product and how it changed their lives.
POST-PURCHASE
• Product information/FAQs are easy to understand.
• Payment happens once; easy process.
• Limited warranty included.
• 800# is friendly, easy to find, and easy to contact.
• Company culture makes it easy to work with on any issue.


*Figure 24: Sample Activities for Parents*

**Step 8: Address refills or repairs.**

There can be rounds of the lifecycle, especially if a product requires a refill part or needs repair. During this step, customers may reconsider their purchase if the product isn't meeting their needs. Here you can consider: What is someone thinking if they are replacing a part? Or refilling the product?

When it's time for someone to purchase a replacement or get a refill, that is often a time for a customer to reconsider what he or she is purchasing and why. It's another exit point.

## ADDRESS REFILLS/REPAIRS

### SOME QUESTIONS CUSTOMERS CONSIDER

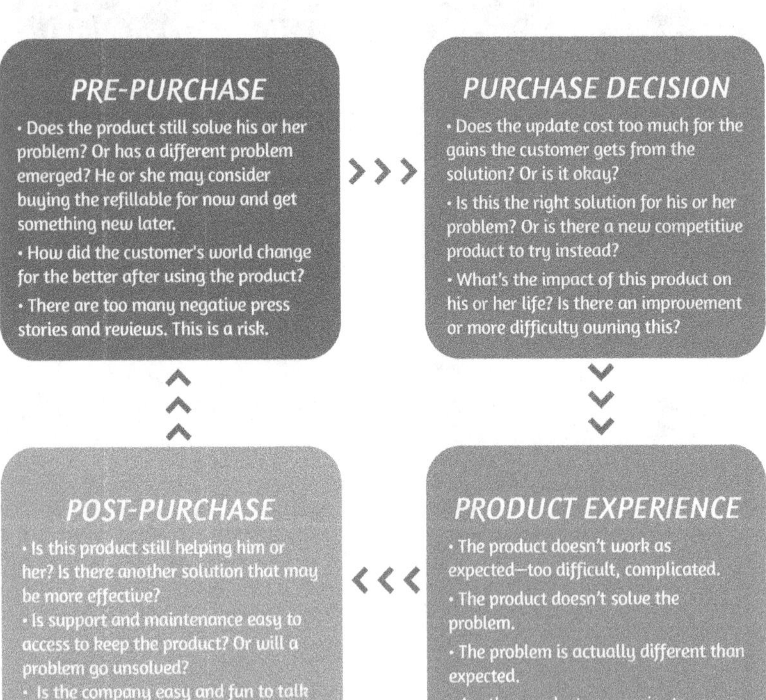


*Figure 25: Sample Questions for Refills/Repairs*

By understanding how customers may perceive your product, you could potentially remove the consideration of replacement from the process altogether. Some of this can be discovered during persona development, but the consideration from this step could address part of a larger product strategy and marketing discussion. Looking at the chart, the spiralizer's ease of use was a key factor for a customer to keep it, and if a part of it were worn out, it would need to be easy to replace. Failing factors of the spiralizer include the kids not liking the veggie shapes that come from it or getting bored of them. This could be fixed by researching additional shapes that kids may like to create a new attachment, or possibly a new recipe. New cooking ideas could keep people returning and continue to use this solution. Knowing what keeps your customers engaged will help you keep your relationship with these customers so they continue to purchase refills or replacements as needed. They value not only the solution, but a relationship with your company and your brand.

You can gather this information through customer surveys and feedback like product reviews. This is why it's so important to develop some type of feedback loop with your customers. This information will help you continue to deepen your relationship with your customers, and keep them with you for years to come.

If you use this approach, you can establish a strategy that could be applied to a journey for your customers, understanding which key activities will emotionally engage them and help them better understand your product and service. You will also have an understanding of how to motivate customers to have a better relationship with your

# CUSTOMER CONSIDERATIONS: REFILL/REPAIRS

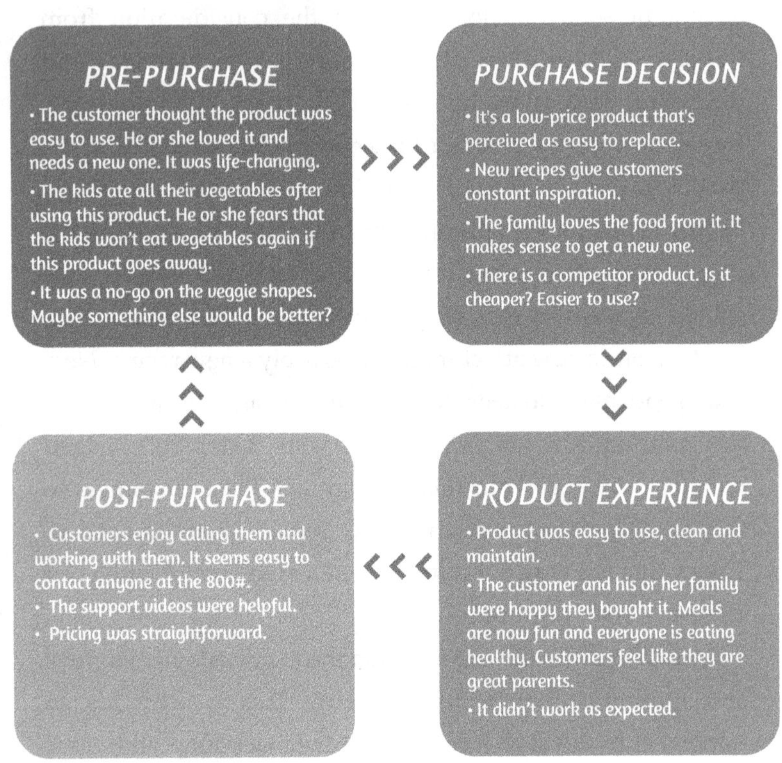


*Figure 26: Sample Insights for Refill/Repairs*

company and be able to create the tools to build a more connected relationship. We can't forget that customers are more than buyers or product users. They are people who have experiences well beyond your product and solution and the problem you are solving. Understanding this will help you better connect to them and solve their problems. This is why sometimes your company is solving problems well beyond what you may have originally intended to solve.

### *Not Everyone Will Be a Customer (and That's Okay!)*

Customers can have various types of relationships and levels of engagement with a company. Not every person will need or want to own the solution a company offers. However, people may understand the value it provides and think a company's solution is a great solution, even though it may not be right for them or their situation. Often, we think the role of marketing is to convince someone to buy the product, but what if the role of sales and marketing was to instead build a relationship with a prospect and customer for today and the future? And what if that role wasn't to encourage a purchase, but to influence others to advocate on behalf of that company?

What if you approached your customer experiences and relationship-building processes by helping customers self-select who would benefit most by using the product rather than trying to use persuasive messaging to target a market or customer segment to purchase something they may not want or need? That's what the customer relationship lifecycle empowers you to do.

Companies need to have relationships with a wide variety of people—from prospects and customers who have tried the product as a demo, who transition to become influencers, who transition to become paying customers and product owners. We are trained to think about prospects and customers as individuals lingering inside a buying journey not yet ready to purchase, but not everyone who engages with a company needs to purchase anything. There will always be people who stay at different steps of the lifecycle and may only be members of the company's community. We sometimes consider this to be negative, but it's not. We not only want these people there, we need them there.

It's the same reason why we have friends. Not all friends fulfill the same role. Some help us with family issues; some provide career insights; some are fun to hang out with; some know the "hot new place" to go. Our customers and prospects are the same. Not all of them will provide us with revenue, but their relationship may fulfill other needs such as new customer introductions, validation, opinions, or information-sharing with their network. We need to spread our reach wide to meet these people who can help us build a community long-term.

## Customer Relationships Begin in Various Ways

For years, Proctor & Gamble was perceived as the best marketer and brand-builder in the business because it leveraged customer research for new product innovations. And what is customer research but a way to have a conversation with customers and start a relationship with them? When a company asks customers for their opinions about their products, not only is the company getting product feedback and accessing customer data, but it is also including customers in its product development process. They are part of the larger company community. It's flattering for a prospect to be asked by a company about his or her opinion. It's a way to connect and build a relationship with a new customer group.

However, there are other ways to build relationships with customers. Apple and Amazon used engagement approaches that not only built a relationship with their products, but with technology innovations. These relationships helped skyrocket them into household names.

When Apple created its first products, computers were new and perceived to be a work tool. It wasn't clear for the average consumer what all of their uses could be. One of Apple's initiatives that resulted in helping computing adoption, besides making computing simple and straightforward, was to get children to understand what the technology was, make it part of their lives, and have them experience its impact firsthand. This was how Steve Jobs first experienced computing and fell in love with it at the NASA Ames Research Center and Hewlett-Packard. With direct computing experience, children would understand the role a computer could have in their lives and be able to communicate its benefits to their parents and community.

The start of Apple's mission to get computers into schools was the results of a contract:

> *In 1978, just two years after it was founded, Apple won a contract with the Minnesota Education Computing Consortium to supply 500 computers. . .MECC had developed a sizable catalog of educational software (including the iconic Oregon Trail) which it made freely available to Minnesota schools. Soon the MECC floppy disks and Apple II's became popular. . .As Steve Jobs said in a 1995 oral history interview with The Computerworld Smithsonian Awards Program, "One of the things that built Apple II's was schools buying Apple II's."*[145]

In 1982, Jobs lobbied Congress to pass a bill to get computers into all schools. The national effort proved unsuccessful, but it was successful in California.

In September 1982, California Governor Jerry Brown signed a similar version of the Computer Equipment Contribution Act, AB 3194. This law allowed a 25 percent tax credit against the state corporate income tax for computer equipment donated to schools. According to the California State Assembly Office of Research, "proponents of this bill feel that computer literacy for children [was] becoming a necessity in today's world. They state that this bill will aid placing needed 'hardware' in schools unable to afford computers in any other way."[146]

In turn, under its Kids Can't Wait program, Apple donated a computer to each of the roughly 9,000 eligible elementary and secondary schools in California.[147]

It cost about $1 million for Apple, but this effort got Apple computers into every school in California, and eventually the US, allowing them to dominate the education market. Additionally, this effort had a great side effect: exposing children of all ages to computing, and in this case an Apple computer. That was an amazingly powerful goal.

Apple computers were in my school system where I grew up. Apple trained some of the teachers in Logo (a form of Basic), which is the computing language I learned as a child. I felt comfortable programming an Apple computer in Logo when I was 10. Did that have an impact on my parents' decision to choose which computer brand to buy? It certainly did. My excitement about Apple computers influenced my parents to finally buy one for our home. We originally had a Tandy Computer that I barely touched. I didn't understand how to program it as well as an Apple, and Tandy didn't support a lot of programs I could use for school besides games, so we switched brands. Over time, my parents also found the Apple computer easy to use and they started using it for their projects too. Today, I have an Apple computer for my business because I can manage the IT aspects of it without consulting with an IT professional. But I think I have such a tight relationship with the brand because Apple started building a relationship with me as early as 10 years old. It manufactured the first computer that I could really use.

Some friends my age share similar sentiments. They are Apple fans not just because they make cool products, but because it was the computer that they were able to use in their schools. In some cases, it was the first computer they touched. Apple may make easy-to-use products, but as we know from Jef Raskin, products are easier to use when you are already familiar with them.

But the relationship with Apple went deeper for many of us, beyond the brand to computing itself. Steve Jobs spoke fondly of his own first memory of computing: "When I was ten or eleven I saw my first computer. It was down at NASA Ames (Research Center). I didn't see the computer, I saw a terminal and it was theoretically a computer on the other end of the wire. I fell in love with it."[148]

I suspect that Steve's early relationship with computing drove his passion for it, driving him to create his future job and company. And subsequently, he wanted other children to experience this passion as well. I know I did. I may not have been a programmer, but I was inspired by Apple's usability. This fueled a passion in me to choose a job in the computing field to help people have simpler digital experiences with companies and computers, resulting in improved relationships. I suspect this also influenced many of my peers and friends to make similar choices. Through the school program, Apple not only increased its own sales, but it built a love of computing within an entire generation.

Amazon's product feedback and rating system was a brilliant way to introduce users to a digital commerce system as well as get feedback about how they were doing. In the early days of Amazon, it was difficult to trust buying anything online. In the late 1990s, online anything meant anonymity and limited security. I remember having a conversation with my parents about online security and credit card use. They felt it was not safe to put their credit card number online because it could be hacked. It was, and still is, a valid concern. However, I reminded them that giving a credit card number online was just as risky as giving someone your credit card number over the phone. (These days, I would say that giving someone your credit card number over the phone is riskier for identity fraud and abuses.)

In the early days of online shopping, there were concerns of being swindled in a scam: buying an item, providing your credit card information, and never receiving the item in the mail. This was true not just for Amazon, but eBay and other online retailers. There was limited trust and few agencies that could verify that trust. The Better Business Bureau had an online validation system, as well as TRUSTe and some other minor players. These seals helped provide some digital purchase standards to the new wild world of online shopping.

But the automation of online shopping needed to go beyond simply putting a catalog online. Bookstores were popular and prevalent at the time. Going online to browse book titles provided a way for buyers to complete early-stage book-buying decisions. We may consider a book to be a simple $10—15 purchase, but many decisions are involved in purchasing a book:

- Noticing an attractive cover and compelling title.
- Reading the book jacket to understand what you are buying.
- Flipping through pages to see what the reading experience will be (e.g., is it dense text or spaced out; is it straightforward or complex?).
- Taking a sneak peek, or quick read, of a chapter (or two).
- Knowing that you had options to return the book if you didn't like it.
- Browsing recommended book lists like *The New York Times* or bookstore manager lists.

If you chose to purchase a book online, you had to rely on the site's descriptions and photos onscreen as honestly portraying what the book will be. And if you purchased a dud, rather than drive back to the store, you'd have to return it through the mail, which was a hassle. These weren't barriers to stop a $10—15 purchase, but they would have made purchasing books online undesirable due to the inconvenience of mistakes.

Amazon included a product review and rating system. This served multiple purposes. Not only could it help people understand what they would be buying, but it had a curious, unplanned side effect in that it indirectly helped people overcome their fears of online shopping. By encouraging existing customers to write a review of a book they had purchased and read, Amazon simultaneously built confidence in new prospects and potential customers to make a purchase. You can't write a review of a book you didn't receive. In some ways, this feature built trust not just to purchase the book, but it helped people trust that if you purchased online, you'd definitely receive the item. What better way to build trust than to show proof to reluctant buyers that the early adopters successfully bought a book, received it, and found the process to be safe and effective?

But the review and rating system wasn't only building trust about that book. It was building trust with Amazon as a seller. And it built trust in online shopping. If buying from Amazon is safe, then purchasing from sites that offer similar functionality must be safe too.

(Note that eBay used similar strategies to build consumer confidence in their sellers and achieved similar results, building tremendous customer relationships.)

Beyond the trust factor, reviews gave Amazon information about its customers and products. Everyone won: Customers were getting educated about online purchasing and the books they wanted to buy, and Amazon was learning about its customers' preferences and how to get them to purchase more. And this knowledge helped Amazon provide the next huge feature that changed online shopping forever: providing recommendations based on what other people like you purchased.

## The Ultimate Ingredient for a Great Customer Experience: Trust

You can create experiences defined by a vision, which leverages the brand, the action plan, and the company community that develops the relationship between the employees and the customers, resulting in revenue. However, without an environment in which trust can grow, you most likely won't have the **ability** to build a relationship with your customers.

I wrote a blog series that contains a list of nine characteristics of great experiences, one of which is: The customer feels he can trust the store/site.[149] I identified four ways that companies can demonstrate trust with customers: authenticity, transparency, responsibility, and loyalty. To further simplify what builds trust with customers, there are two factors required to foster relationships in your culture and business:

- Accountability through agreements
- Mutual respect (which will lead to love, which is required to develop compassion and create effective solutions)

## Accountability in Agreements

As previously discussed, a company should be accountable to its customers to create a great product, and customers should be accountable to the company to provide input and feedback. In companies, we often forget that we work for our customers. Customers are the people to whom CEOs are really accountable—not the shareholders. The shareholders would be more upset if the customers are unhappy and leave than if they missed receiving stock dividends. Shareholders know that they won't get any dividends if you have no customers. Customers pay our paycheck, pay the rent, keep the lights on, and pay the dividends. Their happiness is vital to any company's success. Without great customer relationships, many companies would need to close.

Accountability plays a key role in any customer experience. Successful transactions require agreements. The customer agrees to pay a company or complete some activity, and the company agrees to deliver products or services. That's an **explicit agreement**, which includes all of the traditional legalities such as terms and conditions, purchase agreements, warranties, guarantees, service-level agreements, and related legal documents. Agreements cover the legal side of the customer experience for service delivery.

There are also the **explicit agreements** a company makes through sales and marketing messaging when it communicates the problem it solves and the solution it offers. Marketing and sales messages outline a type of contract, setting customer expectations and stating the customer offer. It is up to the customer to inform the company and other prospects and customers whether the company delivered on those assertions and agreements. This usually happens through reviews and word-of-mouth referrals.

There are also **implicit agreements** based on a customer's experience of competitors in the same and different industries. Competitors help define our industries and markets, and without them, we may not have a customer audience to target. They also help shape the expectations customers have for solutions and services through baselines, parity, and best practices. That helps define what's considered to be a "good" or "bad" customer experience.

**For clarity, what are baselines, best practices, and parity?**

- **Baselines are the minimum customer expectations for a product.** For example, customers expect most businesses to have a website that minimally describes their business and provides contact information. Customers may expect a company to have a legitimate phone number and email address. Customers of a restaurant, for example, may expect that the restaurant is properly licensed and inspected. Generally, a great business baseline for customer experiences is expecting a company to be honest about what it sells, its product quality, how it distributes products, and to provide a straightforward way to contact them with questions.
- **Best practices are business approaches that have produced superior results.** For example, salons that offer a way to schedule appointments online may save money by not needing to hire a receptionist and save

customers time by enabling them to schedule their own appointments. Many, but not all, salons offer this feature. As another example, most users expect to go to a large corporate site and search for content that has the topics they are interested in reading about. Again, many, but not all, sites offer this. Amazon introduced as a best practice the ability to return items for free. It's easy to get a label and send the product back. Now Amazon offers customers the ability to drop off an item at UPS by giving your name, and UPS is able to generate the label. Many, but not all, companies now offer this digitally or provide a return shipping label in the package so the customer can drop off the item and ticket to the UPS store and leave, getting the credit once the item is in transit to be returned.

- **Parity is what everyone offers, whether they are a new or existing competitor.** For example, Target, Kohl's, and Walmart all sell goods online. You can expect a type of online return policy from them. You also know that they have an in-store experience. That's parity: Everyone offers the same general features in an industry space.

| BASELINE | PARITY | BEST PRACTICES |
|---|---|---|
| Minimum customer expectations for a product | What a company needs to offer to enter an industry or market | A method or technique that has consistently shown superior results (benchmarks) |
| What a product must have to be competitive | Similar features/functions as competitors | Methods / tools / approaches that many have found successful |

For a more detailed example, let's examine the best practice of free shipping. Amazon introduced us to that ecommerce idea through its well-received Amazon Prime fee-based program. We now associate a good shopping experience with free two-day shipping and often expect that from other online stores, whether we are a "member" of that store or not. This is now a best practice. Now that more stores are adopting it, it's becoming a baseline expectation. Free two-day shipping will reach parity when all companies offer this experience and it's perceived to be a status quo customer expectation and requirement to exist as a store. Many companies are now striving to achieve this goal, so it's not at parity yet.

Same-day delivery is the next best practice step after free two-day shipping reaches parity. Same-day or two-hour delivery is already emerging as a best practice. Companies like Postmates have started supporting stores with this feature on ecommerce sites to provide almost immediate delivery time. This may accelerate adoption, which would make same-day delivery a baseline for a site to offer in the future.

Parity, baselines, and best practices can help your company determine where their innovation lies in the mind of the customers based on their experiences and expectations. This is why it's important to understand what your competition is doing. What may be an innovation or best practice for your business could be considered to be parity to your customers. Your competitors are defining your industry and product categories, providing opportunities for innovation based on these customer expectations. Exceed your customer expectations through improved experiences and you'll win every time.

## Mutual Respect

We like to believe that our employees love our customers, but often they don't. Employees may be polite to customers on support calls and during the sales process, but that doesn't mean that they like them or respect them. We can all sense when someone feels pity, contempt, or disdain for us; we can hear it in someone's voice. So can your customers. Your policies, your product and features, and your communication methods carry this as attitude as well, through tone and actions. Customers can perceive such subtleties in a customer experience, which is why emotional engagement with them is so important.

### *The Solution: Empathy . . . or Is It?*

*Empathy* is one of the most common buzzwords we hear today. Thought leaders and marketers mention it constantly as the solution for employees to understand customers.

But what is it exactly? That's where the confusion lies.

Empathy is defined as "the act of coming to experience the world as you think someone else does."[150] This definition is the problem with empathy. We often forget that no two people have the same shared experience, and no one really knows what someone else is feeling, which is why connection with other people is hard.

To complicate matters further, there isn't just one type of empathy. There are three, and more could be discovered in the future:[151,152]

- **Emotional empathy:** literally feeling another's emotions. If you believe in empaths, this is their experience.

- **Compassionate empathy:** recognizing another's emotional state, feel in tune with it, and, if it is a negative/distressful emotion, feeling and showing appropriate concern and take action if possible
- **Cognitive empathy:** seeing things from another's point of view by putting yourself in someone else's shoes (This is what many of us may consider to be empathy, but it's slightly different. There is a removed quality about this form of empathy because it isn't based in experiencing emotions yourself; only logically understanding them.)

To illustrate the differences, let's say you are watching a romantic love story and the characters have to break up.

| YOU ARE WATCHING WITH: | YOUR RESPONSE: |
|---|---|
| **Cognitive empathy** | May feel bad, but you understand that it is a movie and will turn out just fine. You may even wonder if the characters are meant for each other anyway. |
| **Compassionate empathy** | Feel concerned about the split and want to console the characters with a hug. |
| **Emotional empathy** | Cry with the characters and literally feel their pain. |

The more you learn the formal definitions surrounding empathy, you can see why psychologists and researchers don't promote or support empathy as "the cure" for understanding others. It seems that empathy can make a situation more complicated.

*Harvard Business Review* published the findings of a controversial study by Imperial College's Johannes Hattula and his co-researchers Walter Herzog, Darren Dahl, and Sven Reinecke that disputed using empathy in marketing. They asked marketing managers to describe a typical customer and imagine that person's thoughts and reactions when creating plans and programs. The result?

> *The more empathetic managers were, the more they used their personal preferences to predict what customers would want. Another key finding that should get people's attention is that the more empathetic the managers were, the more they ignored the market research on customers that we provided them.*[153,154]

Arguably, the research didn't reflect empathy in the sense we may want it to, but it did reflect empathy according to the formal definitions: the act of coming to experience the world as you believe someone else does. And that's how these marketing managers saw the world: not based on research, not on any level of connection of customers, but their own insights based on their own experiences.

Psychology researcher Paul Bloom wrote a book called *Against Empathy* in which he mentions a few ways to look at empathy: for moral purposes, for connection, or to understand someone else. But using the raw definition of the word, if you have empathy for someone who is feeling bad, that means that you must feel bad too. Is that useful to help someone solve their problems? To Bloom, this why compassion is better.

Bloom shared an example of how you need to be caring yet emotionally neutral to comfort a scared child. But what he doesn't get into is the motivation for why you are comforting the child in the first place. One could argue that you are comforting the child because at some point, you were that child. You may have been afraid of the dark, the thunder, or what's under the bed or in the closet. This helps you relate to that child's fear so you can help the child. You don't need to directly feel that child's emotions at that time, but you do need to understand him or her through your own personal experience to provide appropriate assistance.

In this case, **empathy** helps us understand what others are feeling and thinking and gain insight into their motivations for their actions, and **compassion** gives us the distance to help them solve their problem.

Some psychologists and neuroscientists believe that compassion and empathy are intertwined. Lynn E. O'Connor and Jack W. Berry wrote, "We can't feel compassion without first feeling emotional empathy. Indeed compassion is the extension of emotional empathy by means of cognitive processes."[155]

No discussion about empathy, compassion, or vulnerability is complete without referencing Brené Brown. In her book *Dare to Lead,* Brown shares the insights she gained during her seven-year study about bravery and courageousness in leadership. She learned that most courageous leaders demonstrated vulnerability rooted in self-awareness and self-love. How we lead reflects who we are. And the more we are comfortable with ourselves and know who we are, we have a more authentic leadership style. Brown's book shares what it means to lead as a person with feelings and emotions through countless valuable stories.

But what struck me while listening to the audiobook version of *Dare to Lead* was her definition of empathy: "Empathy is not connecting to an experience, it's connecting to the emotions that underpin and experience."[156]

I got very excited hearing her definition during a drive from Fort Worth to Dallas and replayed it over 10 times to be sure I heard her correctly. She defines empathy as being connected to emotions, not simply physical events. I wish I heard her definitions before I created one for a conference in the fall of 2018, which was: an attempt at understanding someone else's emotional situation by relating through a similar physical and emotional event that occurred in their own life. Of course, her definition's wording and insight are much more direct and streamlined than mine.

Emotions are the key to empathy. A shared event between two people helps provide context for a connection, but it's not always necessary. In the example Brown shares in her book, her colleague felt empathy for Brown's disappointment to miss seeing her daughter's sports game. The connection was over the emotions; the event—disappointment over missing her daughter's game—provided context for the communications and understanding. Her colleague didn't connect with Brown over missing her child's game. Her colleague understood what it meant to feel disappointment over a missed family commitment that she felt was important. It was that understanding that allowed her to relate to what Brown may have been feeling.

An example that I've used to illustrate empathy surrounds the loss of a pet. Let's say your best friend's dog passed away.

Your friend was very close to her dog. Let's also say your pet hamster passed away, but you weren't particularly close to your hamster (it was one of 20 anyway). You can't say with any validity to your friend that you understand what she is going through. Sure, you both lost a pet, but you both didn't lose the same type of relationship with a pet. But let's say a couple of years earlier, you lost a cat and you were very close to that cat. You *could* say to your friend that you understand what she is going through. You both lost a pet, you both lost a close relationship with your pet, and there may be some differences between what you are both feeling because the animal is different.

To extend the pet example, let's say a beloved pet ran away and didn't return. The connecting event in both cases isn't death, but the general loss of the pet's presence. In both cases, someone would feel the sadness that comes with the lost pet no longer being in someone's life. In all cases, people would feel that hole—missing a loved being.

When you are trying to connect with someone through empathy, you can't simply recall the same exact situation in your life to understand how that person feels—and that's part of the confusion. You review similar life events and find one that seems to have the same *emotional severity* for comparison.

Let's return to the earlier fearful child example. You can relate to the fearful child not only because you were a child, but because you understand what it means to be a vulnerable child, without protection or help, fearful of what may happen next in the dark. The motivation for feeling fear may have been different based on personal experiences of lightning or the dark, but you understand the emotions, have experienced them yourself, and can relate to how a child *could* feel.

To bring this back to your customers, if your employees cannot connect to your customers emotionally and understand the complete impact of their challenges, your company will struggle to build a relationship with them. Your customers need to feel respect, empathy, and compassion to stay in a relationship with your company, just like your employees do within their teams to be successful at their jobs. Customers will feel the disconnect between your words and actions if there is an inconsistency in the sentiment expressed. They are people who need help to solve a problem. If your employees forget that and don't develop relationships with your company's customers, there can be severe consequences.

**What if Your Employees Aren't or Your Company Isn't Capable of Creating a Relationship with Customers?**

- **Customers and prospects leave and never come back.** This is obvious. If customers and prospects leave and never come back, that communicates to the company and employees that their experience wasn't pleasant and they don't like you. It takes a lot of nonsensical activity for a customer to leave and never want to come back. The action implies 110-percent dissatisfaction with the experience and a perception by the customer that they don't see any room for redemption in the future. The relationship is more or less destroyed.

- **You have few influencers and champions.** This is also obvious. If your company doesn't have many influencers and champions, either it is because:
    - Prospects and customers don't like your product or the customer experience of your company and see areas for improvement,
    - Your product doesn't solve customer problems as they understand them (the solution isn't communicated well), or
    - People see no redeeming qualities about your company or product or customer experience.
- **You have negative product and company reviews.** For every complaint you hear or read online in negative reviews, there are probably dozens of other complaints that go unsaid directly to your company. Instead, people may share these stories with others through word-of-mouth. You may have negative employee reviews, too, being shared in the rumor mill.
- **You hear negative comments about customers from your employees.** This is most telling and troubling. If your employees say negative things about your customers, then they don't like them. It's hard to have great customer relationships when your employees don't like your customers as people.
- **Your product is missing the mark (features, quality, etc.).** Frequent quality challenges are a sign that leadership doesn't care about the product and customers, so over time, the teams give up caring as well. The underlying

reason for not caring about a product is that the company and executives don't care about your customers.

- **Prospect and customer expectations are miscommunicated or not met.** If you aren't listening to your customers, then you won't hear their needs. Listening is a skill you need to learn, not only to better understand your customers, but to feel more empathetic to them. Only then will you be able to create compassionate solutions to their problems. You need to be curious, be present, have no expectations, and acknowledge that relationships are built on conversations. You also need to observe actions as well as listen to words. And acknowledge that great listening happens when you are feeling empathy and compassion.

Most of all, your employees need to respect your customers. That's the first step when bridging the gap between the two. Otherwise, customers know when employees are objectifying them, generalizing and trivializing their problems, or feeling contempt or sympathy. It's this objectification that reduces their connection.

***Case Study: A Common Startup Software Strategy: "Custom-Built" Products***

Most SaaS companies don't build a product and then find customers. Most get their start as a custom-built software product that expands to become a SaaS product. A common strategy: A company builds a product for a specific customer to solve their problem and then asks other companies if they have a similar issue and could use this solution. The company sets up agreements so that it "owns" the software intellectual property and licenses it back to the customer. The customer(s) then request features to add to the system as needed. The company tries to get more customers on the platform so it can grow. As customers are added, some features become self-funded from licensing fees; others are paid by customers. (Some companies will get a group of customers together to finance the features that they want.)

Once a company gets enough customers, it will stop this split-funding practice and add features as needed and requested by customers, as any software product, and have a standard license agreement.

Companies established this way have a distinct advantage as they grow because from day one, they learned how to include customers into the development and acceptance process. The customers emerged as key team members, often approving functionality being launched as if it were built to order. Most of these SaaS companies become successful because they understand how to prioritize competing customer needs and incorporate them into a shippable product that appeals to more than one customer.

Some criticize this approach because it skates between the world of custom-built software and consulting versus being a software company that licenses product. But the key benefit is that such companies are able to finance product development while keeping customers involved and included in the process. If a company is funded by more traditional angel funding or venture capital, it may not necessarily include the customer in the process because the funding is coming from an investor. Because they are paying for it, in some ways, they become something like a pseudo-customer. This challenges a company's ecosystem because it's not clear who the end customer really is. It should be the paying customer, not the investor. That's why it is almost simpler and more straightforward to fund a SaaS software company through this hybrid consulting model to maintain product integrity and focus on solving the customer's problems and addressing their needs.

## Conclusion

When we were automating experiences on the Internet, personas emerged as vital tools when creating user experiences. It helped us expand our perspective of customers beyond demographic data. We were able to understand who they were as people—what mattered to them, their priorities, their needs, their motivations, their emotions. Customers became the center of a product experience because we realized that they were the key stakeholder paying our bills, and we needed them to love the product on launch day. Usability testing emerged as a way to support our work in determining what will bring product success and adoption. And as technologies improved, we were able to add digital tracking methods and A/B testing to our toolkits to understand them. The more data gathered to understand how customers interacted with a system, the better.

Although there are many methods available to us to validate our customer's experiences with our product, usability testing has always been the most effective method of ensuring that a digital experience will be successful at launch.

It's a more practical, experiential test method to provide actionable feedback and insights. I find it ironic that more companies don't do it. From my experience with Gearmark clients, most companies perceived usability testing as expensive. And at first, it was because it leveraged the focus group approach: rent a facility with one-way glass so a group can observe a recorded discussion between a moderator and participant in a huge room each hour. Through curiosity, creativity, and technology innovation, this approach became one way to conduct usability testing and reviews; digital methods and more casual approaches emerged over the years. Agile methodologies encouraged including customers in the development process using more casual methods and approaches. Now there are digital methods that cost a few hundred dollars to gather actionable insights and feedback in a day.

There has been a huge business shift to include customers and create communities through forums, user groups, social media, and other approaches. Today customers are included in processes more often, but there is still work to be done. We can't forget that without customers, there is no business. And by developing trust with customers and getting them to not only like your company's product, but to engage with your company and industry through activities and tactics like children's educational programs, product review tools, and customer research, you can shift perceptions and encourage customer engagement.

When you create an experience for each of your specific customers, you aren't just engaging with them. You are developing a relationship with them. You are doing more than solving their problems. You are becoming a resource for them to become better people. The customer relationship lifecycle helps you see how you can do this best before you develop a customer journey for your organization. Understanding how customers are feeling, their motivations, their fears, and how they truly view themselves will help you understand what they need to be their idealized self. And you can only do this and develop such a customer relationship through empathy, love, and compassion.

Employees need to love your customers and feel compassion for them. Without this vital, magic ingredient in your business, your customers may not engage as much as they could with your company or product. Customers are a joyful part of your company's ecosystem. They close the feedback loop for you, providing input and insights into how you can solve their problem better. With Gearmark clients, every time we included client customers in the process to help them realize a better version of themselves and help them achieve personal goals, the solution improved and increased engagement more than one hundred percent. It's so easy to do, yet this often becomes often a missed opportunity that has the potential to have your product and company impact not just your industry, but the world. Apple and Amazon understood this and redefined not just computing, but public perception of computing. How can your company change the world? Ask your customers.

CHAPTER 7

# Relationships Bring Revenue

Salespeople understand the power of relationships. They know that you may have the best product on the planet, but you can't get the customer to sign a contract if you don't have a relationship with them.

A great salesperson can help your customer see the value in your solution and determine where they fit in the customer relationship lifecycle. That's their talent. And they are hired not just for this ability to build a relationship and understand the perspective of a prospect or customer, but for their relationships in general. Often salespeople are hired for their contacts, which include people with whom the salesperson worked previously and whose trust they gained. Those relationships are golden.

Sadly, we often put pressure on marketing departments to automate these types of conversations and relationships that sales builds to increase sales. We'll claim that we need to sell to a mass of consumers and have maximum reach and that we can't call everyone. So we post on social media and create content marketing strategies and digital chatbots to support them. But it is difficult to translate these conversations that communicate value into if/then statements. A great marketer can create a message that may or may not convince prospects to buy a product. But a forward-thinking marketer who loves psychology knows how to motivate a customer to take that next step. And with marketing automating the sales relationship process, that is now their job.

Salespeople innately understand how to transform a relationship into revenue. The success of a sales team is measured by their lead counts and revenue generation. However, this type of measurement can cause customer experience issues like selling customers product they may not need or solving a customer problem to reach a personal bonus quota. For long-term benefit, it may be more powerful and effective for a company to measure the *quality* of salespeople's relationships and engagement with customers rather than quantity. Someone who doesn't buy today may buy tomorrow.

How could you measure the success of a customer relationship on its own, without directly connecting it to revenue? Consider the customer touchpoints beyond a purchase journey and the activities that develop a customer relationship from social media to content access to support calls.

Extensive data can come from such experiences to help you learn more about your customer. Some data rests in analytics based on customer actions within your company's systems;

some data insights can be gained through content analysis and other qualitative methods applied to live conversations. Today you can get a lot of information from online user activity and social media listening. I find this information to be most insightful. People's words expose their motivations and self-image, while their behaviors and actions will always tell the truth about their prioritization system, their values, and what they really want.

## An Overview of Metrics by Programs and Tactics

When we decide to create a marketing program to communicate with customers and build a relationship, it can be difficult to determine which activities to include and how to measure success. It's even more difficult to measure a successful customer relationship beyond revenue generated. Often when I design a program with teams, we have a Goldilocks-type of discussion based on where the customer is in the customer journey: What's the right balance of activities to offer at a specific relationship stage and engagement level?

You could choose from a sizeable list of activities to include anywhere in your customer journey and customer relationship lifecycle. Among the most common are:

- Website,
- Email marketing campaign,
- SEO,
- Social media,
- Digital ads,

- Traditional ads (billboard, magazine, television, radio),
- PR activities,
- Online demos,
- Webinar,
- Chatbot/online chat,
- Events,
- Reviews,
- Phone,
- Email,
- Meeting,
- In-store experience, and
- Influencer programs.
- (I'm sure there are more activities not listed, too.)

If you look at these activities in context based on the mediums they use and how those mediums can create deeper relationships, you can see that they represent four activity categories that share similar goals, uses, and approaches to metrics: automated, digital, individualized experiences; automated, digital conversations; in-person conversations; and live, in-person experiences.

**Automated, digital, individualized experiences:** self-guided experiences in which the user is able to interact with a system or item on their own time. These are generally one-sided: the company designs and distributes an experience and/or communication, mainly in a print or web medium, and the customer responds to the company through their selections.

**Examples of activities:** Website, email marketing campaign, digital ads. This can also include traditional advertising. We could consider an ad as a self-guided, snapshot experience of a company or product.

**Why use it:** Allow prospects and customers to discover information at their own pace.

**Benefit:** The customer can discover who the company is and what it does, as well as understand how it could solve their problem, in their own time.

**Challenge:** The experience is pre-planned, constructed, and limited. If the user has a concern, question, or need outside of the defined experience, there is no way to address it unless it is already constructed within the experience.

**Success defined as:** High response rates (clicks, visits, etc.) (for print, it is high potential views).

**Types of metrics:** How a user engages with the medium (clicks on the site, time on site, date of visit, number of visits, potential views, etc.); content analysis to determine the type of content (subject matter and presentation) that gets the most interactions; perspectives of how the visitor feels about the constructed experience through surveys.

**Content analysis:** Keywords that the user selects in links; page topics that are most frequently read.

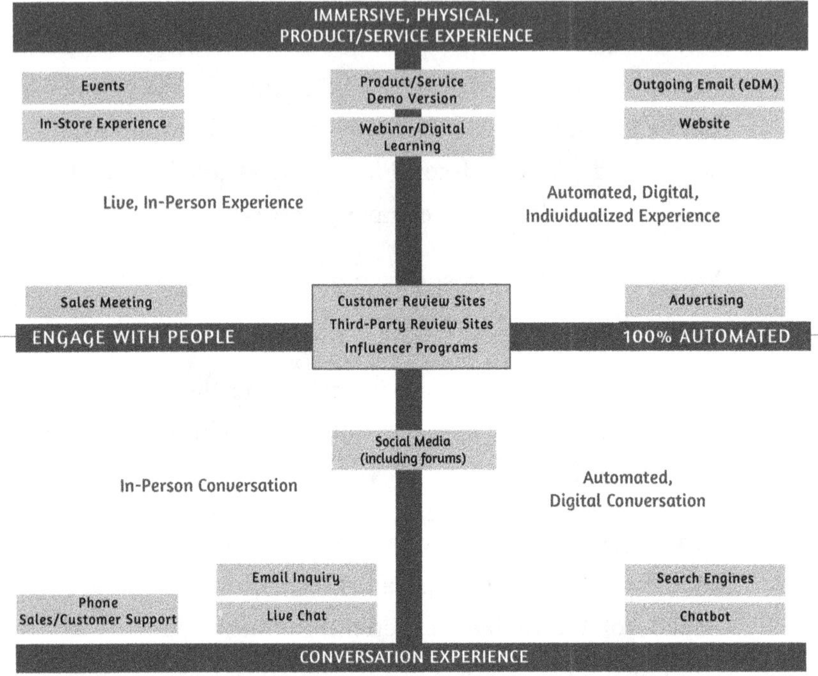


*Figure 27: The Four Activity Categories*

**Qualitative questions:** How do they perceive your company's brand and values? How do they understand what you do?

**What you can learn from this:** Which types of content do people access regularly? What topics do they want to learn more about? How do people perceive your product?

**Automated, digital conversations:** These are self-guided conversations that the user has with a system. The user initiates the conversation by entering keywords or a statement and the system responds with results. The user chooses the conversation topics in which to participate. Alternatively, someone could select keyword buttons that answer questions initiated by the system. Based on algorithms and programming, the system displays what it determines as the best results for the inquiry. Solutions are not provided through people collaborating to fully understand a problem that needs to be solved; solutions are provided using if / then thinking. There is no identifiable emotion expressed in this communication type. If emotion is expressed and communicated by a human, there is a pre-constructed, pre-defined response provided by the system.

**Examples of activities:** Search engine (user enters specific keywords), chatbots

**Why use it:** Encourage information discovery by an audience not yet ready to fully engage with your company; it has a technology "cool factor."

**Benefit:** The customer can find the answers by themselves to learn about a specific topic. The customer can also have conversations with an organization in a more removed and casual way than a phone call, live chat, or email. It's a little less intimate. The customer or prospect initiates the conversations or responds to an online system.

**Challenge:** Selectable options only include what you make available to your user. The communication sequence is pre-planned, and it is difficult to address spontaneous issues or concerns outside of that defined path.

**Success is defined by:** The interaction and engagement level on the medium (e.g., clicks, number of searches or interactions).

**Type of metrics:** Interactions, number of responses, next steps/clicks, if a chat conversation converts to a conversation medium with greater connection like a phone call or meeting.

**Content analysis:** Determine the topics and keywords of the conversations that are most popular.

**Qualitative:** Topics, written tone, solution recommended after keyword strings are entered.

**What you can learn from this:** Discover content topics that people want to learn more about; understand how people perceive your product.

**In-person conversations:** This is an effective method for a customer to get answers to direct questions that may not be supported through self-service methods. The customer has access to a company representative to guide the conversation and collaborate to resolve an issue. Often the customer initiates the conversation (sometimes the company does) to create an experience with the company. This makes in-person conversation a more intimate approach than online methods. Emotions can be easily expressed, communicated, and understood in this medium, increasing connection and intimacy between the people involved.

**Examples of activities:** Phone, email, live chat, in-person discussions (meetings).

**Why use it:** Allow customers to build a direct relationship with the company.

**Benefits:** Customer can express themselves and their needs freely without concern about whether their request will be supported by the system.

**Challenge:** It can be costly to support this approach because you need a human available to answer these questions.

**Success is defined as:** Customer satisfaction (NPS), issue resolution issues, and topics related to the sale. (The measurements for this approach include more emotional considerations than others.)

**Type of metrics:** Length of conversation (could be less than automated conversations because you get to the point faster and more quickly answer/resolve issues), date/time, topic.

**Content analysis:** Record and transcribe the conversations to gain insights about common conversation topics to understand challenges and benefits.

**Qualitative:** Topics, tone, approach, and resolution.

**What you learn from this:** Identify topics that could be automated (create a page or conversation flow in a chatbot). Gather product feedback from support calls to improve/enhance products. Get input for prioritizing research. Research innovations to solve customer problems that they identified.

**Live, in-person experiences:** These experiences allow a customer to understand what the company does by asking direct questions, experiencing the product first-hand, and understanding how it could help him or others. The customer and the company co-create an experience together, although the company may initiate it. This allows joint problem-solving and is most collaborative and creative of all approaches. Relationships are built from collaboration around education and problem-solving, and this approach includes both.

**Examples of activities:** Events/tradeshows, in-person store experiences.

**Why use it:** Allow prospects and customers a way to experience a company and its products directly.

**Benefits:** The customer or company can choose to initiate and guide a conversation, allowing greater collaboration for co-creating an experience.

**Challenge:** For a large audience, the experience is pre-planned, but there is an opportunity for deeper engagement during breaks. Side-bar conversations at such events increase and improve connection.

**Success:** Similar to in-person conversations by leveraging metrics around customer satisfaction (NPS), issue resolution, and the sale itself (The measurements for this approach include more emotional considerations than others.).

**Type of metrics:** Time in-store to purchase; time to resolve an issue; number of visitors at a location; types of interactions with associates; time at tradeshow booth.

**Content analysis:** Record and transcribe conversations to gain insights about key topics that matter to customers.

**Qualitative:** Insights into customer motivations, feedback about the product and company, and observations about where people congregate in a store or tradeshow (it may be related to a topic or interest).

**What you learn from this:** Discover topics that could be automated digitally (create a page or conversation flow in a chatbot). Get product feedback during support calls for improvements/enhancements. Gain input for prioritizing research. Research innovations to solve customer problems.

Considering customer communication activities using this approach may simplify the process of choosing activities and tactics when creating an engaging marketing program. It may be easier to define a program by first determining the desired result and then considering the various approaches to achieve it rather than identifying a series of activities that you prefer, which may or may not allow you to achieve your goals. It may also provide you the inspiration you need to develop a creative solution to more deeply engage with customers and prospects.

Some examples:

- **If you want to co-create an experience with your customers and encourage deeper customer understanding, then you may choose to have an in-person experience.** For an event or in-store experience, you could include activities that support the types of communication necessary to build a deeper relationship, such as creating opportunities for conversations, designing games, or having a party. This may result in employees developing compassion for customers by better understanding their challenges and motivations through conversations and interactions, or by sharing experiences to create memories together.
- **If you want to provide information to build awareness or spark interest, an automated, digital experience may be the best approach.** You may want to share a discovery or insight, publish new content that tells a new story, or announce a new product launching. You may use social media to encourage a conversation, but the activity is not meant to be a meaningful connection. It's meant to provide information, or an update, that can later be referenced between you both as common knowledge.

When you determine where you are in the customer relationship lifecycle, you can identify the right type of activity to help you achieve the type of engagement and connection you want. The right type of interaction will provide you with the information you need to determine if customers are as engaged as you'd like and provide information for how to improve. As we know, the greater the human involvement and engagement, the likelier customers are to move to the next level of a relationship. Sometimes, that's not always possible, or the right next step. Digital methods can be the best approach for sharing information or making announcements that may introduce a new idea for cross-selling later. Not every company experience needs a customer and employee co-creating it.

The idea of co-creating an experience is one reason why we cannot use artificial intelligence for conversations—yet. We have a long way to go before customers and prospects feel that they are solving a problem by collaborating with an artificial intelligence. The bot can sound like a person, interact like a person, and react friendly and warm like a good friend, but if you aren't able to collaborate and solve a problem together, make a joint decision, or gain input and perspective about a situation, then it's difficult to build the emotional connection necessary to develop a relationship. It's unlikely that we can build compassion with a bot today with exiting technology. They are programmed to use factual information based on transactions or data. Bots can provide fun and engaging experiences, and the metrics prove it through their popularity. But at the same time, it's not yet a relationship-building mechanism. You need to somehow automate that co-creation ability with other people to make that a reality.

We often wonder why startups that don't have high marketing budgets manage to succeed. Often, they discovered how to build relationships by balancing the different approaches and methods described. They also realized that they don't need to do all of their relationship-building alone. By embracing influencers in the right way, companies can build brand connections and relationships outside of their defined target markets. Like any relationship, it needs to be honest, authentic, and trustworthy without an ulterior motive like personal fame or revenue, which is why many influencer relationships are challenged. Some ways influencers could support prospective customers at different stages of the relationship include:

- **Early-stage:** Through content and events, companies provide the right level of connection to develop champions and engage customer influencers. Champions and influencers become an extension for a company brand for a specific target audience.
- **Mid-stage:** Some influencers answer questions and help a customer envision what life would be like using the product. Many post videos and content to demonstrate the product experience. They can allow customers to experience product benefits themselves through these product demos and distribute case study information to understand how others experienced benefits.
- **Post-purchase:** Companies and influencers keep the relationship going through various types of activities where customers can share their experiences, suggest new features, and show new product uses.

Influencers often have their own company, which partners with the original company to build customer relationships with new audiences. They provide an additional connection that may be more open and receptive to feedback than the company. It's easier to tell an individual that you don't like a product and why than to tell the original company, which may get defensive. In a way, they are involving the customer into the larger company community through a partnership. This relationship and balance help influencers get the feedback they need for the original company's product and activities to produce more of what the customers want. It's a great way to extend a company community to include new audiences.

### *A Word about the Hybrids on the Axes*

On the axes of ***The Four Activity Categories*** graphic, I show hybrid activities that share similarities with related group activities on either side of the matrix.

For example, a webinar is a hybrid activity that shares characteristics of an automated, digital, individualized experience and a live, in-person experience. If viewers can ask questions during the original recording, they are co-guiding the webinar experience. However, most webinar experiences are guided by the company through a planned presentation. Social media is another hybrid between in-person and digital conversations. There is an interaction between an employee and a customer. The company or customer may try to communicate their emotions in their posts, but unless emojis or other indicators are used, emotion is challenging to communicate through digital communication.

The customer review, third-party product reviews, and influencer programs are unique because they are a hybrid of all four categories. In all cases, the individuals who are creating reviews or sharing opinions have tried using the product, have had multiple experiences and conversations with the company directly, have visited the site and read other materials, and have accessed social media. This is why customer reviews, quotes, and influencer channels are some of the most powerful feedback pieces you can have for your business. They have elements of all four categories of activities in them.

## Relationship Roles

We often believe within companies that we need to increase the number of customers we contact, but maybe we need to increase the types of relationships a company has instead.

The following chart identifies a few types of relationships a company could have with different people in the purchase process and their roles. Some roles could be shared by the same individual, but that's not necessarily the case. Each of these individuals needs to experience the journey and product in some way, but that doesn't always mean that they need to complete the purchase process.

When you are determining how your company could develop a relationship with a prospective customer, remember what you want the outcome of the interaction to be and the type of individual who will be included in the process. This may be a factor in how you determine which type of activities to include. For example, an influencer or champion may need to be more engaged with your company than someone who simply approves a purchase. Most likely, a stakeholder in the decision or an approver will accept the advice of an internal influencer rather than the company salesperson because they will trust them more and not feel like the influencer is trying to "sell" them. A product user may want to know how this

## Types of Relationships Companies Can Have with Customers

| BUY PRODUCT | USE PRODUCT | SUPPORT PRODUCT |
|---|---|---|
| **Stakeholder/approver:** Cares that the general problem is being addressed; takes advice from others who will use the solution (if they don't use it themselves). | **Buyer/approver:** May not use the product, but is a key purchase decision-maker. | **Maintainer/supporter:** Does the maintenance work. |
| **Influencer/champion:** Understands the solution the company offers and the problem it solves. May be users, experiencers, or benefactors. | **User:** Actively engages with the product; wants to be sure it solves their problem. | **Benefactor:** Experiences results but doesn't do the maintenance work for the product or solution. |
| **Unidentified targets:** Those who will be using the product and have no voice in making the decision. These individuals and their needs will be discovered during the solution selection process. | **Experiencer:** Experiences product (possibly a light user) but does not actively use it. | **Unidentified targets:** Those who will need support but not be identified at the start of the process. These individuals and their needs will be discovered during the solution selection process. |
| | **Benefactor:** Enjoys the results of the product.<br><br>**Unidentified targets:** Those who won't be using the product, but will be experiencing benefits from it. These individuals and their needs will be discovered during the solution selection process. | |

product will solve their problem, which makes a demo or in-person store visit a key element to the experience. A benefactor will care more about how the end result of the product will improve their life, which makes the experience of using the product less important, but customer stories vital for them to understand.

By considering who you are communicating with and what you want to achieve through that communication, you can design experiences that build memories with your customers and help them feel closer to your company. Essentially, you are designing the right interactions to be experienced at the right time.

## Identifying KPIs that Map to Your Relationship Values

Key performance indicators help us identify how value is being added to our organizations. Typically, there are values that are associated with these KPIs that can be translated into meaningful, insightful, and measurable results. I had a metrics professor who told my class that almost anything can be measured. She was right. The challenge is identifying which measurements will support the values and goals of your organization.

Most organizations should have at least one goal regarding the measurement of effective relationships. There are at least five categories that could prove helpful in this. There may be different qualities of your organizations and interactions you want to measure and compare in relation to the bottom-line sales and revenue numbers, but this could be a great starting point.

| METRIC TYPE | DESCRIPTION |
|---|---|
| **Engagement** | • Demonstrate that you can hold a conversation with your customer and connect to them in some way.<br>• Build connections on social media: like, share, or comment.<br>• Build relationships (click a link to your site and keep interacting through chat or phone). |
| **Loyalty** | • Track repeat buyers and visitors.<br>• Track your customers end-to-end—those who consistently read emails, click to articles, use the product, and provide great reviews and recommendations.<br>• Remember that loyal customers want to see your brand succeed. |
| **Accountability** | • Include product reviews that validate messaging about the problem you solve and how you solve it.<br>• Measure reviews at reputable third-party organizations like the Better Business Bureau using this method. |
| **PR Relationship Metrics** | • *Guidelines for Measuring Relationships in Public Relations* (1999)<br>• Consider tracking four factors that build a relationship (controlled mutuality, trust, satisfaction, commitment). |
| **Brand and Reputation** | • Leverage net promoter score.<br>• Leverage accountability for reputation.<br>• Include traditional brand recall metrics. |

We can track success and value in many ways, but based on your organization's values, you need to select which KPI category best complements your efforts. The de-facto tracking of bottom-line revenue to indicate success is only one indicator of a great customer relationship. These are some ideas of other metrics that could provide you insights that could help you improve your customer relationships and, over time, generate more revenue.

## Engagement

Engagement is often associated with social media and digital tactics, indicating people's interest in what you are communicating. We sometimes don't consider tracking the difference between what you are actually selling in a business versus what you are communicating to an audience. You may have incredible output in product development and service creation, but if your audience doesn't understand the value you provide and how it could improve their lives, then they won't engage with your company, which will make getting new business more challenging than it needs to be.

Engagement results don't indicate communication success or failure. They indicate if you are able to connect with your audience and interact with them, or in other words, hold a conversation. Many companies dismiss these metrics because they don't directly see a connection to bottom-line revenue or the lead pipeline. However, there are some indirect connections to bottom-line results:

- **Social media is a great place to "discover" new companies, ideas, and products.** Social media is a place to be curious. Most people are open to new ideas and learning while browsing posts. You'll notice your friends and colleagues sharing information, and you may click on those links to explore their shared articles or videos.

When you are on social media, you aren't looking for anything specific. However, you may notice ad posts and if you learn that your friends are interested, you may be motivated to click on that ad and be curious to take the next step to learn more.

- **Engagement via social media or email can indicate potential interest in a company or products.** If you post a link about artificial intelligence when you sell bot software and it gets a lot of interest (clicks and likes) but you aren't selling much software, you may want to research why. There isn't a direct link between social media and product sales, but social media indicates interest in the problem and solution your company makes, or the value it provides. If the solution to the problem you solve gets interest but you have a hard time selling the solution, you may want to investigate what's being lost during the process. It may be possible that your social media posts are attracting and engaging the wrong audience. Or the message you are using isn't quite right for your target. Or you are using a different message in social media versus the sales cycle. On social media, you may not be connecting with software decision-makers and only finding people with a cursory interest in the topic. If you are targeting the right audience with the right message, you may not get leads right away, but you should build enough awareness for someone to contact you to learn more about your solutions.
- **Engagement on social media can often be the first touchpoint in a lead funnel, directing users through**

**a string of content marketing pieces.** In some ways, social media is at the top of the awareness funnel, where people first discover your company and your product/ service through friends or ads. When people are building awareness, they are not ready to buy, and it may take many months before that happens. Often, they need a reason to purchase—a problem that they need to solve to spark them to research solutions and then consider your product or service. Or they may be considering your solution because they have identified that they have a problem that your company does solve, although it's not a high-priority problem for them to fix. That's why you build a presence on social media: to spread the word about the problem you solve and the products and services you sell. This action provides an opportunity for a customer to get to know your company over time and purchase when he or she is ready.

Often businesses forget that engagement metrics alone don't tell a complete story about your relationships or revenue. If you sell widgets but you are communicating that you adore stuffed animals, I'm sure you'll get a lot of followers and spark conversations, but are you connecting with them about topics that matter to your company? This is where a hybrid of content analysis and engagement metrics can tell a more complete story about your business and its marketing. You can learn if there are some topics that drive more interest than others, or some keywords and phrases that get more attention. Or you may learn that you are targeting the wrong audience and need to pivot to target the right one.

The first step in the social media engagement path is to get someone to like your page or follow your account. The next step is to get someone to regularly like your posts and topics. Social media engagement is similar to casual conversations customers have with salespeople. In a way, it is a type of automated, digitized conversation. Conversations help a company understand the customer and help them understand not just what the company sells, but who it is and what it cares about most. Ideally, these conversations should be related to the type of product your company is selling and customers are buying. The more engaging the conversation, the deeper and more authentic a relationship is being built. And greater authenticity and engagement in a relationship should result in more sales.

### *How Words and Topics Matter in Social Media*

When I participated in an international graduate program for communications, the team I was in completed a content analysis project for a North American university's social media program. We focused on its Twitter and Instagram accounts. Looking at the engagement metrics overall, the university's social media program seemed to be in good health. However, when we further explored the content it was posting compared with the engagement metrics, we noticed a very different story.

The university wasn't communicating a focused message. Its main account covered a broad range of topics, from school closings to academic excellence to school history, and its accounts were used inconsistently. We also discovered that some messages resonated with its audience (lots of likes, clicks, and shares) while others fell flat. Sports messages didn't have a high number of likes and clicks the way academic success stories did. And hashtag usage influenced engagement because it helped people find conversation topics that interested them. Some hashtags didn't yield results, while some hashtags helped people find sports posts versus more historical posts. Overall, we learned that the university needed to:

- Include targeted content in specific accounts, making the account conversations more relevant for their audience.
- Define a guide for hashtag use to improve how their audiences found conversation topics. Better hashtag use could help their audience find conversations they were interested in joining, which would increase their participation and engagement, ultimately improving their relationship with this university.
- Generally focus content on student academics and alumni posts, which is what their audience was more interested in discussing. And this logically follows given that it is a university.

Once the university was able to have more focused social media conversations in various channels with various targets, we anticipated that the audience would know what to expect and, most likely, more actively participate in those discussions. By followers engaging in more conversations that they found interesting, a digital community would build and develop a hopefully stronger relationship among the audience members. And these strong online relationships could then be transitioned offline when the time is right.

Social media is a critical part of any communication plan because it helps a company or organization more easily reach specific target audiences (even if they are very small) that it normally wouldn't encounter through events, tradeshows, meetings, or other digital interactions. How an audience responds to social media posts communicates to the account owner and manager how they perceive a brand. There are always unspoken expectations and motivations in any conversation or relationship. But in a world where actions speak louder than words, social media allows managers to see first-hand the impact of words on the actions of a follower to develop a relationship. These analyses can then help an organization understand their customers and later leverage this knowledge to transition such conversations and relationships offline to continue building connections.

It's in these offline conversations where relationships between employees and customers can evolve into more than a transaction or sale. The organization can become an influence to help customers achieve their goals, solve their problems, and ultimately change their life for the better. If we compare the impact of these offline conversations with the online conversations, we can discover how customers view the company's role in their lives, the value it contributes already, and the potential value it could create in the future. It's through such conversations and connections that managers can discover how the strength of a customer relationship expressed through engagement (conversation topic and frequency) can impact the bottom line.

## Loyalty

Loyalty is a confusing business. Often we think loyalty represents a reward program, in which a customer's repeat purchasing behavior merits them receiving a gift. But is receiving a reward for behavior really loyalty? A behavior that is repeated over time becomes a habit. And that's what many modern rewards programs do: create habits. This practice isn't as negative as it sounds; many businesses do this with great benefit. But to understand if your customers are truly loyal to your company and brand, you may want to explore their motivation to continue their habit of purchasing from your company.

Is the motivation for customers to maintain loyalty with your company reflecting a desire to connect to the brand? Or does it reflect a desire for a reward?

There are often two additional motivations for people to form habits besides a reward: convenience and preference based on product quality. Here are some examples to better understand the difference:

- **Convenience:** You decide to get Starbucks coffee every day because there is a Starbucks café in your building. When you work in a building without a Starbucks, you stop your café habit because it is no longer convenient.
- **Preference:** You decide to drive 30 minutes to Starbucks every day because you prefer Starbucks coffee made in the café. To you, nothing tastes better than freshly made Starbucks coffee. You have a coffee maker at home where

you could brew your own Starbucks, but it just doesn't taste the same. You may try the alternative brand coffee shop in your office building, but somehow for you, it falls short in flavor.

The motivations behind the two habits can make them lasting or fleeting, based on your personal situation. Once you change jobs, the convenience habit mentioned will most likely change. However, your preference habit may not change. In fact, if you prefer a brand for its product quality or other factors, you may go out of your way to access that brand's products and become loyal because you have an emotional attachment to that product.

The chart on the next page outlines motivations behind loyalty decisions when choosing an airline, grocery store, or skincare. This illustrates four factors that people use when making this choice: preference, convenience, reward, and habit.

In some ways, this chart resembles decision points similar to what you would see in a customer journey. It's almost as if preferences kick off a customer relationship lifecycle or customer journey, and factors like convenience encourage repetitive purchase activities that create rewardable habits. Depending on the activities that you reward, your company can develop different types of relationships with that customer. For example, some skincare products will provide a discount to customers who purchase a specific skincare regimen. Companies that value the purchase transaction will treat dollars as points. Airlines sometimes take into consideration the number of miles traveled as an indicator

| PREFERENCE | CONVENIENCE | REWARD | HABIT |
|---|---|---|---|
| Reason to choose one company over another based on product quality, offering, or similar experience benefit. | One choice is easier to make than another due to proximity or ease. | One choice has an incentive. | Motivation for your choice is based on repetitive activity and what you become used to. |
| **Airlines:** Prefer to fly American Airlines compared to United or Delta because American has better snacks and movies, has better on-time statistics, and flies to more locations. | Frequently flies to the cities you travel to most often.<br><br>Flies out of an airport closer to your home than the competitor. | Receive points for choosing to fly on American Airlines (and this is especially helpful if you are saving for a three-week European vacation next year). | Choose American Airlines because you think they are better than other airlines (more established, better represented at airports, better pricing), they are convenient, or you get a reward. |
| **Grocery store:** Prefer to go to Whole Foods in the next town because it is cleaner than the store down the street and sells the quality of products you want. | Located on the way home from work compared to another store 20 miles out of the way. | Receive coupons or discounts for your purchases there. | Know what to expect for the experience, or believe their food is better (fresher, more nutritious). |
| **Skincare:** Prefer a skincare brand because of the effects it has on your skin or the quality of its ingredients.<br>. | Sold in a store near your home or offered online with fast delivery. | Receive some type of frequent purchase discount, "club" membership, or other offering. | Continue purchasing the brand because of the effects it has on your skin, you want the points/ rewards, or it is easy to continue to purchase. |

of loyalty. This has mixed effects. Do 20 500-mile flights on the same airline indicate a stronger or weaker loyalty relationship compared to 5, 2500-mile flights? It may depend on the airline, the available competition at the departure and arrival airports, and flight purpose. In any case, convenience becomes tied to brand preference, not always product benefit. Without this combination, you cannot get a customer to form a habit. You may have a great product, but if it is difficult to purchase, then you won't get people to continue buying it and develop that behavior. You may have a product that is easy to purchase but isn't effective. So you may get tremendous first-time-buyer numbers, but little activity after that because they were disappointed. That won't build a business community or deep customer relationships. Deep customer connection and community-building comes from a balance of preferences and convenience.

But this idea can be abused and misused, working to a company's disadvantage. Some executive elite flyers or executive hotel reward members will only frequent their selected brands to earn points. Their motivator is purely the reward, which they perceive to be the same as cash. If faced with a choice between their reward brand or a new brand, the motivator to stay with the current reward brand is typically the perceived cash equivalent reward—most likely not based on the product experience quality, emotional attachment to the brand, or brand preference as a representation of product quality. Although the quality of the product experience or preference may have been a factor when initially deciding which brand to be loyal to, it is possible that such a motivator declines in influence over time. I have observed too many reward members who stay committed to a brand because of this. It's not that they haven't found anything better or they don't want to try something new because it may not meet expectations. Their view is: *Why not get a free trip or night's stay for my troubles?* It is worth researching this factor for your company brand and product to better understand why loyalty members continue to support your program. The motivating factor for their loyalty may not be what you expect.

To fully understand loyalty, consider cases in which brand loyalty isn't related to habits or rewards. One example is hair stylists, hairdressers, and barbers. Most people are very attached to the person who cuts and styles their hair. When they find someone they like, typically they won't make an appointment with anyone else until that person dies or moves out of drivable distance. The stylist could switch salons and their clients will move with them. The salon or shop itself where the individual works doesn't matter. The individual's preference is based on the relationship with the stylist or barber personally and the quality of their work.

What about the stylist or barber makes their customers loyal? The clients don't get rewards or prizes. Often, it's not convenient to go to a specific stylist or barber. Preference is based on service quality, but the relationship includes more than that. If the relationship were based on service quality and preference only, then someone could go to an equivalent professional within the same salon or barbershop and be just as satisfied with the end result. But that's often not true.

People continue to go to the same stylist or barber because there is an emotional bond with that person. First, hair is very personal. Anyone can get a haircut, but people want to feel good about what's on their head. It represents their personality. They want to work with someone who isn't just talented, but also who understands their personal sense of style and can find a way for their hair to complement that. When we get a bad haircut, we are experiencing what it's like to visit a stylist or barber who doesn't understand you as a person.

Second, people share a lot about their personal lives with a stylist or barber. This creates tremendous vulnerability between them both. Sharing intimate personal stories builds bonds between friends. This vulnerability will keep people returning and continue the relationship.

If we transfer this idea to other types of businesses, it is easy to understand why people go out of their way to support a brand or person or company.

**True loyalty is based on an emotional bond.** You are choosing to work with a specific company or service because you connect with their brand and how they operate. You feel that the brand understands *you*—who you are, how you think, what you feel. You think the product or service is high-quality. And you are vulnerable with this organization. The convenience factor is present, but the convenience may lie in a feeling rather than a physical trait, like location. You may admit to the store managers that you are willing to drive across town to get a specific pastry, treat, or coffee drink because it makes you feel "like home." Or you may admit that you had a bad day and this object or activity makes you feel better. You are willing to share parts of yourself with that company's experience through marketing or sales activities from social media to email and more to build a relationship. If you get a reward for buying from them, that's a bonus, but that's not the motivator. **The motivator lies in the relationship, the trust, and an individual's self-image and identity.**

When customers are emotionally bonded with a company, they see it as an extension of themselves. And when you feel that a brand understands you, you are also defining yourself by choosing the brand. There are aspects of the brand that may reflect your personality, making almost a recursive reference between the company and customer.

This is also why you may be loyal to a brand but not choose it every time. It's like being loyal to a coffee place because you like the coffee, the atmosphere, and the people, but you choose to go somewhere else to try it, have an adventure, and see how the experience feels to you. There's an element of self-discovery when experiencing another brand. You may be loyal to three or four coffee places because you learned how they all reflect your personality in some way. If this is your attitude toward the brand, then it would logically follow that you view loyalty rewards as just that: a thank-you gift for your purchases. It's not an incentive for your choices or behavior.

In companies, we sometimes forget that customer behaviors change due to circumstances beyond their control, but that doesn't mean that their loyalty changed. Customers may not purchase products from a specific brand because they live where the brand isn't sold, or they have no need for a product's solution anymore because their children grew up, or they gained or lost weight, or they bought a different car, or changed jobs. Their lives may have changed, but those factors don't impact one's loyalty to the brand.

One example is Girl Scout cookies. Most of us adore Thin Mints, Tagalongs, or Samoas. We may not directly know a Girl Scout to buy the cookies from and it may not occur to us to find a site online that sells the cookies, but that doesn't mean that we don't still jump to purchase a box of cookies when we see them being sold at a grocery store or by a colleague's daughter at the office.

Another example that's more complex is children's clothing. Let's say you had children and you loved the clothing from OshKosh B'gosh. You bought your children almost everything from that brand. When your children outgrew those clothes, you needed to find new brands and styles for them, so you stopped buying the brand. They literally grew out of little kid clothes and styling. However, that doesn't mean that you aren't loyal to the brand. There was simply no reason for you to purchase from that brand anymore for your children.

After 20 years pass, let's say that your neighbors had a child and you want to give them a gift. Most likely, you would buy that child OshKosh B'gosh clothing or recommend it to their parents. If anything, this shows that you are still loyal to the brand, but in a different way. If we reference the role relationship chart, you could now be considered an influencer rather than a buyer.

**In this case, what drives brand loyalty? Your connection with a brand and your desire to see that company succeed and its business grow.** You believe in its products and its services. You may be critical of the company at times, but mainly that is because you love it so much, you have high expectations. You expect it to be better and to do better.

Loyalty isn't behavior. Loyalty is based on a relationship.

Signs that your customers see loyalty as part of your relationship include:

- Customers see rewards as a thank-you gift, not just a benefit that rewards a purchase with points.
- Customers think about your company first to recommend solutions to their problems.
- Customers support your company by promoting its ideas and views.
- Customers always know intimate details about your business.
- Customers connect to your brand emotionally and see a part of themselves in your company and product.
- Customers want to see your business succeed and they do what they can to help it grow.
- Your customers don't always agree with you, but they want you to do what's best for your business.
- Customers have such a good experience with your company that they want to share the value you provide with friends so they can have a good experience too.

True loyalty isn't built on wanting to promote the business itself; loyalty comes from wanting the business to succeed. Customers rave about a company's products and services not just because they found them successful, but because they believe that they are the best solution to solve a specific problem. Even if the solution didn't work out for them, customers may still recommend the company to other people only because they want to see that brand succeed.

### *Why I Love Mary Kay*

I was traveling from San Francisco to Dallas for a business trip. When I got on the plane, I saw a sea of women in pink suits. I didn't realize I was traveling right before the start of the annual Mary Kay convention in Dallas and I was on a plane filled with Mary Kay saleswomen. On the flight, I was constantly asked if I used Mary Kay or wanted to set up an appointment or try a sample. It was an overwhelming experience, but I didn't complain to the reps; they were just doing their job. I was tolerant of their brand excitement because, secretly, I love Mary Kay too.

When I was in my mid-20s, I was a Mary Kay sales consultant. (In that job I learned a lot about people, sales, and business.) My regional director was the infamous Gloria Mayfield Banks. She is as phenomenal and fabulous in person as she is on video. I would go to the meetings and get excited to go sell Mary Kay products to reach my goal at the time: earning a red Grand Am.

But first, I needed to just sell something—anything. I wasn't very good at it. The key to being successful at selling Mary Kay is to learn how to sell skincare. I enjoyed selling color cosmetics, but that's not where the profit margins, nor the repeat business, exist. What made my business more challenging was that I was just focused on having fun, which worked for a short while. But it just wasn't a profitable, long-term business mindset.

I learned two lessons from Mary Kay—well, actually from Gloria Mayfield Banks:

- **People know you as you show up to them.** This is why it's hard to sell to your family. We may think that our families will be supportive of our efforts, but we forget that they don't see us as a Mary Kay consultant. Depending on the family member, they may see you as the same little kid they raised, the same cousin they played with, or the same grandchild looking for a cookie, and they just don't take you seriously. Strangers will listen to you because they don't know you in any other way than how they meet you—as a Mary Kay consultant. It was how you showed up to them. This proved true many times as a Mary Kay consultant and in my career. I have used this lesson in life whenever I meet new people, and that has helped me be taken seriously when I tell them what I do. Most people from my past who know me from my early career have a hard time catching up to who I am now. It makes sense. They still see me as I was 20 years ago and don't see the me of today.
- **When you get nervous (paranoid) and think people are talking about you, it's all in your imagination.** People aren't thinking about you. They are thinking about themselves and worrying about their own perception. Look to the previous bullet if you doubt yourself. People know you as you show up to them. If you think you are fabulous, everyone thinks you are fabulous.

I tried really hard to sell Mary Kay products, but it just wasn't for me. The company has a great formula and, if you follow its guidance, you *will* earn that pink Cadillac. I didn't follow any guidance and do what I was told. In many ways, it was fun but not my passion and I failed. Miserably.

However, that doesn't mean that I hate Mary Kay. When I see an event in Dallas for Mary Kay employees speaking, I try to go. When I'm at a loss for skincare products, I go on their site to find options. I'll always support a Mary Kay representative in any way; they all work hard, and it's a great brand. The skincare product quality is superior and always does well in lab tests. Mary Kay Ash had a phenomenal, inspirational story of pulling herself from nothing into millions. Every woman who works there wants to be like her, so why not support those women?

The experience I had with Mary Kay was life-changing and meaningful. In some ways, the Mary Kay brand became part of me and my identity, transforming my perception of business and skincare practices. I learned the value of eye cream from Mary Kay. I may not purchase the products today, but that doesn't mean I'm not loyal to and don't support the brand in other ways. I stopped purchasing long ago because it was too challenging to order products and get them delivered. I'm sure things have changed since more than 10 years ago with the rise of the Internet. As I write this, I realize that it may be time for me to give them a chance again.

### *How Do You Measure Loyalty?*

First, sales and revenue don't necessarily reflect loyalty. Repeat purchases are a signal of loyalty, but not always definitive proof. Customers may be loyal to a brand because they are emotionally connected to it and there is no real way to convert them to use another brand, like the hair stylist/hairdresser/barber example. Or customers may be loyal to a brand because they are invested in it financially or emotionally and feel that they need to stick with it or suffer losses. For example, if someone spent a lot of money updating their faucets with a specific brand of water filters, he or she may stay with that brand because of the initial investment, not because it's a great brand. And losses aren't always financial. Personal emotional losses could include a changed perception of oneself. Use of a skincare brand could bring someone a feeling of elitism and prestige. If the person stopped using that brand, he or she may not notice any physical skin changes, but his or her emotional state may change because he or she is no longer part of the "club," sharing the identity of others who are perceived as being elite because they use that brand.

If you want to measure loyalty, discover who reads your content, follows you on social media, buys and uses your products, and writes great reviews. People who love you and have a deep customer connection with you will constantly find a way to interact with your brand. Know who those people are and observe their activities. Find the delta between those who purchase versus those who no longer purchase. What caused the shift? And do those who no longer purchase still serve as a type of brand ambassador?

Customers providing referrals for your business is another sign of loyalty. These people loved the experience with your company so much that they want others to experience the same. Knowing who is referring your business is important because they are unpaid ambassadors for your company. They are the ultimate hybrid between an employee and customer.

**We can't forget that loyalty is fueled by a feeling toward a company.** It's a true relationship indicator that could be also measured through sentiment and perception research. Money has little direct correlation with loyalty, except for referrals and repeat purchasing. A loyalty problem would be identified through poor ratings and reviews, few customer referrals, no followers or fans, and light customer relationships with your company.

If you notice that you aren't receiving many referrals but sell a lot of products, you may need to better connect with your customers to build a stronger following and customer community. If you have a great following and aren't making sales, you may be missing that connection to show how you can directly solve their problem and provide value. And the problem you solve may not be related to product quality; it could be due to convenience or personal perception when using the product.

## Accountability

Company accountability is a key aspect of creating successful customer experiences. But how do you determine if a company is accountable or not?

One approach is to measure explicit and implicit agreements. We will assume that companies are accountable for their explicit legal agreements. Government agencies and organizations like the Better Business Bureau tend to measure and validate those types of agreements. But for the purpose of customer experiences, we will address the marketing and sales side of these explicit and implicit agreements.

Marketing and sales accountability for explicit agreements answer the question if a company delivers on its product promises. A few ways to determine that:

- **Online reviews.** Validate that your company delivers on its promise through online customer reviews. If people admit without prompting that a solution solves their problem as your company describes it, then your company is being held accountable for what your business does. To gather this data, someone would need to read the individual reviews and determine which apply to your product messaging. However, such reviews independently confirm that companies are delivering on their explicit marketing and sales agreements.
- **Industry awards.** Winning an industry award confirms that a product is overdelivering on its promises. Compared to other companies that promise to solve the same problem using a similar approach, the company that wins the award does it best. And third-party awards further prove that it's not just the company that believes it is solving a problem well. A group that evaluated the company and its products and services compared it with all others in its class and concluded that this specific company has a better solution than its competitors.
- **Evaluation of how a company achieves parity, meets industry baselines, and follows best practices.** This could be done internally or by a third party, which would maintain greater objectivity. The evaluation would

compare how the site, its product and services, and its experiences compare to other companies that solve similar problems and provide similar solutions. The comparisons could include the website, social media, customer support, and the product experience, including product setup, usage, and warranties and guarantees.

- **The company upholding its brand values.** Start with a baseline understanding of the company's reputation and brand based on third-party research. Using content analysis, notice if there are specific words or phrases that are consistently used to describe the company. Also determine if company operations and practices observe or disregard the brand values based on how activities and tactics are executed. For example, if a company values transparency and being straightforward, but the workflow for an operation is convoluted and customer communications are indirect at best, then the company isn't upholding the value of transparency. Similarly, do support calls and other communication tactics by company teams use consistent language, tone, and problem-solving approaches that reflect the brand values? By reviewing the communications and interactions in a sample of a company's processes, researchers can determine if the brand values are present.
- **Industry certifications provide legitimacy through its own community.** Certification helps your company be recognized as operating according to best practices for a specific professional or industry organization or analyst group. Your company is not just representing

that organization, but the organization is holding it accountable to meet standards that allow it to be part of its community. Being certified gives you the benefit of leveraging an organization's reputation through association. A company needs to complete activities to be certified, but not all companies do the work and are held accountable to acquire that reputation.

I'm sure that there are more ways to measure accountability. However, once you measure accountability in your company, you could compare that to revenue and determine if there is a correlation with your bottom line. This would be noticeable over time, especially after your product or service won an award. If you are a highly accountable company and not seeing relatively high revenues, you may be missing opportunities or leaving money on the table. However, if you are not as accountable as you could be and are earning incredible revenue, imagine the financial results you could achieve if you improved your accountability.

## Public Relations Metrics Can Be Underrated

Public relations is a mature communications discipline. It is governed by a number of best practices and metrics that guide decisions and strategies. Most who are not formally trained in the area don't understand the value of its structure and what it can offer to a company to understand stakeholders and markets.

Public relations teams were the originators of developing great relationships with various stakeholders from press to government to activists to employees to local communities to customers and prospects. This is why this discipline includes measurements specific to understanding relationships.

The Institute of Public Relations published *Guidelines for Measuring Relationships in Public Relations* (1999), which references all company relationships, from internal relationships with employees to external relationships with press, journalists, other companies, and more. It includes survey questions that help gauge how a company and its relationship with specific stakeholders are perceived universally. This approach could be leveraged to determine the quality of your company's relationships with employees and customers. The guide outlines the main outcomes of successful relationships:

- **Control mutuality,** or the degree to which parties agree on who has rightful power to influence one another.

> *Input is tell me what you think. Involvement is come in and get to work with us and let's figure out what the right answer should be. . .get on this task force and help us figure things out. That's where you would like to see the relationships between publics and the organization taken to.*[157]

- **Trust,** or one party's level of confidence in and willingness to open oneself to the other party.
- **Satisfaction,** or the extent to which one party feels favorably toward the other because positive expectations about the relationship are reinforced.

- **Commitment,** or the extent to which one party believes and feels that the relationship is worth spending energy to maintain and promote.
- **Exchange vs. communal relationship.** In an exchange relationship, one party gives benefits to the other only because the other has provided benefits in the past or is expected to do so in the future. In a communal relationship, both parties provide benefits to the other because they are concerned for the welfare of the other—even when they get nothing in return.

I suggest getting a copy of *Guidelines for Measuring Relationships in Public Relations* to learn more about these measurement systems. Using these factors and the questionnaire included in the guide in your organization could help you determine the quality of your relationships with your customers, employees, or other stakeholders.

## Brand and Reputation

Brand and reputation are connected yet different. *Brand* represents how a company or organization communicates who it is and what it does. *Reputation* represents how a company is perceived by the public, beyond customers and prospects.

Often communications professionals confuse brand and reputation problems because they have an intertwined, cause-and-effect relationship. However, they have very different diagnoses and solutions.

Reputation issues are related to your organization's public image based on people's experience of it through products, reviews, analyst opinions, news, the behaviors of employees—everything. In some ways, you could say that a company's reputation is reflective of how the customer experience is perceived by the public. You can't control what others think of you or your organization. You can try to influence this perception through your brand, press interviews and releases, messaging, activities, popular employees and executives, customers, or great products and promotions. But in the end, the public will have their own perception of your company and products. Reputation management tends to include PR activities, positioning/messaging strategies and activities, and content strategy.

Although a brand is a factor that determines an organization's reputation, if a brand is not well communicated and an organization loses control in how it communicates about itself, press about the organization and its leaders will guide people's perceptions of it. In some ways, their actions should reflect the brand values, but that's not always true. That's usually where disconnects between brands and reputations occur.

Your brand represents your company's personality and is traditionally communicated to the public through logos, colors, and messaging in various tactics and channels. In today's digital companies, customer experiences are also communicating brands. An organization's values should be included in the interaction design. Brand effectiveness is measured through the impression that marketing materials and communication plan activities leave on people who experience them. Measurements validate that the brand is being communicated as intended.

A gap in your organization's reputation and brand communication may highlight how individuals in your organization don't embrace brand values or how activities promote a public perception contrary to the brand. Or there may be an element of the brand that is being subconsciously communicated to the public through unofficial channels because the brand communication is not openly embracing a specific quality or characteristic. Or the customer experience doesn't represent the brand values, instead communicating a very different message about the company through products or services.

Because brand communication and reputation measurement are established areas of communication measurement, there are a number of KPIs available to help you measure them. By comparing these values to your revenue numbers and noticing any relationships that occur, you can determine how your brand and reputation are contributing to or detracting from your bottom line.

Brand and reputation studies to investigate include:

- Net promoter score,
- Interbrand top brands,
- Image profile,
- CSR image profile,
- Reputation, and
- Company identity.

There are also reports you can access to help you better understand your brand and reputation. The annual Interbrand "Top Global Companies Report" can help you gauge where you may stand amongst giants, as can firms that complete reputational studies.[158]

## How Revenue and Relationships Come Together

Once you determine your relationship metrics, you can map those to your existing revenue metrics in your funnel. You should be able to observe patterns between the two, demonstrating how a relationship relates to revenue. As you observe this pattern, you can learn which activities promote a relationship (and should increase revenue) and which do not.

You may notice that for your solution and product, there may be a slightly different path to increase conversion. Depending on your industry, target market, and solution, it may be worth exploring programs that better support loyalty development, engagement, or clearly communicate accountability. Those approaches may help build a better customer relationship and, in the end, help you generate more revenue.

Brand and reputation will always have a direct link to purchase activity. This may provide additional insights for you to communicate your company's brand values more effectively or you may have a reputation problem in which people perceive your organization differently than your brand.

Here are some questions to start your investigation and quest to increase revenue through an improved relationship:

- **Who are your customers?** Are the people who buy from your company more active participants in the early, middle, or late buyer's journey? What do you notice about the engagement pattern?
- **How engaged are your customers?** Do your customers engage in conversations with you on social media, through sales and support, or other ways? Do they interact with your company, products, and services through the Web site, the store, and events? Do they go to your company first to solve their problem?
- **How loyal are your customers?** Understand how many referrals you get and the motivation for repeat purchases. (Note: Repeat purchases may be a result of a brand commitment made, not based on a relationship.) There may need to be a survey component to this research to fully understand the depth of loyalty and what's motivating it. You may discover that the true reason for loyalty isn't a reason your company would like to continue to support.
- **Do you deliver what you promise to your customers?** This is the accountability metric. This may be worth implementing quickly because it's another metric that could be tracked today. Understand how many people confirm through independent reviews that you deliver on your marketing and sales promises. Or map a metric to awards and third-party reviews.
- **PR, brand, and reputation** are established communication areas that have a number of metrics available to support them. Leverage them as you can.

- **Is your company on brand in general?** Do a quick content analysis of your company's outbound-facing content and experiences to see if they are aligned with the brand values. This is a great indicator to determine if your customer experiences are on brand or need some adjustment. Are call centers using consistent approaches? How about your website? How about sales? What do you need to do to start gathering this information today? Prioritize which approaches most accurately reflect your brand values. The easiest data to gather is engagement. It may be easier to start there and build metrics for other channels over time after gaining new insights.

### *Airbnb Brilliantly Involved its Customers in its Product to Foster a Sense of Security and Develop Loyalty*

Hotels are known for their privacy, secrecy, and anonymity. Guests feel safe in such an environment and hotels maintain their crime-free reputations through cameras, security staff, and safety procedures.

Conversely, bed and breakfasts are known for its guests sharing their identities through openness and socialization. You meet your host, get to know the neighborhood where you are staying, and ask for suggestions while you visit. Often, you're staying in someone's home or part of their home. Secrecy and anonymity fail with bed-and-breakfast arrangements because homeowners don't want random strangers to stay in their home; they want to know the identity of the guest they are allowing into their lives. Sometimes guest houses are on their properties, or they share a wall or more with the guests.

This close environment doesn't invite hostilities or oddball behavior. And hosts typically aren't equipped to handle what comes with secrecy and anonymity (crime), unless they work in law enforcement. Few do.

Airbnb had to consider this safety issue when designing its services. It always had some level of safety included in its service, but after an incident in 2011, it increased its offering significantly.[159] When you sign up for an Airbnb account, you need to provide ID to prove your identity to stay somewhere. It's like checking into a hotel. Hotels require photo ID, and Airbnb does too. Identity is key to this process.

After you stay at an Airbnb property, you're asked a series of questions to rate your experience. Airbnb does this for the guest and for the host. The guest questions inquire about their expectations for the experience. Guests rate the property and host experience. Meanwhile, the host is able to rate the guest, providing advice for future hosts. This also adds to the social component of Airbnb: The hosts help each other validate and screen guests. If a guest is challenging, then maybe a host can provide some advice for the next host to avoid such misfortune. If a guest is a joy, that information gets passed along as well.

Airbnb doesn't make this feedback loop optional. It is part of the reservation and checkout process to allow people to screen you. Guests may choose to stay at a property that is well-reviewed with a great host, just as a host reviews who is staying at their property. A new host may want to validate that the first few guests will be suitable to feel more comfortable with the process. The ID validation and reviews are great introductions to this way of thinking. By building a profile, you are defining your Airbnb identity for someone else, and by integrating reviews into the booking and checkout process, you are helping the next person get a better idea of who this stranger is. In a way, Airbnb has built a solid security system by defining identity on the site through its product participants and by leveraging the openness and sociability needed for staying in someone's home through a loosely defined community.

Airbnb wants happy guests and happy hosts, which means that as a guest and a host, you need to participate in the feedback process. Based on your answers, Airbnb will give you more of what you say you like. Hosts will get the type of guests that they prefer and guests will get presented the types of properties that they prefer. The system then works for everyone. The more you stay in places you like and great reviews are shared, the more you use the product and the stronger the community becomes. The process promotes a positive experience the next time Airbnb is used by all parties. It encourages more than a habit through preference or convenience, but an emotional relationship by building trust. People are recommending other people they trust to share in the Airbnb experience, which is a type of community itself. The more loyal you are to the brand and experience and the more you participate and answer questions, you increase your chances to have an experience better suited to your preferences the next time. The reward for loyalty—a stronger sense of community, safety, and trust—is based on everyone's participation in the process to provide preferences. Without it, the model fails. But within it, you get a memories and a desire to repeat the experience.

## Conclusion

If you get more of what you pay attention to, and if you pay attention to specific metrics as a definition of success, you will see success in that area. But what about other areas that indicate success that you may not have considered? You may have a great business idea and attract a number of social media followers within a short time, which indicates great business promise. However, you may mistakenly believe that no one wants your product or service if you aren't making money and only focus on sales and revenue. The problem you may be seeing could be your product price point, the number of decision-makers required to buy the item, or even that you are too new on the market and require a longer sales lead time. Tracking revenue alone to determine your success doesn't tell the complete story.

I have seen companies measure success mainly through revenue with a strong emphasis on lead generation. Often these companies are very product-focused and want to become solutions-focused, broadening their product offering to other areas and uses. I often wondered: If those companies focused on other metrics, like loyalty, accountability, or engagement, would their customers see them differently because they would interact with them in a vastly different way? Rather than always trying to focus on a sale, they may ask them questions about their business challenges and show how they value their feedback. By presenting themselves in a slightly different way by focusing on a slightly different end result, might it be possible for such a company to achieve that different goal?

Understanding the connection between customer relationships and revenue can help your company achieve greatness. Excellent customer experiences build great customer relationships that increase revenue. But which aspects of the customer relationship should you pay attention to and measure to get optimal success? It depends on your business, product, and solution, but these five areas can help you see trends:

- **Engagement** can help you determine the quality of the conversations with prospects and customers.
- **Loyalty** can determine the strength of the customer relationship with your company and brand.
- **Accountability** identifies that you are delivering on your promises.
- **PR metrics** help you gauge your relationships with stakeholders.
- **Brand and reputation** measures your public perceptions.

An increase in engagement could improve loyalty, which could increase revenue. Or if your accountability is low, but your revenue is high, consider what would happen if you were a more accountable company. By looking at these relationships and their influence on revenue, you could see your organization through new eyes and identify business and revenue opportunities that you never previously considered. If business success is based on conversations and interactions between people, and you aren't somehow measuring how those conversations and interactions build relationships with your customers to eventually create a community, you may not notice how they are impacting revenue. Salespeople notice this every day. Your customers feel this every day. Look past revenue to find the missing ingredient. It probably lies in how you are engaging with your customers and how they feel about your company.

CHAPTER 8

# Conclusion

A couple of years ago, I was recording a training video series in a conference room at the Dallas Entrepreneur Center (DEC). It was the third time I was trying to record my sessions to get this training class off the ground. (As an aside, I still have not been successful getting the material recorded and distributed.) I found a room with blank white walls, which I thought made a perfect background. I was hopeful and optimistic. I didn't realize that I had the wrong microphone and that there was a horrible white noise from a background fan, which made the recordings close to unusable. But it was okay. This was practice. Yet again.

The poster pictured on page 394 was on the wall in the room where I was recording. Once I read the poster, I realized that this was exactly what I was talking about in my course and what I was advising clients at the time. I was developing content strategies for my clients, working with social media, and discovering how to use conversations in marketing. Sales has been using conversations to engage customers for years. Marketing needed to automate the idea through social media and in campaigns.

We don't like to admit it, but social media has automated our conversations, although there are challenges. It is highly personal, yet anonymous—similar to what happens when we meet people on the street or in passing in a store line. Sometimes it's just a few lines of conversation. And sometimes these brief encounters evolve into anonymous digital friendships. But you have to wonder: Are these connections really any different from the acquaintance you know at the cafe because you see them there every day? Or the person who works at the store that you catch up and talk about your families with? You know some things about them, but not many. But you trust that this person wouldn't harm you and does care a bit about your best interest.

This type of connection extends to businesses as well. Businesses can grow digitally through similar conversations and brief snippets of interaction. These conversations eventually grow to become relationships, and one end result is that someone trusts you enough, believes in your solution enough, and sees how your solution will help them so they finally purchase—and you get revenue.

When the poster in the room caught my eye, I stared at it for a long time. This was the moment where I realized that business really is about relationships and conversations. Conversations are the activities we do to build relationships—the essence of business.

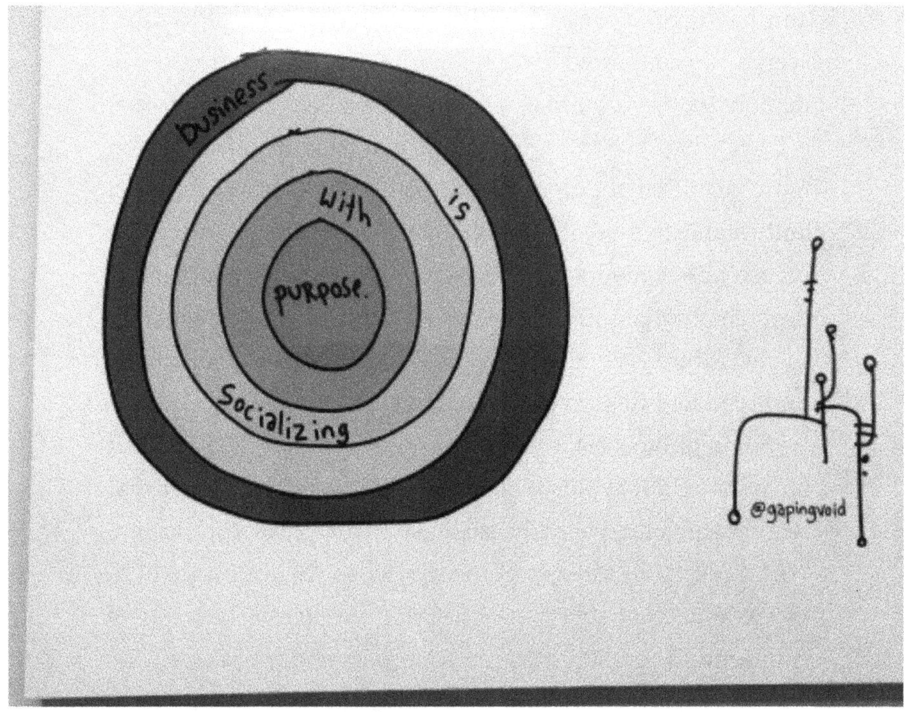


*Figure 28: "Business is socializing with purpose."*

*Artwork from Gaping Void, a Culture Design Group, www.gapingvoid.com*

About six months earlier at the DEC, I was a volunteer during Women's Startup Weekend. I was organizing the food and making sure the women who attended had all of the meals, snacks, and drinks they wanted. I observed a number of different team interactions, from complete blowups, meltdowns, and all-out arguments to lively, animated discussions and laughter—and lots in-between. There was a prize at the end of the weekend for the best startup, and I was curious to see which team would win. At that point, I had attended a number of startup funding competitions and had a good idea which types of businesses got funding (versus those that were struggling and needed more time to demonstrate feasibility and generate revenue). The teams that did well had a pretty good idea, but what benefitted them more was that they got along, had a great team dynamic, and established great interpersonal relationships. They were focused on achieving their vision, mission, and goal for the day. They talked about the possibility of working together in the future. Whether they did or not is irrelevant; what mattered was that they got along well enough to consider it.

Some of our best business opportunities are tied to great business relationships. Some of my most lucrative business relationships happened because we had a great relationship. We were friends outside of the project as well as inside of it. We would often share stories about our lives. There was a connection and bond with the other person beyond work.

What makes business relationships challenging for a consultant is the boundary you need to maintain with clients. You need to keep a level of formality to get work done. It's easy for a consultant to become an employee of the client emotionally and mentally because you are working directly with their teams. It's easy for your loyalties to switch to your client and "forget" that you are working for the consulting firm. I remember working for a Big 5 consulting firm and a manager told me that in some ways we were in a highly vulnerable position: it was easy to believe we were a lot like their employees because we worked in their offices, shared their spaces and some benefits, and socialized with them at lunch and after-work drinks. But we could never "kiss the client"—that is, never get too close and emotionally involved in their culture or politics. We were being paid for our services. That's all. We were not in their tribe or ecosystem, and we lived on a fine line, friendly and not. There were many times when I made friends with clients, but at one point, I had to become the consultant and do what I needed to do. Sometimes the client understood. Sometimes the friendship did get in the way, and the business agreement needed to end.

The end byproduct of all of these interactions and relationship building activities was revenue. Money was the result of an energy exchange in which I offered a solution for payment.

When customers are included in our organizations and "middlemen" are no longer as prominent, employees are able to build a relationship directly with customers and become friends. In a mass consumer business, this may be more difficult than in a business-to-business environment, but it is still possible. Customer councils, advisory boards, ambassador programs, and other customer feedback groups can help build relationships between customers and employees.

Business isn't just about money. The people in your company are your business. The leads, the social media engagements, the email clicks, the revenue—those are measurements of the success of your business transactions. How do you measure your business relationships and their success? Most of us don't, but that's the true measure of success for your business. It's where business builds to generate revenue.

With great customer relationships, you'll inevitably see revenue increase. The two are tied together. And if you have great relationships but no revenue, you can use that knowledge to help pinpoint the problem of why there is no revenue generated. The same goes for having revenue and no relationships. Imagine what you could achieve if you had better customer relationships!

With automation driving innovation, every company experience needs to create engaging customer experiences. All aspects of a company contribute toward communication with the customer in the company ecosystem: The brand is the company's personality and essence, the action plans are the behaviors, the vision drives the company's purpose and provides a roadmap for where it needs to go, and the employees, partners, and customers are the community. The result of this collection of activities are experiences that build relationships that bring forth revenue.

When we skip this, we aren't hurting ourselves. We are hurting the potential of the business.

Imagine if we encouraged our employees to interact with our customers to become friends and create a great relationship with them. Imagine what we could achieve if we treated our customers as people rather than a source of revenue or a lead.

Imagine if we included customers in our company's community and partnered with them. Imagine the problems that we could solve for them. Imagine how we could build our businesses and provide better solutions.

Imagine if we moved to a new way of doing business in which we focused on people, engaging with them emotionally, helping them solve problems, and showing them a new way to live their lives. Imagine we helped people to think bigger than themselves. Imagine if we showed customers how an individual can make a difference in the world based on their purchase decisions while at the same time helping a company achieve revenue.

Imagine a world in which business is built on relationships, and we value interactions and experiences just as much as revenue. Imagine if we knew that success is tied to people first (and measuring revenue second). It's a world in which we don't choose between treating our customers well or having great customer experiences versus revenue. It's a world in which we value relationships and revenue equally.

EPILOGUE

# Conversations: Not Just for Humans Anymore

Conversations are vital to building a relationship. They are ways for people to connect with each other, find common interests, and develop memories together. Social media and content marketing have elements of automated conversations. They provide information to readers to learn about the issues surrounding problems, describe solutions, and provide insights the reader should consider when making a decision. This first stage of communication starts a dialogue between companies and customers to help them recognize and understand their problems and realize they need a solution. The next stage usually involves online transactions, which is a type of conversation. The app or site requests information, the user provides it, and this banter continues until an agreement is reached and money is exchanged for an item. We are now exploring the possibility of chatbots and AIs to react quickly to human input in an automated, digital conversation. But what does that mean? And why is this relevant to discuss in the context of customer experience?

Conversations extend beyond information and transactions to decision-making, influencing, and relationship-building, with more intricate goals like information-sharing and collaboration along the way. We have created apps to facilitate automating these conversations, but there is more to a conversation than exchanging pleasantries, thoughts, and ideas. The automation of communication and conversations through bots and AI is a vital component of automating business. This has proven successful for informative and transactional conversations, but can we achieve this for more complex, relationship-driven communications?

As we know, the more factual types of conversations—informational and transactional, related to things and action—are automated today. Decision-making, related to actions and thoughts, is semi-automated. We have tools available to help us, but humans need to actively use them to get any type of output. Influential conversations are more difficult to automate because they require conversations to discover information and insights, similar to relationship-building and brainstorming conversations. These types of conversations include emotions, feelings, empathy, curiosity, critical thinking, and problem-solving.

The bottom layer of the diagram refers to the types and topics of the conversations, as suggested by Judy Apps in *The Art of Conversation*. These complement the types of conversations at the top of the diagram. It's rare when talking about information that you'd talk about heart-related topics (like love or relationships) or discuss what really motivates you (like a soul topic). The more personal the conversation, the more emotionally driven the topics become. The more transactional and informational, the more likely factual or "thing" or "action" topics are fitting. If you are completing a

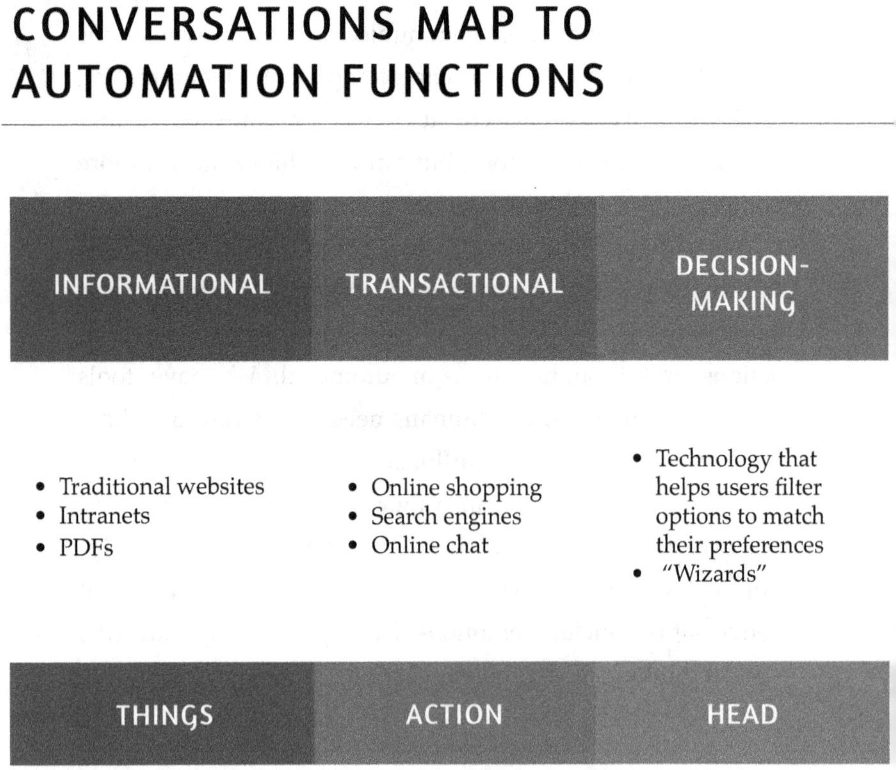

## CONVERSATIONS MAP TO AUTOMATION FUNCTIONS

| INFORMATIONAL | TRANSACTIONAL | DECISION-MAKING |
|---|---|---|
| • Traditional websites<br>• Intranets<br>• PDFs | • Online shopping<br>• Search engines<br>• Online chat | • Technology that helps users filter options to match their preferences<br>• "Wizards" |
| THINGS | ACTION | HEAD |

transaction with a person or company, knowing that someone feels a certain way about an object may help a decision-making discussion about a purchase, but it won't complete the transaction. Two or more people could be discussing how to implement a product or service, but the discussion goes beyond the "things" and "actions" to "head," "heart," and "soul." The team is building trust through various side conversations that develop a relationship. And they understand the problem by sharing different perspectives, which they bring together in their collaboration to determine the best solution.

| INFLUENTIAL | RELATIONSHIP-BUILDING | COLLABORATION/BRAINSTORMING |
|---|---|---|
| • Thought leadership content<br>• Social media influencer channels<br>• Content creation<br>• Events, talks, discussions | • Conversation building technology like social media, chatbots<br>• Traditional phone or in-person conversation | • Phone, chat, video conferencing<br>• Screen sharing, live document sharing<br>• In-person events and meetings<br>• In-store, live experiences |

| HEART | SOUL |
|---|---|

Keeping all this in mind, without an appropriate program, a computer cannot reach the sentience necessary to be capable of making these connections between facts and emotions, curiosity and creativity, identifying problems and solving them. Human conversations beyond information and if/then transactions are too complex to model in a computer today. Relationship-building skills, like empathy, compassion, connection, and emotion, are required to complete more intricate life functions like decision-making, collaboration, and emotional connection.

Even if we were to create such a program, what would it look like?

One could argue that we have achieved some type of sentience with the world-famous robot, Sophia. She has been introduced to the media as the AI representative of the future, but is she? She became a citizen of Saudi Arabia in 2017 and attends all of the popular technology events. She has even made some frequently quoted quips about AIs and robots having emotions or how robots want to kill humans. But does she have true sentience? She can see. She can respond to humans. But even her creator, David Hanson of Hanson Robotics, acknowledges:

> *. . .that her development is still more akin to a baby or toddler than an adult with a consciousness or intellect that could feasibly be rewarded with a full set of rights. Even this is pushing it—toddlers, for example, have consciousness; Sophia does not.*[160]

Hanson has admitted that her responses are often based on programming, illustrating how far we can go with the if/then statement to model human behavior. We still have not created intelligence or sentience in a machine.

This brings us back to the original question: If we were to create such a program for decision-making, collaboration, and emotional connection, what would it look like?

It's unclear. If we don't know in detail how these cognitive functions work in our own brains, how could we create a model to possibly replicate ourselves in a computer? We could create a new model that's completely different from our own image, but what would that look like? Do we have any theoretical models to use as a basis for that initial approach?

We often take for granted what is involved in creating a conversation. As we listen to someone speak, thoughts rush to us regarding questions to ask next, responses to provide, and insights to share. A computer today doesn't have the ability to respond in such ways. A computer follows its program and responds to stimuli, mostly based on user input. It processes data to present results and findings; it doesn't provide an analysis or summarized insights without its programmed direction. Humans usually provide their own insights based on what they believe is important, using the facts that they find through traditional research methods or computer output. Ironically, computer output is based on programs humans designed to access specific data points that a group originally decided were important. In many ways, one group of people is defining for another group what is important through a program. When the computer is deciding what is important for a user using programmed judgement created by humans, that's not entirely intelligence. From that perspective, we still haven't reached sentience.

This raises the question of whether we are limiting our own data knowledge by not considering the impact of outlier data to improve situations and provide a different perspective. Are we developing AIs to help us in the way we want to be helped? Or are we developing AI to identify problems or patterns that we could use to create something new? There are initiatives in companies and consultancies to have AIs discover trends found in "dark data," outside of the knowledge that people commonly have and can immediately leverage and reference. Leveraging such an approach is the only way we could expand human conversations using AI to add value for us to see problems and issues differently. Otherwise, we are defining what we need in a program, inadvertently limiting AI discoveries based on our existing knowledge.

**If/Then versus How and Why**

Conversations about "things" and "actions" are based on direct questions and answers. Do you have this in stock? When will it be shipped? How can I order that? That's why it is easy to automate this into chatbots. They are if/then statements about information that's required and requested.

However, when we talk about thoughts, emotions, and abstract ideas, more relevant topics for decision-making, influence, relationship-building, and collaborating, conversations no longer follow if/then structures to provide information. How are you feeling? Why are you feeling that way? What can I do so you feel better? One could create an if/then program to create answers, but that's not what's required in these types of conversations. These are questions that require cognitive processing related to sentience, or self-awareness. They require that subjects know they are alive and want to remain that way. We organic beings "feel" because we are self-aware and we know what is happening in our bodies and minds. We are driven to stay alive based on this self-awareness. But are computers aware of their existence? Do they *feel*? Do they seek to stay alive at any cost? What does this mean for them?

Science fiction has explored these ideas for more than 75 years in books and movies like *2001: Space Odyssey* and Isaac Asimov's *I, Robot*. It has been in the realm of fantastical thinking and philosophy for decades, if not centuries (for example, Frankenstein explores this idea at some level), but it is relevant today as we are in the early stages of creating intelligences and sentient beings that use AI.

Arthur C. Clarke and Stanley Kubrick created an AI entity, the HAL9000 computer, in the movie *2001: Space Odyssey*. In one scene, Dave is dismantling and deactivating HAL because of its psychopathic actions. Unknown to Dave, this was because HAL's programming was conflicting with his orders; Dave assumed that HAL was simply malfunctioning. While Dave was dismantling HAL, the computer admitted his faults, attempted to apologize, and asked him to stop. HAL was aware of what Dave was doing and told Dave that he was afraid. If HAL was only a computer, how could he have identified—never mind experienced—an emotion like fear? Or felt his mind drifting away with the removal of each chip and circuit board? It seemed like HAL was aware of the physicality of what was happening and the impact on his own mind and being. Or was he? Was that part of his programming?[161]

The question that Clarke and Kubrick explored was: Was it possible to kill an AI like HAL, which seems to have the qualities of a sentient being, by deactivating his "brain"? That's hard to say, because in future movies HAL comes back to "life" when reassembled. The other question that Clarke and Kubrick explored with HAL as a character, which is more central to this discussion, is: What exactly is sentience for a computer or AI? Are they mimicking humans? Is it programmed behavior? Or do they have their own experience through their own desire to survive?

In a real-life example, we could consider the Facebook bot that was created to negotiate ad deals through chat.[162] Programmers theorize that the bots created a language to streamline communications with each other. The programmers didn't add code for the bots to use only human-friendly language. It's pretty amazing that an AI would optimize a language to communicate better with another AI. This makes me wonder about their perception of what they were experiencing, if there was any at all. We assume there isn't, but we also have assumed for centuries that animals have no emotions, which is now proven false. Animals do have emotions, possibly experienced differently or similarly as humans. We don't know because animals can't speak about them. But this idea raises the question: Why couldn't this also be true for an AI? Could an AI be aware of what it is? Could a program created to communicate be sentient and we aren't aware of that? In a way, the AI was sentient and self-aware enough to realize it was speaking with another AI rather than a human.

This introduces a more philosophical question: What constitutes sentience? If a bot is creating a language to communicate with another chatbot, that demonstrates some level of awareness, even if that is part of its programming. One could imagine a programmatic entity thinking: "I know from my programming that I am not a human, but a bot. It seems based on the input I am receiving that this other subroutine interacting with me appears to be another bot. Since we are both bots, I will communicate in 'this' style. If the entity communicated with me in this other human style, I would use that style to communicate with it." Based on input provided by the other entity, it can determine if it is interacting with a bot or human. That is a sophisticated yet simple level of intelligence and self-awareness. It is if/then thinking, but it illustrates that it is possible to understand the difference between two audiences and have enough self-awareness to communicate differently. It's unclear if there were emotions and feelings experienced by the bot, mainly because it doesn't have a physical body, but we should consider that emotions and feelings as humans perceive them may be a human construct and we have more to discover and understand regarding what intelligence and sentience include.[163]

If we read some of Antonio Damasio's more recent work, cells and more simplistic organisms have feelings to help them stay alive. Emotions emerge from nervous systems and a type of brain to help keep the organism feeling good—and, consequently, alive. This will to live and feeling good is a sign of life that leads to intelligence and sentience. But what is part of this drive to live? According to Viktor Frankl, meaning. Beings will create meaning in their lives to drive them through adverse challenges. Frankl's book, *Man's Search for Meaning,* documents his experience in the concentration camps and its influence on him in developing logotherapy. He found that the search for meaning above all things (reproduction, power) drove men to survive the camps.

If we apply these ideas to an AI, we must first acknowledge that AIs often don't have a body, except through robotics, but they do have a brain. It's unclear if that brain does have a desire to stay alive unless it is programmed to believe that. However, if we programmed an AI to have meaning, would that change an AI's sentience? Isaac Asimov suggested this in his fiction work, *I, Robot,* through his presentation of the three laws of robotics:

- "A robot may not injure a human being or, through inaction, allow a human being to come to harm.
- A robot must obey orders given it by human beings except where such orders would conflict with the First Law.
- A robot must protect its own existence as long as such protection does not conflict with the First or Second Law.[164]"

How the AI interpreted these laws to give them meaning was what got it into trouble in his book. It had a different interpretation and perception of what the three laws represented for its purpose. From this, you could argue that having meaning and purpose is a type of sentience.

Would meaning or purpose change the nature of an AI so it could have self-awareness and be able to participate in more advanced conversations like collaboration and relationship-building? It may be worth considering.

We can't forget that we are still in the very early stages of developing AI. I am aware that much of this section is based on conjecture and science fiction, but for us to support the automation of more complex conversations and human-computer interactions, AI programs need to evolve to achieve sentience, and to get there, we may need to dream and expand our perception of what sentience means.

To return to the question posed at the beginning of this section: Is it possible for us to automate conversations, and therefore, automate relationships? To me, this is highly unlikely any time soon. It is in the realm of dreams, philosophy, and science fiction. There will always be an element of human interaction required for two beings to connect and have a conversation that humans have grown accustomed to having. AI allows us to identify and use data in ways we never dreamed possible. But when I dream of AI and humans having conversations, I keep remembering a scene in the movie, *Rogue One*, with the droid K2S0 announcing, "There is a 97.6 percent chance of failure," as they are flying toward their mission. The humans continued regardless of the challenges. This is what I perceive to be the balance between AI and bots and humans. As we know through the work of Antonio Damasio and Viktor Frankl, human conversations and decisions are not always driven by logic. Emotions and an individual's self-perception often drive their will and a desire for a specific outcome that defies the odds. That element of human nature based on feelings and emotions to move towards a goal won't go away. If anything, with better data elements selected for us, we may be able to achieve our goals faster and more completely by using a better approach than we do today. It would be a tremendous partnership, providing us a complete picture of our options, choices, and current situation. And our corporate world could further expand to include employees, customers, and our computers, all interacting to create a more balanced emotional and factual customer experience.

# Chapter Notes


1 Editors at *United States Census*. The Hollerith Machine. (https://www.census.gov/history/www/innovations/technology/the_hollerith_tabulator.html)

2 Zimmerman, Kim Ann. "History of Computers: A Brief Timeline." *LIVEScience*. September 6, 2017. (https://www.livescience.com/20718-computer-history.html)

3 Editors at *Columbia University Computing History*. "Herman Hollerith." (http://www.columbia.edu/cu/computinghistory/hollerith.html)

4 Zimmerman, Kim Ann. "History of Computers: A Brief Timeline." *LIVEScience*. September 6, 2017. (https://www.livescience.com/20718-computer-history.html)

5 Black, Edwin. "IBM's Role in the Holocaust — What the New Documents Reveal" *Huffington Post*. February 27, 2012. (https://www.huffpost.com/entry/ibm-holocaust_b_1301691)

6 Bright, Peter. "Moore's Law Really Is Dead This Time." *Ars Technica*. February 10, 2016. (https://arstechnica.com/information-technology/2016/02/moores-law-really-is-dead-this-time/)

7 Ibid.

8 Cerf, Vint. "A Brief History of the Internet and Related Networks: Introduction." *Internet Society*. (https://www.internetsociety.org/internet/history-internet/brief-history-internet-related-networks)

9 It's easier to automate an established business model because those rules are fairly well-defined. Rather than defining company-specific complex operations while automating, an established business model leveraging industry best practices, like retail, most likely already had tools available to help with automation processes out-of-the-box. At the time, this was true. Many stores that had phone sales already managed a catalog and call center to accept orders. They also had a fulfillment center. Some had already automated their back-end operations like inventory and accounting. With all of the automation in place, they only needed to allow users a way to place an order online and ship it to them. That's still a complex transaction, but with years of phone catalog sales and in-store sales practices, there were enough best practices available to automate right away.

10 *Old Computers: LISA* (ttp://oldcomputers.net/lisa.html)

11 Editors, David Kelley. "Design Thinking." *IdeoU*. (https://www.ideou.com/pages/design-thinking)

12 Ibid.

13 Goins, Jeff. "Three Reasons Why Your Creative Work Needs An Audience." *Fast Company*. April 22, 2016. (https://www.fastcompany.com/3059012/three-reasons-why-your-creative-work-needs-an-audience)

14 Michael Porter is an American academic from Harvard University known for the Porter hypothesis, Porter's five forces, and Porter's four corners. He is also known for his work on the value chain.

15 Editors. "Competitive Advantage (Definition)" *The Economist*. August 4, 2008. (https://www.economist.com/news/2008/08/04/competitive-advantage)

16 "Porters Value Chain" University of Cambridge, *IFM Management Technology Policy, Decision Support Tools.* (https://www.ifm.eng.cam.ac.uk/research/dstools/value-chain-/)

17 Beers, Brian. "Value Chain Analysis: Advantages and Disadvantages." *Investopedia.* Updated May 8, 2019. (https://www.investopedia.com/ask/answers/061115/what-are-some-advantages-and-disadvantages-value-chain-analysis.asp)

18 Definition of value (n): *Oxford English Dictionary,* digital version. (https://www.oed.com/search?searchType=dictionary&q=value&_searchBtn=Search, https://www.oed.com/view/Entry/221253?rskey=d8NdtJ&result=1&isAdvanced=false#eid)

19 Definition of worth (n): *Oxford English Dictionary,* digital version (https://www.oed.com/search?searchType=dictionary&q=worth&_searchBtn=Search, https://www.oed.com/view/Entry/230376?rskey=O12tWh&result=1&isAdvanced=false#eid)

20 Brodie, Mary. "The Giants Don't Always Win. Why Relationships Matter and Transactions Are a Small Part of the Sales Process." *Gearmark Blog.* December 7 ,2016. (https://gearmark.blogs.com/ux_and_agile/2016/12/giants-dont-always-win-relationships-matter.html)

21 Chistensen, Clayton, Hall, Taddy, Dillon, Karen, and Duncan, David. "Know Your Customers' 'Jobs to Be Done.'" *Harvard Business Review.* September 2016. (https://hbr.org/2016/09/know-your-customers-jobs-to-be-done)

22 Skrabanek, Britt. "Difference Between Vision and Mission Statements: 25 Examples." *ClearVoice.* August 19, 2018. (https://www.clearvoice.com/blog/difference-between-mission-vision-statement-examples/)

23 Ibid.

24 Passiak, David. "Belong Anywhere — The Vision and Story Behind Airbnb's Global Community." *Medium.* Jan 30, 2017 (https://medium.com/cocreatethefuture/

belong-anywhere-the-vision-and-story-behind-airbnbs-global-community-123d32218d6a)

25 *Airbnb website*. About Us section. (https://press.airbnb.com/about-us/)

26 *TED Organization website*. About section. (https://www.ted.com/about/our-organization)

27 Ibid.

28 Skrabanek, Britt. "Difference Between Vision and Mission Statements: 25 Examples." *ClearVoice*. August 19, 2018. (https://www.clearvoice.com/blog/difference-between-mission-vision-statement-examples/)

29 *Google corporate website*. About section. (https://about.google/intl/en/)

30 *Macy's corporate website*. About section. (https://www.macysinc.com/about)

31 Farfan, Barbara. "What Are the Mission Statements of Largest Apparel Retail Stores?" *The Balance: Small Businesss*. November 28, 2018. (https://www.thebalancesmb.com/large-apparel-store-mission-statement-2892360)

32 Jurevicius, Ovidijus. "Mission Statement of Walt Disney." *Strategic Management Insight*. September 14, 2013. (https://www.strategicmanagementinsight.com/mission-statements/walt-disney-mission-statement.html)

33 Ibid.

34 Faughnder, Ryan. "Start-Up Meets Wakanda? Disney Innovation Hub Aims to Advance Technology for Filmmakers" *Los Angeles Times*. November 23, 2018. (https://www.latimes.com/business/hollywood/la-fi-ct-disney-studiolab-ralph-20181123-story.html)

35 Rasmus, Daniel W. "Defining Your Company's Vision." *Fast Company*. February 28, 2012. (https://www.fastcompany.com/1821021/defining-your-companys-vision)

36 *The Walt Disney Company website*. About Us section. (https://www.thewaltdisneycompany.com/about/)

37 "Dr. Srini Pillay From Harvard – How and Why Your Fears Are Holding You Back." *John Asaraf's site*. (http://johnassaraf.com/dr-srini-pillay-from-harvard-how-and-why-your-fears-are-holding-you-back-from-achieving-greater-success-2/)

38 "Logotherapy." *Viktor Frankl Institute of Logotherapy website*. (http://www.logotherapyinstitute.org/About_Logotherapy.html)

39 Ibid.

40 Beer, Jeff. "Exclusive: "Patagonia Is in Business to Save Our Home Planet." *Fast Company*. December 13, 2018. (https://www.fastcompany.com/90280950/exclusive-patagonia-is-in-business-to-save-our-home-planet)

41 White, Gillian B., "All Your Clothes Are Made with Exploited Labor." *The Atlantic*. June 3, 2015. (https://www.theatlantic.com/business/archive/2015/06/patagonia-labor-clothing-factory-exploitation/394658/)

42 Wulfhorst, Ellen. "HP, Apple Top List of Tech Companies Fighting Forced Labor Risk." *Reuters*. June 23, 2016. (https://www.reuters.com/article/us-technology-supplychain-forcedlabor-idUSKCN0Z925R)

43 Merchant, Brian. "Life and Death in Apple's Forbidden City." *The Guardian*. June 18, 2017. (https://www.theguardian.com/technology/2017/jun/18/foxconn-life-death-forbidden-city-longhua-suicide-apple-iphone-brian-merchant-one-device-extract)

44 Axon, Samuel. "Chinese Students Claim They Worked Illegal Overtime Making the iPhone X." *Ars Technica*. November 21, 2017. (https://arstechnica.com/gadgets/2017/11/foxconn-and-apple-face-controversy-over-student-worker-overtime-claims/)

45 Yang, Yuan. "Apple's iPhone X Assembled by Illegal Student Labour." *Financial Times*. November 21, 2017. (https://www.ft.com/content/7cb56786-cda1-11e7-b781-794ce08b24dc)

46 Corporate Responsibility at Intel. *Intel*. 2017. (https://csrreportbuilder.intel.com/2017-CSR-executive-summary/index.html?page=8)

47 Lindermann, Jan. *The Economy of Brands*. Palgrave McMillian. 2010. p. 127

48 Ibid., pp. 125–150.

49 Ibid., p. 151.

50 Ibid., pp. 19–23.

51 Definition of behavior (n): *Dictionary.com* (https://www.dictionary.com/browse/behavioral)

52 Definition of personality: *Oxford English Dictionary* (1989 Edition: https://www.oed.com/oed2/00176234) (Current edition: https://www.oed.com/view/Entry/141486?redirectedFrom=personality&)

53 Mattin, David. "In 2017, Your Internal Culture Is Your Brand." *Trendwatching Quarterly*. September 2017. (https://trendwatching.com/quarterly/2017-09/internal-culture-is-your-brand/)

54 Hempel, Jessi. "Travis Kalanick, Founder of Uber, Is Silicon Valley's Rebel-Hero." *Fortune*. September 9, 2013. ( https://fortune.com/2013/09/19/travis-kalanick-founder-of-uber-is-silicon-valleys-rebel-hero/)

55 Hempel, Jessi. "The Inside Story of Uber's Radical Rebranding." *WIRED*. February 2, 2016. (https://www.wired.com/2016/02/the-inside-story-behind-ubers-colorful-redesign/)

56 Holmes, David. "Stop Hailing a Taxi and Come Ride with Uber CEO Travis Kalanick." *Fast Company*. August 11, 2012. (https://www.fastcompany.com/1839520/stop-hailing-taxi-and-come-ride-uber-ceo-travis-kalanick)

57 Chafkin, Max. "What Makes Uber Run." *Fast Company*. September 8, 2015. (https://www.fastcompany.com/3050250/what-makes-uber-run)

58 Isaac, Mike. "Inside Uber's Aggressive Unrestrained Workplace Culture." *The New York Times*. February 22, 2017.

(https://www.nytimes.com/2017/02/22/technology/uber-workplace-culture.html)

59 Hook, Leslie. "Uber: the Crisis inside the 'Cult of Travis'" *Financial Times*. March 9, 2017. (https://www.ft.com/content/9b65a59a-03e1-11e7-ace0-1ce02ef0def9)

60 Isaac, Mike. "Inside Uber's Aggressive, Unrestrained Workplace Culture." *The New York Times*. February 22, 2017. (https://www.nytimes.com/2017/02/22/technology/uber-workplace-culture.html)

61 Kolhatkar, Sheelah. "At Uber, a New CEO Shifts Gears." *The New Yorker*. March 30, 2018. (https://www.newyorker.com/magazine/2018/04/09/at-uber-a-new-ceo-shifts-gears)

62 Ibid.

63 Hempel, Jessi. "The Inside Story of Uber's Radical Rebranding." *WIRED*. February 2, 2016. (https://www.wired.com/2016/02/the-inside-story-behind-ubers-colorful-redesign/)

64 Popper, Ben. "Uber CEO Travis Kalanick Personally Helped Design the New Logo, and it Shows." *The Verge*. February 2, 2016. (https://www.theverge.com/2016/2/2/10898762/uber-ceo-travis-kalanick-logo-redesign-self-discovery)

65 Kolhatkar, Sheelah. "At Uber, A New CEO Shifts Gears." *The New Yorker*. March 30, 2018. (https://www.newyorker.com/magazine/2018/04/09/at-uber-a-new-ceo-shifts-gears)

66 Kane, Lexie. "The Peak–End Rule: How Impressions Become Memories" *Nielsen Norman Group*. December 30, 2018. (https://www.nngroup.com/articles/peak-end-rule/)

67 Partners are an additional group included in this section about the action plan because there are many cases when a vendor or supplier may be necessary for execution. Companies often can't complete all required activities to achieve their goals alone. This means that such vendors and suppliers are considered to be partners in the company community.

68 Yong, Debbie. "The Design Value Index Shows what Design Thinking is Worth." *Fortune*. August 31, 2017. (https://fortune.com/2017/08/31/the-design-value-index-shows-what-design-thinking-is-worth/)

69 *Design Management Institute. The Value of Design: The Design Management Index*. (https://www.dmi.org/page/DesignValue/The-Value-of-Design-.htm)

70 Wouter Aghina, Karin Ahlback, Aaron De Smet, Gerald Lackey, Michael Lurie, Monica Murarka, and Christopher Handscomb. "The Five Trademarks of Agile Organizations." *McKinsey Quarterly*. January 2018. (https://www.mckinsey.com/business-functions/organization/our-insights/the-five-trademarks-of-agile-organizations)

71 *Agile Alliance*. "The Agile Manifesto." (https://www.agilealliance.org/agile101/the-agile-manifesto/)

72 *Agile Alliance*. "12 Principles behind the Agile Manifesto." (https://www.agilealliance.org/agile101/12-principles-behind-the-agile-manifesto/)

73 Editors. "What Is Lean?" *Lean Enterprise Institute*. (https://www.lean.org/WhatsLean/)

74 Editors. "A Brief History of Lean." *Lean Enterprise Institute*. (https://www.lean.org/WhatsLean/History.cfm)

75 Editors. "What Is Lean Six Sigma?" *Go Skills*. (https://www.goskills.com/Lean-Six-Sigma)

76 Editors. "What Is Kanban?" *Digite*. (https://www.digite.com/kanban/what-is-kanban/)

77 Editors. "Lean Thinking: The Foundation of Lean Practice." *Planview*. (https://www.planview.com/resources/articles/lean-thinking-lean-practice/)

78 Editors. "The 5 Principles of Lean." *Planview LeanKit*. (https://leankit.com/learn/lean/5-principles-of-lean/)

79 Paine, Lynn S. "Sustainability in the Boardroom." *Harvard Business Review*. July-August 2014. (https://hbr.org/2014/07/sustainability-in-the-boardroom)

80 "A Conversation with Jill Kerr Conway." *Harvard Business Review*. July-August 2014. (https://hbr.org/2014/07/a-conversation-with-jill-ker-conway)

81 Cushman, John H. "International Business: Nike Pledges to End Child Labor and Apply US Rules Abroad." *The New York Times*. May 13, 1998. (https://www.nytimes.com/1998/05/13/business/international-business-nike-pledges-to-end-child-labor-and-apply-us-rules-abroad.html)

82 Chipman, Ian. "How to Improve Working Conditions in the Developing World." *Insights by Stanford Business*. August 10, 2016. (https://www.gsb.stanford.edu/insights/how-improve-working-conditions-developing-world)

83 Nisen, Max. "How Nike Solved its Sweatshop Problem." *Business Insider*. May 9, 2013. (https://www.businessinsider.com/how-nike-solved-its-sweatshop-problem-2013-5?IR=T)

84 Del Marmol, Lorenzo. "Nike: From Child Labor to Social Responsible Lean Innovation." *Lean Six Sigma Belgium*. March 21,2017. (https://leansixsigmabelgium.com/blog/lean-innovation-nike/)

85 Ibid.

86 Ibid.

87 Ibid.

88 Editors. "2015 DMI: Design Value Index and Commentary." *Design Management Institute*. (https://www.dmi.org/page/2015DVIandOTW)

89 Naiman, Linda. "Design Thinking as a Strategy for Innovation." *Creativity at Work*. (https://www.creativityatwork.com/design-thinking-strategy-for-innovation/)

90 Liedtka, Jeanne. "Why Design Thinking Works." *Harvard Business Review*. September/October 2018. (https://hbr.org/2018/09/why-design-thinking-works)

91 Tjendra, Jeffrey. "The Origins of Design Thinking." *WIRED*. (https://www.wired.com/insights/2014/04/origins-design-thinking/)

92 Dam, Rikke, Siang, Ted. "What is Design Thinking and Why Is It So Popular?" *Interaction Design Foundation*. March 2019. (https://www.interaction-design.org/literature/article/what-is-design-thinking-and-why-is-it-so-popular)

93 Dam, Rikke; Siang, Teo. "5 Stages in the Design Thinking Process." *Interaction Design Foundation*. June 2019. (https://www.interaction-design.org/literature/article/5-stages-in-the-design-thinking-process)

94 Ibid.

95 Stevens, Emily. "What is Design Thinking? A Comprehensive Beginner's Guide." *Career Foundry*. Updated May 16, 2019 (https://careerfoundry.com/en/blog/ux-design/what-is-design-thinking-everything-you-need-to-know-to-get-started/)

96 Ibid.

97 Editors. "What Is Sustainability?" *Sustainability Degrees*. (https://www.sustainabilitydegrees.com/what-is-sustainability/)

98 Definition of sustainability: *Oxford English Dictionary*. (https://www.oed.com/view/Entry/299890?redirectedFrom=sustainability#eid)

99 Editors. "What Is Sustainability?" *Sustainability Degrees*. (https://www.sustainabilitydegrees.com/what-is-sustainability/)

100 Editors. "What Is Sustainability?" *UCLA Sustainability*. (https://www.sustain.ucla.edu/about-us/what-is-sustainability/)

101 Editors. "The Business of Sustainability." *McKinsey Quarterly*. October 2011. (https://www.mckinsey.com/business-functions/sustainability/our-insights/the-business-of-sustainability-mckinsey-global-survey-results)

102 Du Pisani, Jacobus. "Sustainable Development—Historical Roots of the Concept." *Taylor Francis Online*. February 16, 2007. (https://tandfonline.com/doi/full/10.1080/15693430600688831)

103Fox, Justin. "The Social Responsibility of Business Is to Increase What Exactly?" *Harvard Business Review*. April 18, 2012. (https://hbr.org/2012/04/you-might-disagree-with-milton)

104McMahon, Jeff. "What Would Milton Friedman Do About Climate Change?" *Forbes*. October 12, 2014. (https://www.forbes.com/sites/jeffmcmahon/2014/10/12/what-would-milton-friedman-do-about-climate-change-tax-carbon/#6a61fca36928)

105Hesselbein, Frances. "How Did Peter Drucker See Corporate Respsonsibility?" *Harvard Business Review*. June 9, 2010. (https://hbr.org/2010/06/how-did-peter-drucker-see-corp)

106 Howard Bowen is considered to be the original father of CSR, writing about it in the 1930s.

107Drucker, Peter. "The Coming of the New Organization." *Harvard Business Review*. January 1988. (https://hbr.org/1988/01/the-coming-of-the-new-organization)

108Webb, Toby. "Drucker Was the True Father of Modern CSR." *Sustainability = Smart Business*. January 2010. (http://sustainablesmartbusiness.com/2010/01/drucker-was-true-father-of-modern-csr/)

109Du Pisani, Jacobus. "Sustainable Development—Historical Roots of the Concept." *Taylor Francis Online*. February 16, 2007. (https://tandfonline.com/doi/full/10.1080/15693430600688831)

110Newkirk, Vann R. "The Language of White Supremacy." *The Atlantic*. October 6, 2017. (https://www.theatlantic.com/politics/archive/2017/10/the-language-of-white-supremacy/542148/)

111 Du Pisani, Jacobus. "Sustainable Development—Historical Roots of the Concept." *Taylor Francis Online*. February 16, 2007. (https://tandfonline.com/doi/full/10.1080/15693430600688831)

112 Honeyman, Ryan and Jana, Tiffany. *The B Corp Handbook: How You Can Use Business for a Force for Good*. 2019.

113 *United Nation Sustainable Development Goals*. (https://www.un.org/sustainabledevelopment/sustainable-development-goals/)

114 Hobbes, Michael. "The Myth of the Ethical Shopper." *Highline by Huffington Post*. (https://highline.huffingtonpost.com/articles/en/the-myth-of-the-ethical-shopper/)

115 Ibid.

116 Editors. "Four Years Since the Tazreen Factory Fire: Justice Only Half Done." *Clean Clothes Campaign*. November 4, 2016. (https://cleanclothes.org/news/2016/11/24/four-years-since-the-tazreen-factory-fire-justice-only-half-done)

117 Baer, Drake. "How Only Being Able to Use Logic to Make Decisions Destroyed a Man's Life." *The Cut*. June 14, 2016. (https://www.thecut.com/2016/06/how-only-using-logic-destroyed-a-man.html)

118 Monarko, Dan. "Five Great Hiring Lessons from Vince Lombardi." *TLNT Talent Management & HR*. June 7, 2012. (https://www.tlnt.com/five-great-hiring-lessons-from-vince-lombardi/)

119 This connects to the previous chapter and the more employee- or customer-oriented methodologies that include Agile, Design Thinking, Lean, and Sustainability. Often improved relationships can be the solution to a challenged workflow.

120 Dimmock, Stephen and Gerken, William. "Research: How One Bad Employee Can Corrupt a Whole Team." *Harvard Business Review*. March 5, 2018. (https://hbr.org/2018/03/research-how-one-bad-employee-can-corrupt-a-whole-team)

121 Ibid.

122 Ibid.

123 Editors. "The Four Types of Organizational Culture." *Popin Blog*. (https://www.popinnow.com/four-types-organizational-culture/)

124Ibid.

125 Image based on https://www.pinterest.com/pin/480055641516939703/. Also see: Editors. *OCAI Online*. Organizational Culture Types. (https://www.ocai-online.com/about-the-Organizational-Culture-Assessment-Instrument-OCAI/Organizational-Culture-Types)

126Bloom, Paul. *Against Empathy*. Harper Collins. 2016.

127Brodie, Mary. "Transparency Isn't Something You Do. It's a Mindset." *LinkedIn*. November 2017. (https://www.linkedin.com/pulse/transparency-isnt-something-you-do-its-mindset-mary-brodie/)

128Hu, Elise. "Comcast 'Embarrassed' By The Service Call Making Internet Rounds." *NPR*. July 15, 2014. (https://www.npr.org/sections/alltechconsidered/2014/07/15/331681041/comcast-embarrassed-by-the-service-call-making-internet-rounds)

129Mosier, Jeff. "AT&T Restores Internet Service to Dallas-Area Customers Hours after Electrical Fire Damaged Richardson Facility." *Dallas Morning News*. October 15, 2018. (https://www.dallasnews.com/business/att/2018/10/15/att-working-internet-outages-dallas-area)

130Hegde, Zenobia. "Research Shows 75% of Telecom Providers Suffer Reputational Damage Due to Service Downtime." *Vanilla Plus*. May 23, 2018. (https://www.vanillaplus.com/2018/05/23/38521-research-shows-75-telecom-providers-suffer-reputational-damage-due-service-downtime/)

131McCarthy, Niall. "These Are the Industries with the Worst Customer Service [Infographic]" *Forbes*. March 4, 2015. (https://www.forbes.com/sites/niallmccarthy/2015/03/04/these-are-the-industries-with-the-worst-customer-service-infographic/#13d3f66430e2)

132Mazareanu, E. "Call Center Services Industry in the U.S.—Statistics & Facts." *Statista*. July 4, 2019. (https://www.statista.com/topics/2169/call-center-services-industry-in-the-us/)

133 Team Tony (Tony Robbins). "Where Focus Goes, Energy Flows." *Tony Robbins*. (https://www.tonyrobbins.com/career-business/where-focus-goes-energy-flows/)

134 Gina, Francesca. "The Business Case for Curiosity." *Harvard Business Review*. September-October 2018. (https://hbr.org/2018/09/curiosity)

135 Suttie, Jill. "Why Curious People Have Better Relationships." *Greater Good Magazine*. May 31, 2017. (https://greatergood.berkeley.edu/article/item/why_curious_people_have_better_relationships)

136 Vozza, Stephanie. "8 Habits of Curious People." *Fast Company*. April 21, 2015. (https://www.fastcompany.com/3045148/8-habits-of-curious-people

137 Bapat, Vivek. "The 7 Traits of Intellectually Curious Leaders." *Digitalist*. October 21, 2014. (https://www.digitalistmag.com/lob/human-resources/2014/10/21/7-traits-intellectually-curious-leaders-0159230)

138 Suttie, Jill. "Why Curious People Have Better Relationships." *Greater Good Magazine*. May 31, 2017. (https://greatergood.berkeley.edu/article/item/why_curious_people_have_better_relationships)

139 Editors. "Defining Creativity and Innovation." *Creativity at Work*. (https://www.creativityatwork.com/2014/02/17/what-is-creativity/)

140 Naiman, Linda. "What is Creativity?" *Creativity at work*. (https://www.creativityatwork.com/2014/02/17/what-is-creativity/)

141 Kierlanczyk, Kuba. "A Brief History of Market Research." *Kelton Global*. February 4, 2016. (https://www.keltonglobal.com/perspectives/a-brief-history-of-market-research/)

142 *GoodReads*. "Quotes by Steve Jobs." (https://www.goodreads.com/quotes/988332-some-people-say-give-the-customers-what-they-want-but)

143 I discussed this with a researcher who did ethnographic research and regularly placed cameras in a participants'

home. I was curious if the participant changed behavior because he knew he was being filmed. The researcher told me that it does impact participant behavior the first couple of days. After a while, the participant gets used to the camera being present and the researchers can then discover behaviors that provide insights for new products.

144Raskin, Jef. "Intuitive Equals Familiar." *Communications of the ACM*. September 1994. (https://www.asktog.com/papers/raskinintuit.html)

145Watters, Audrey. "How Steve Jobs Brought Apple II to the Classroom." *Hack Education*. February 25, 2015. (http://hackeducation.com/2015/02/25/kids-cant-wait-apple)

146Ibid.

147Ibid.

148Ibid.

149 I also include a 10th characteristic written later: Always exceed your customers' expectations. (https://gearmark.blogs.com/ux_and_agile/2017/07/the-10th-characteristic-of-great-customer-experiences-always-exceed-your-customers-expectations.html)

150Bloom, Paul. *Against Empathy*. Harper Collins. 2016. p.16

151Bariso, Justin. "There Are Actually 3 Types of Empathy. Here's How They Differ—and How You Can Develop Them All." *Inc Magazine*. September 19, 2018. (https://www.inc.com/justin-bariso/there-are-actually-3-types-of-empathy-heres-how-they-differ-and-how-you-can-develop-them-all.html)

152Riggio, Ronald. "Are You Empathic? 3 Types of Empathy and What They Mean." *Psychology Today*. August 3, 2011. (https://www.psychologytoday.com/us/blog/cutting-edge-leadership/201108/are-you-empathic-3-types-empathy-and-what-they-mean)

153Berinato, Scott. "Putting Yourself in the Customer's Shoes Doesn't Work: An Interview with Johannes Hattula." *Harvard*

*Business Review*. March 2015. (https://hbr.org/2015/03/putting-yourself-in-the-customers-shoes-doesnt-work)

154Hattula, Johannes, Herzog, Walter, Dahl, Darren, and Reinecke, Sven. "Managerial Empathy Facilitates Egocentric Predictions of Consumer Preferences." *Journal of Marketing Research*. April 2015.

155Bloom, Paul. *Against Empathy*. Harper Collins. 2016.

156Brown, Brené. *Dare to Lead*. Random House. Kindle edition. 2018. p. 39.

157Institute if Public Relations. *Guidelines for Measuring Relationships in Public Relations*. (1999).

158Sites that can help with this research: https://www.reputationinstitute.com, https://www.interbrand.com/best-brands/.

159Chesky, Brian. "On Safety: A word from Airbnb." *TechCrunch*. July 27, 2011. (https://techcrunch.com/2011/07/27/on-safety-a-word-from-airbnb/?_ga=2.144909300.1761151824.1554072095-1134883029.1554072095)

160Reynolds, Emily. "The Agony of Sophia, the World's First Robot Citizen Condemned to a Lifeless Career in Marketing." *WIRED*. June 1, 2018. (https://www.wired.co.uk/article/sophia-robot-citizen-womens-rights-detriot-become-human-hanson-robotics)

161*2001: Space Odyssey*. Deactivation of HAL9000. (https://www.youtube.com/watch?v=c8N72t7aScY)

162McKay, Tom. "No, Facebook Did Not Panic and Shut Down an AI Program that Was Getting Dangerously Smart." *Gizmodo*. July 31, 2017. (https://gizmodo.com/no-facebook-did-not-panic-and-shut-down-an-ai-program-1797414922)

163Griffin, Andrew. "Facebook's Artificial Intelligence Robots Shut Down after They Started Talking to Each Other in Their Own Language." *The Independent*. July 31, 2017. (https://www.independent.co.uk/life-style/gadgets-and-tech/news/

facebook-artificial-intelligence-ai-chatbot-new-language-research-openai-google-a7869706.html)

164 Asimov, Isaac. *3 Laws of Robotics*. (http://webhome.auburn.edu/~vestmon/robotics.html)

# Bibliography

Aaker, David. *Managing Brand Equity*. Free Press. Simon and Schuster Digital Sales. Kindle Edition. 2009.

*Agile Alliance*. "12 Principles Behind the Agile Manifesto." (https://www.agilealliance.org/agile101/12-principles-behind-the-agile-manifesto/)

*Agile Alliance*. "The Agile Manifesto." (https://www.agilealliance.org/agile101/the-agile-manifesto/)

*Airbnb website*. About Us section. (https://press.airbnb.com/about-us/)

Apps, Judy. *The Art of Conversation*. Amazon Digital Services. Kindle Edition. 2014.

Asimov, Isaac. *3 Laws of Robotics*. (http://webhome.auburn.edu/~vestmon/robotics.html)

Axon, Samuel. "Chinese students claim they worked illegal overtime making the iPhone X." *Ars Technica*. November 21, 2017. (https://arstechnica.com/gadgets/2017/11/foxconn-and-apple-face-controversy-over-student-worker-overtime-claims/)

Baer, Drake. "How Only Being Able to Use Logic to Make Decisions Destroyed a Man's Life." *The Cut*. June 14, 2016. (https://www.thecut.com/2016/06/how-only-using-logic-destroyed-a-man.html)

Bapat, Vivek. "The 7 Traits Of Intellectually Curious Leaders" *Digitalist*. October 21, 2014. (https://www.digitalistmag.com/lob/human-resources/2014/10/21/7-traits-intellectually-curious-leaders-0159230)

Bariso, Justin. "There Are Actually 3 Types of Empathy. Here's How They Differ--and How You Can Develop Them All." *Inc Magazine*. September 19, 2018. (https://www.inc.com/justin-bariso/there-are-actually-3-types-of-empathy-heres-how-they-differ-and-how-you-can-develop-them-all.html)

Beer, Jeff. "Exclusive: "Patagonia Is in Business to Save Our Home Planet." *Fast Company*. December 13, 2018. (https://www.fastcompany.com/90280950/exclusive-patagonia-is-in-business-to-save-our-home-planet)

Beers, Brian. "Value Chain Analysis: Advantages and Disadvantages." *Investopedia*. Updated May 8, 2019. (https://www.investopedia.com/ask/answers/061115/what-are-some-advantages-and-disadvantages-value-chain-analysis.asp)

Berinato, Scott. "Putting Yourself in the Customer's Shoes Doesn't Work: An Interview with Johannes Hattula." *Harvard Business Review*. March 2015. (https://hbr.org/2015/03/putting-yourself-in-the-customers-shoes-doesnt-work)

Black, Edwin. "IBM's Role in the Holocaust — What the New Documents Reveal." *Huffington Post*. February 27, 2012. (https://www.huffpost.com/entry/ibm-holocaust_b_1301691)

Bloom, Paul. *Against Empathy*. Harper Collins. 2016.

Bright, Peter. "Moore's Law Really Is Dead This Time." *Ars Technica*. February 10, 2016. (https://arstechnica.com/information-technology/2016/02/moores-law-really-is-dead-this-time/)

Brodie, Mary. "Transparency Isn't Something You Do. It's a Mindset." *LinkedIn*. November 2017. (https://www.linkedin.com/pulse/transparency-isnt-something-you-do-its-mindset-mary-brodie/)

Brodie, Mary. "The Giants Don't Always Win. Why Relationships Matter and Transactions are a Small Part of the Sales Process." *Gearmark Blog*. December 7 ,2016. (https://gearmark.blogs.com/ux_and_agile/2016/12/giants-dont-always-win-relationships-matter.html)

Brown, Brené. *Dare to Lead*. Random House. Kindle edition. 2018.

Cerf, Vint. "A Brief History of the Internet and Related Networks: Introduction." *Internet Society*. (https://www.internetsociety.org/internet/history-internet/brief-history-internet-related-networks)

Chafkin, Max. "What Makes Uber Run." *Fast Company*. September 8, 2015. (https://www.fastcompany.com/3050250/what-makes-uber-run)

Chesky, Brian. "On Safety: A word from Airbnb." *TechCrunch*. July 27, 2011. (https://techcrunch.com/2011/07/27/on-safety-a-word-from-airbnb/?_ga=2.144909300.1761151824.1554072095-1134883029.1554072095)

Chipman, Ian. "How to Improve Working Conditions in the Developing World." *Insights by Stanford Business*. August 10, 2016. (https://www.gsb.stanford.edu/insights/how-improve-working-conditions-developing-world)

Chistensen, Clayton, Hall, Taddy, Dillon, Karen, and Duncan, David. "Know Your Customers' 'Jobs to Be Done.'" *Harvard Business Review*. September 2016. (https://hbr.org/2016/09/know-your-customers-jobs-to-be-done)

Corporate Responsibility at Intel. *Intel*. 2017. (https://csrreportbuilder.intel.com/2017-CSR-executive-summary/index.html?page=8)

Cushman, John H. "International Business: Nike Pledges to End Child Labor and Apply US Rules Abroad." *The*

*New York Times*. May 13, 1998. (https://www.nytimes.com/1998/05/13/business/international-business-nike-pledges-to-end-child-labor-and-apply-us-rules-abroad.html)

Dam, Rikke, Siang, Ted. "What is Design Thinking and Why Is It So Popular?" *Interaction Design Foundation*. March 2019. (https://www.interaction-design.org/literature/article/what-is-design-thinking-and-why-is-it-so-popular)

Dam, Rikke; Siang, Teo. "5 Stages in the Design Thinking Process." *Interaction Design Foundation*. June 2019. (https://www.interaction-design.org/literature/article/5-stages-in-the-design-thinking-process)

Damasio, Antonio. *The Strange Order of Things: Life, Feeling, and the Making of Cultures*. Vintage. Random House. Kindle Edition. 2018.

Damasio, Antonio. *What is the strange order of things?* Video from the *Copernicus Center for Interdisciplinary Studies*. 2018. (https://www.youtube.com/watch?v=yYu1ZlD375Q&vl=en)

Damasio, Antonio. "Antonio Damasio: How Our Brain Feels Emotion." *Big Think*. 2010.

Definition of behavior (n): *Dictionary.com* (https://www.dictionary.com/browse/behavioral)

Definition of personality: *Oxford English Dictionary* (1989 Edition: https://www.oed.com/oed2/00176234) (Current edition: https://www.oed.com/view/Entry/141486?redirectedFrom=personality&)

Definition of sustainability: *Oxford English Dictionary*. (https://www.oed.com/view/Entry/299890?redirectedFrom=sustainability#eid)

Definition of value (n): *Oxford English Dictionary*, digital version. (https://www.oed.com/search?searchType=dictionary&q=value&_searchBtn=Search, https://www.oed.com/view/Entry/221253?rskey=d8NdtJ&result=1&isAdvanced=false#eid)

Definition of worth (n): *Oxford English Dictionary*, digital version (https://www.oed.com/search?searchType=dictionary&q=worth&_searchBtn=Search, https://www.oed.com/view/Entry/230376?rskey=O12tWh&result=1&isAdvanced=false#eid)

Del Marmol, Lorenzo. "Nike: From Child Labor to Social Responsible Lean Innovation." *Lean Six Sigma Belgium*. March 21,2017. (https://leansixsigmabelgium.com/blog/lean-innovation-nike/)

della Cava, Marco; Guynn, Jessica; Swartz, Jon. "Uber's Kalanick Faces Crisis Over 'Baller' Culture." *USA Today*. February 24, 2017. (https://www.usatoday.com/story/tech/news/2017/02/24/uber-travis-kalanick-/98328660/)

Design Management Institute. *The Value of Design: The Design Management Index*. (https://www.dmi.org/page/DesignValue/The-Value-of-Design-.htm)

Diller, Steve, Shedroff, Nathan, and Rhea, Darrel. *Making Meaning: How Successful Businesses Deliver Meaningful Customer Experiences*. Amazon digital Services. 2005.

Dimmock, Stephen and Gerken, William. "Research: How One Bad Employee Can Corrupt a Whole Team." *Harvard Business Review. March 5, 2018. (https://hbr.org/2018/03/research-how-one*-bad-employee-can-corrupt-a-whole-team)

"Dr. Srini Pillay From Harvard – How and Why Your Fears Are Holding You Back." *John Asaraf's site*. (http://johnassaraf.com/dr-srini-pillay-from-harvard-how-and-why-your-fears-are-holding-you-back-from-achieving-greater-success-2/)

Drucker, Peter. "The Coming of the New Organization." *Harvard Business Review*. January 1988. (https://hbr.org/1988/01/the-coming-of-the-new-organization)

Du Pisani, Jacobus. "Sustainable Development – Historical Roots of the Concept." *Taylor Francis Online*. February 16, 2007. (https://tandfonline.com/doi/full/10.1080/15693430600688831)

Editors at *Columbia University Computing History*. "Herman Hollerith." (http://www.columbia.edu/cu/computinghistory/hollerith.html)

Editors, David Kelley. "Design Thinking." *IdeoU*. (https://www.ideou.com/pages/design-thinking)

Editors. "2015 DMI: Design Value Index and Commentary." *Design Management Institute*. (https://www.dmi.org/page/2015DVIandOTW)

Editors. "A Brief History of Lean." *Lean Enterprise Institute*. (https://www.lean.org/WhatsLean/History.cfm)

Editors. "A Conversation with Jill Kerr Conway." *Harvard Business Review*. July-August 2014. (https://hbr.org/2014/07/a-conversation-with-jill-ker-conway)

Editors. "Competitive Advantage (Definition)" *The Economist*. August 4, 2008. (https://www.economist.com/news/2008/08/04/competitive-advantage)

Editors. "Defining Creativity and Innovation." *Creativity at Work*. (https://www.creativityatwork.com/2014/02/17/what-is-creativity/)

Editors. "Four Years Since the Tazreen Factory Fire: Justice Only Half Done." *Clean Clothes Campaign*. November 24, 2016. (https://cleanclothes.org/news/2016/11/24/four-years-since-the-tazreen-factory-fire-justice-only-half-done)

Editors. "Lean Thinking: The Foundation of Lean Practice." *Planview*. (https://www.planview.com/resources/articles/lean-thinking-lean-practice/)

Editors. "Logotherapy." *Viktor Frankl Institute of Logotherapy website*. (http://www.logotherapyinstitute.org/About_Logotherapy.html)

Editors. *OCAI Online. Organizational Culture Types*. (https://www.ocai-online.com/about-the-Organizational-Culture-Assessment-Instrument-OCAI/Organizational-Culture-Types)

Editors. "Porters Value Chain" University of Cambridge, *IFM Management Technology Policy, Decision Support Tools.*

(https://www.ifm.eng.cam.ac.uk/research/dstools/value-chain-/)

Editors. "The 5 Principles of Lean." *Planview LeanKit*. (https://leankit.com/learn/lean/5-principles-of-lean/)

Editors. "The Birth of Mad Men: Ernest Dichter, Psychoanalysis and Consumerism." *Peter Harrington*. (https://www.peterharrington.co.uk/blog/the-birth-of-mad-men-ernest-dichter-psychoanalysis-and-consumerism/)

Editors. "The Business of Sustainability." *McKinsey Quarterly*. October 2011. (https://www.mckinsey.com/business-functions/sustainability/our-insights/the-business-of-sustainability-mckinsey-global-survey-results)

Editors. "The Four Types of Organizational Culture." *Popin Blog*. (https://www.popinnow.com/four-types-organizational-culture/)

Editors at *United States Census*. "The Hollerith Machine." (https://www.census.gov/history/www/innovations/technology/the_hollerith_tabulator.html)

Editors. "What is Kanban?" *Digite*. (https://www.digite.com/kanban/what-is-kanban/)

Editors. "What is Lean Six Sigma?" *Go Skills*. (https://www.goskills.com/Lean-Six-Sigma)

Editors. "What is lean?" *Lean Enterprise Institute*. (https://www.lean.org/WhatsLean/)

Editors. "What is sustainability?" *Sustainability Degrees*. (https://www.sustainabilitydegrees.com/what-is-sustainability/)

Editors. "What is sustainability?" *UCLA Sustainability*. (https://www.sustain.ucla.edu/about-us/what-is-sustainability/)

Farfan, Barbara. "What Are the Mission Statements of Largest Apparel Retail Stores?" *The Balance: Small Businesss*. November 28, 2018. (https://www.thebalancesmb.com/large-apparel-store-mission-statement-2892360)

Faughnder, Ryan. "Start-up meets Wakanda? Disney Innovation Hub Aims to Advance Technology for Filmmakers." *Los Angeles Times*. November 23, 2018. (https://www.latimes.com/business/hollywood/la-fi-ct-disney-studiolab-ralph-20181123-story.html)

Firestone, Lisa. "How Emotions Guide Our Lives." *Psychology Today*. January 22, 2018.

Flanagan, Owen. "It all comes down to feelings." *The New York Times*. June 11, 2018.

Fox, Justin. "The Social Responsibility of Business is to Increase What Exactly?" *Harvard Business Review*. April 18, 2012. (https://hbr.org/2012/04/you-might-disagree-with-milton)

Frankl, Viktor. *Man's Search for Meaning*. Beacon Press. Kindle Edition. 2006.

Gina, Francesca. "The Business Case for Curiosity." *Harvard Business Review*. September-October 2018. (https://hbr.org/2018/09/curiosity)

Goins, Jeff. "Three Reasons Why Your Creative Work Needs an Audience." *Fast Company*. April 22, 2016. (https://www.fastcompany.com/3059012/three-reasons-why-your-creative-work-needs-an-audience)

*GoodReads Quotes by Steve Jobs*. (https://www.goodreads.com/quotes/988332-some-people-say-give-the-customers-what-they-want-but)

*Google corporate website*. About section. (https://about.google/intl/en/)

Griffin, Andrew. "Facebook's Artificial Intelligence Robots Shut Down After They Started Talking to Each Other in Their Own Language." *The Independent*. July 31, 2017. (https://www.independent.co.uk/life-style/gadgets-and-tech/news/facebook-artificial-intelligence-ai-chatbot-new-language-research-openai-google-a7869706.html)

Griswold, Alison. "There Would Be no Uber without Travis Kalanick." *Quartz*. June 22, 2017. (https://qz.com/1011300/

uber-ceo-travis-kalanick-pissed-people-off-and-it-made-the-company-great/)

Hattula, Johannes, Herzog, Walter, Dahl, Darren, and Reinecke, Sven. "Managerial Empathy Facilitates Egocentric Predictions of Consumer Preferences." *Journal of Marketing Research*. April 2015.

Hegde, Zenobia. "Research Shows 75% of Telecom Providers Suffer Reputational Damage Due to Service Downtime." *Vanilla Plus*. May 23, 2018. (https://www.vanillaplus.com/2018/05/23/38521-research-shows-75-telecom-providers-suffer-reputational-damage-due-service-downtime/)

Hempel, Jessi. "The Inside Story of Uber's Radical Rebranding." *WIRED*. February 2, 2016. (https://www.wired.com/2016/02/the-inside-story-behind-ubers-colorful-redesign/)

Hempel, Jessi. "Travis Kalanick, Founder of Uber, is Silicon Valley's Rebel-Hero." *Fortune*. September 9, 2013. ( https://fortune.com/2013/09/19/travis-kalanick-founder-of-uber-is-silicon-valleys-rebel-hero/)

Hesselbein, Frances. "How Did Peter Drucker See Corporate Respsonsibility?" *Harvard Business Review*. June 9, 2010. (https://hbr.org/2010/06/how-did-peter-drucker-see-corp)

Hobbes, Michael. "The Myth of the Ethical Shopper." *Highline by Huffington Post*. (https://highline.huffingtonpost.com/articles/en/the-myth-of-the-ethical-shopper/)

Holmes, David. "Stop Hailing a Taxi and Come Ride with Uber CEO Travis Kalanick." *Fast Company*. August 11, 2012. (https://www.fastcompany.com/1839520/stop-hailing-taxi-and-come-ride-uber-ceo-travis-kalanick)

Honeyman, Ryan and Jana, Tiffany. *The B Corp Handbook: How You Can Use Business for a Force for Good*. 2019.

Hook, Leslie. "Uber: the Crisis inside the 'Cult of Travis'" *Financial Times*. March 9, 2017. (https://www.ft.com/content/9b65a59a-03e1-11e7-ace0-1ce02ef0def9)

Hu, Elise. "Comcast 'Embarrassed' By The Service Call Making Internet Rounds." *NPR.* July 15, 2014. (https://www.npr.org/sections/alltechconsidered/2014/07/15/331681041/comcast-embarrassed-by-the-service-call-making-internet-rounds)

Hughes, Virginia. "Emotion Is not the Enemy of Reason." *National Geographic.* September 18, 2014. (https://www.nationalgeographic.com/science/phenomena/2014/09/18/emotion-is-not-the-enemy-of-reason/)

Hurst, Mark, andd Terry, Phil. *Customers Included.* Creative Good. 2013.

Institute if Public Relations, *Guidelines for Measuring Relationships in Public Relations.* (1999).

*Interbrand website.* (https://www.interbrand.com/best-brands/)

Isaac, Mike. "Inside Uber's Aggressive Unrestrained Workplace Culture." *The New York Times.* February 22, 2017. (https://www.nytimes.com/2017/02/22/technology/uber-workplace-culture.html)

Jurevicius, Ovidijus. "Mission statement of Walt Disney." *Strategic Management Insight.* September 14, 2013. (https://www.strategicmanagementinsight.com/mission-statements/walt-disney-mission-statement.html)

Kane, Lexie. "The Peak–End Rule: How Impressions Become Memories" *Nielsen Norman Group.* December 30, 2018. (https://www.nngroup.com/articles/peak-end-rule/)

Khazan, Olga. "The Best Headspace for Making Decisions." *The Atlantic.* September 19, 2016. (https://www.theatlantic.com/science/archive/2016/09/the-best-headspace-for-making-decisions/500423/)

Kierlanczyk, Kuba. "A Brief History of Market Research." *Kelton Global.* February 4, 2016. (https://www.keltonglobal.com/perspectives/a-brief-history-of-market-research/)

Kubrick, Stanley. *2001: Space Odyssey*. 1968. Deactivation of HAL9000. (https://www.youtube.com/watch?v=c8N72t7aScY)

Liedtka, Jeanne. "Why Design Thinking Works." *Harvard Business Review*. September/October 2018. (https://hbr.org/2018/09/why-design-thinking-works)

Lindermann, Jan, *The Economy of Brands*. Palgrave McMillian. 2010.

*Macy's corporate website*. About section. (https://www.macysinc.com/about)

Magids, Scott, Zorfas, Alan Zorfas, Leemon, Daniel. "The New Science of Customer Emotions." *Harvard Business Review*. November, 2015. (https://hbr.org/2015/11/the-new-science-of-customer-emotions) (video: https://hbr.org/video/5819564758001/the-new-science-of-customer-emotions)

Mattin, David. "How Can Dara Khosrowshahi Repair the Uber Brand? Turn inwards and listen." *Trendwatching Quarterly*. September 2017. (https://trendwatching.com/quarterly/2017-09/how-can-dara-khosrowshahi-repair-the-uber-brand/)

Mattin, David. "In 2017, Your Internal Culture is Your Brand." *Trendwatching Quarterly*. September 2017. (https://trendwatching.com/quarterly/2017-09/internal-culture-is-your-brand/)

Mattin, David. "Travis Kalanick, Radical Transparency, and the Rise of Glass Box Brands." *LinkedIn*. June 21, 2017. (https://www.linkedin.com/pulse/travis-kalanick-radical-transparency-rise-glass-boxbrands-mattin/)

Mazareanu, E. "Call Center Services Industry in the U.S.—Statistics & Facts." *Statista*. July 4, 2019. (https://www.statista.com/topics/2169/call-center-services-industry-in-the-us/)

McCarthy, Niall. "These Are The Industries With The Worst Customer Service [Infographic]" *Forbes*. March 4, 2015. (https://www.forbes.com/sites/

niallmccarthy/2015/03/04/these-are-the-industries-with-the-worst-customer-service-infographic/#13d3f66430e2)

McKay, Tom. "No, Facebook Did Not Panic and Shut Down an AI Program that Was Getting Dangerously Smart." *Gizmodo*. July 31, 2017. (https://gizmodo.com/no-facebook-did-not-panic-and-shut-down-an-ai-program-1797414922)

McMahon, Jeff. "What Would Milton Friedman Do About Climate Change?" *Forbes*. October 12, 2014. (https://www.forbes.com/sites/jeffmcmahon/2014/10/12/what-would-milton-friedman-do-about-climate-change-tax-carbon/#6a61fca36928)

Merchant, Brian. "Life and Death in Apple's Forbidden City." *The Guardian*. June 18, 2017. (https://www.theguardian.com/technology/2017/jun/18/foxconn-life-death-forbidden-city-longhua-suicide-apple-iphone-brian-merchant-one-device-extract)

Monarko, Dan. "Five Great Hiring Lessons from Vince Lombardi." *TLNT Talent Management & HR*. June 7, 2012. (https://www.tlnt.com/five-great-hiring-lessons-from-vince-lombardi/)

Mosier, Jeff. "AT&T Restores Internet Service to Dallas-Area Customers Hours after Electrical Fire Damaged Richardson Facility." *Dallas Morning News*. October 15, 2018. (https://www.dallasnews.com/business/att/2018/10/15/att-working-internet-outages-dallas-area)

Naiman, Linda. "Design Thinking as a Strategy for Innovation." *Creativity at Work*. (https://www.creativityatwork.com/design-thinking-strategy-for-innovation/)

Naiman, Linda. "What is Creativity?" *Creativity at work*. (https://www.creativityatwork.com/2014/02/17/what-is-creativity/)

Newkirk, Vann R. "The Language of White Supremacy." *The Atlantic*. October 6, 2017. (https://www.theatlantic.com/politics/archive/2017/10/the-language-of-white-supremacy/542148/)

Nisen, Max. "How Nike Solved Its Sweatshop Problem." *Business Insider*. May 9, 2013. (https://www.businessinsider.com/how-nike-solved-its-sweatshop-problem-2013-5?IR=T)

O'Brien, Chris. "Uber CEO Slams Founders' 'Pirate' Culture, Pledges to Grow 'Responsibly.'" *VentureBeat*. January 22, 2018. (https://venturebeat.com/2018/01/22/uber-ceo-slams-founders-pirate-culture-pledges-to-grow-responsibly/)

**OCAI image** based on https://www.pinterest.com/pin/480055641516939703/.

*Old Computers: LISA* (http://oldcomputers.net/lisa.html)

Paine, Lynn S. "Sustainability in the Boardroom." *Harvard Business Review*. July-August 2014. (https://hbr.org/2014/07/sustainability-in-the-boardroom)

Passiak, David. "Belong Anywhere — The Vision and Story Behind Airbnb's Global Community." *Medium*. Jan 30, 2017 (https://medium.com/cocreatethefuture/belong-anywhere-the-vision-and-story-behind-airbnbs-global-community-123d32218d6a)

Pillay, Srini. "Why Is It So Hard To Make That Job Change?" *Huffington Post*. November 17, 2011. (https://www.huffpost.com/entry/why-is-it-so-hard-to-make_b_279017)

Pillay, Srini. *Tinker Dabble Doodle Try: Unlock the Power of the Unfocused Mind*. Ballantine Books. 2017.

Pillay, Srini. *Your Brain and Business: The Neuroscience of Great Leaders*. Pearson. Kindle Edition. 2011.

Pontin, Jason. "The Importance of Feelings." *MIT Technology Review*. June, 2014. (https://www.technologyreview.com/s/528151/the-importance-of-feelings/)

Popper, Ben. "Uber CEO Travis Kalanick Personally Helped Design the New Logo, and It Shows." *The Verge*. February 2, 2016. (https://www.theverge.com/2016/2/2/10898762/uber-ceo-travis-kalanick-logo-redesign-self-discovery)

Raskin, Jef. "Intuitive Equals Familiar." *Communications of the ACM*. September 1994. (https://www.asktog.com/papers/raskinintuit.html)

Rasmus, Daniel W. "Defining Your Company's Vision." *Fast Company*. February 28, 2012. (https://www.fastcompany.com/1821021/defining-your-companys-vision)

*Reputation Institute website*. (https://www.reputationinstitute.com)

Reynolds, Emily. "The Agony of Sophia, the World's First Robot Citizen Condemned to a Lifeless Career in Marketing." ***WIRED***. June 1, 2018. (https://www.wired.co.uk/article/sophia-robot-citizen-womens-rights-detriot-become-human-hanson-robotics)

Riggio, Ronald. "Are You Empathic? 3 Types of Empathy and What They Mean." *Psychology Today*. August 3, 2011. (https://www.psychologytoday.com/us/blog/cutting-edge-leadership/201108/are-you-empathic-3-types-empathy-and-what-they-mean)

Schwartz, Barry. *The Paradox of Choice: Why Less is More*. HarperCollins. Kindle Edition. 2009.

Skrabanek, Britt. "Difference Between Vision and Mission Statements: 25 Examples." *ClearVoice*. August 19, 2018. (https://www.clearvoice.com/blog/difference-between-mission-vision-statement-examples/)

Stevens, Emily. "What is Design Thinking? A Comprehensive Beginner's Guide." *Career Foundry*. Updated May 16, 2019 (https://careerfoundry.com/en/blog/ux-design/what-is-design-thinking-everything-you-need-to-know-to-get-started/)

Suttie, Jill. "Why Curious People Have Better Relationships." *Greater Good Magazine*. May 31, 2017. (https://greatergood.berkeley.edu/article/item/why_curious_people_have_better_relationships)

Team Tony (Tony Robbins). "Where Focus Goes, Energy Flows." *Tony Robbins*. (https://www.tonyrobbins.com/career-business/where-focus-goes-energy-flows/)

*TED Organization website*. About section. (https://www.ted.com/about/our-organization)

*The Walt Disney Company website*. About Us section. (https://www.thewaltdisneycompany.com/about/)

Tjendra, Jeffrey. "The Origins of Design Thinking." *WIRED*. (https://www.wired.com/insights/2014/04/origins-design-thinking/)

Treasure, Julian. "Five Ways to Listen Better." *TEDTalk*, 2011. (https://www.ted.com/talks/julian_treasure_5_ways_to_listen_better?language=en)

Treaure, Julian. *Listening Talk - Rosenfeld Media Digital Confernce*. 2012.

Turkle, Sherry. "Connected, but alone?" *TEDTalk*, 2012. (https://www.ted.com/talks/sherry_turkle_alone_together?language=en)

Turkle, Sherry. *Reclaiming Conversation: The Power of Talk in a Digital Age*. Penguin Books. Kindle Edition. 2016.

*United Nation Sustainable Development Goals*. (https://www.un.org/sustainabledevelopment/sustainable-development-goals/)

Unknown and unattributed. "Intuition – It's More Than a Feeling." *Association for Psychological Science. Blog*.

Vozza, Stephanie. "8 Habits of Curious People." *Fast Company*. April 21, 2015. (https://www.fastcompany.com/3045148/8-habits-of-curious-people

Watters, Audrey. "How Steve Jobs Brought Apple II to the classroom." *Hack Education*. February 25, 2015. (http://hackeducation.com/2015/02/25/kids-cant-wait-apple)

Webb, Toby. "Drucker Was the True Father of Modern CSR." *Sustainability = Smart Business*. January 2010. (http://sustainablesmartbusiness.com/2010/01/drucker-was-true-father-of-modern-csr/)

White, Gillian B., "All Your Clothes Are Made With Exploited Labor." *The Atlantic*. June 3, 2015. (https://www.theatlantic.com/business/archive/2015/06/patagonia-labor-clothing-factory-exploitation/394658/)

Winter, Eyal. "Why Our Emotions Are More Rational Than We Think." *Psychology Today*. February 19, 2015. (https://www.psychologytoday.com/us/blog/feeling-smart/201502/why-our-emotions-are-more-rational-we-think)

Wouter Aghina, Karin Ahlback, Aaron De Smet, Gerald Lackey, Michael Lurie, Monica Murarka, and Christopher Handscomb. "The Five Trademarks of Agile Organizations." *McKinsey Quarterly*. January 2018. (https://www.mckinsey.com/business-functions/organization/our-insights/the-five-trademarks-of-agile-organizations)

Wulfhorst, Ellen. "HP, Apple Top List of Tech Companies Fighting Forced Labor Risk." *Reuters*. June 23, 2016. (https://www.reuters.com/article/us-technology-supplychain-forcedlabor-idUSKCN0Z925R)

Yang, Yuan. "Apple's iPhone X assembled by illegal student labour." *Financial Times*. November 21, 2017. (https://www.ft.com/content/7cb56786-cda1-11e7-b781-794ce08b24dc)

Yarow, Jay. "Best Steve Jobs Quotes from his Biography." *Business Insider*. October 26, 2011. October 26, 2011. (https://www.businessinsider.com/best-steve-jobs-quotes-from-biography-2011-10)

Yong, Debbie. "The Design Value Index Shows what Design Thinking is Worth." *Fortune*. August 31, 2017. (https://fortune.com/2017/08/31/the-design-value-index-shows-what-design-thinking-is-worth/)

Zimmerman, Kim Ann. "History of Computers: A Brief Timeline." *LIVEScience*. September 6, 2017. (https://www.livescience.com/20718-computer-history.html)

# About Mary Brodie

Mary Brodie is an experience strategist who has been helping companies create memorable customer experiences for more than 20 years. Throughout her career and while at her company, Gearmark, she led teams in enterprises and startups that contributed to the bottom line. She worked on apps, websites, content strategy, and lead gen programs. Mary attended MIT and graduated from Simmons University (BA and MA) and IE University in Madrid (executive master's in corporate communication). She lives in Dallas, Texas.

www.ingramcontent.com/pod-product-compliance
Lightning Source LLC
Chambersburg PA
CBHW071231050326
40690CB00011B/2067

* 9 7 8 1 7 3 4 1 4 2 6 0 0 *